"Donna Besel is one of the bravest and most honest writers I know. The high quality of her prose provides the reader with safe entry to what is a harrowing but essential read. We owe her much gratitude for having the courage to write it." —GERARD BEIRNE, author of *In a Time of Drought and Hunger*

"In *The Unravelling*, Donna Besel tells an important story with an unsentimental, fearless voice, of a family riven as much by the original crime as by the slow-turning wheels of justice." —DENISE CHONG, author of *The Concubine's Children*

"After a childhood of abuse and years of suffering its aftermath, author Donna Besel courageously sets out to free herself and her family members from the suffocating denial and the lies that threaten to crush them all. While family ties are strained beyond endurance, and delays in the twisted court system protect the perpetrator and torture the victims, Besel keeps fighting, wisely draws strength from her love of her children, her friends, and the natural world, and survives to tell this harrowing, heart-breaking story of terrible losses and a lonely, valiant quest for justice in an unjust world." —CATHERINE HUNTER, author of *After Light*

"With courage and conviction, Donna Besel details the crushing personal, familial, and social effects of justice denied when she and some of her siblings decide, as adults, to confront and expose their father as an abuser. Both conscientious record and cris de coeur, *The Unravelling* speaks powerfully for all victims of sexual abuse. In its honest acknowledgement of pain, it also offers pathways to healing and hope." —SUSAN OLDING, author of *Big Reader*

"Donna Besel's battle for acknowledgment of the evils that infected her childhood is illumined in *The Unravelling* by the sheer strength of her lucid, straightforward, voice. Besel carries us along an eye-opening journey, one of healing and remarkable endurance." —HARRIET RICHARDS, author of *Waiting for the Piano Tuner to Die*

"A shattering story and an essential one, told with consummate honesty and courage." —JOAN THOMAS, author of *Five Wives*

The Unravelling

~

*Incest and the
Destruction of a Family*

DONNA BESEL

Printed and bound in Canada at L'Imprimerie Gauvin. The text of this book is printed on 100% post-consumer recycled paper with earth-friendly vegetable-based inks.

COVER AND TEXT DESIGN: Duncan Noel Campbell
COPY EDITOR: Marionne Cronin
PROOFREADER: Caley Clements
COVER PHOTO: "Family—circa 1955" by kuco / Adobe Stock

Library and Archives Canada Cataloguing in Publication

TITLE: The unravelling : incest and the destruction of a family / Donna Besel.

NAMES: Besel, Donna, author.

SERIES: Regina collection.

DESCRIPTION: Series statement: The Regina collection

IDENTIFIERS: Canadiana (print) 20210233826 | Canadiana (ebook) 20210235640 | ISBN 9780889778436 (softcover) | ISBN 9780889778443 (PDF) | ISBN 9780889778450 (EPUB)

SUBJECTS: LCSH: Besel, Donna. | LCSH: Besel, Donna—Family. | LCSH: Incest victims—Canada—Biography. | LCSH: Adult child sexual abuse victims—Canada—Biography. | LCSH: Trials (Incest)—Canada. | LCGFT: Autobiographies.

CLASSIFICATION: LCC HV6570.9.C3 B47 2021 | DDC 362.76092—dc23

University of Regina Press

University of Regina, Regina, Saskatchewan, Canada, S4S 0A2
TEL: (306) 585-4758 FAX: (306) 585-4699
WEB: www.uofrpress.ca

10   9   8   7   6   5   4   3   2   1

We acknowledge the support of the Canada Council for the Arts for our publishing program. We acknowledge the financial support of the Government of Canada. / Nous reconnaissons l'appui financier du gouvernement du Canada. This publication was made possible with support from Creative Saskatchewan's Book Publishing Production Grant Program.

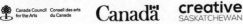

In memory of my mother, Violet England.
She stayed, but left us far too soon.

Contents

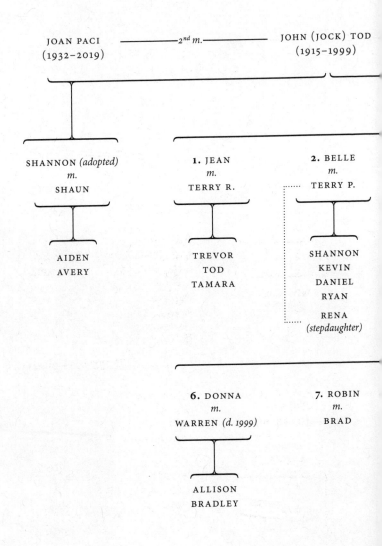

JOAN PACI —————2nd m.————— JOHN (JOCK) TOD
(1932–2019)   (1915–1999)

SHANNON *(adopted)*
m.
SHAUN

AIDEN
AVERY

1. JEAN
m.
TERRY R.

TREVOR
TOD
TAMARA

2. BELLE
m.
TERRY P.

SHANNON
KEVIN
DANIEL
RYAN

RENA
(stepdaughter)

6. DONNA
m.
WARREN *(d. 1999)*

ALLISON
BRADLEY

7. ROBIN
m.
BRAD

Family Tree

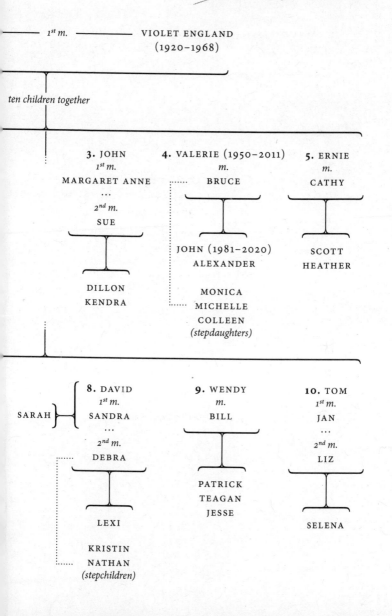

1st m. ——— VIOLET ENGLAND
(1920–1968)

ten children together

3. JOHN
1st m.
MARGARET ANNE
...
2nd m.
SUE

DILLON
KENDRA

4. VALERIE (1950–2011)
m.
BRUCE

JOHN (1981–2020)
ALEXANDER

MONICA
MICHELLE
COLLEEN
(stepdaughters)

5. ERNIE
m.
CATHY

SCOTT
HEATHER

SARAH

8. DAVID
1st m.
SANDRA
...
2nd m.
DEBRA

LEXI

KRISTIN
NATHAN
(stepchildren)

9. WENDY
m.
BILL

PATRICK
TEAGAN
JESSE

10. TOM
1st m.
JAN
...
2nd m.
LIZ

SELENA

Confusion, indecision, fear, these are my weapons.

The one means that wins the easiest
victory over reason: terror and force.

—ADOLF HITLER

Prologue

CALL ME "INCESTED."

I earned that name. I struggled long and hard to be able to say those words.

I cannot speak for husbands, children, sisters, brothers, cousins, wives, ancestors, friends, or any of the hundreds involved; I speak only for myself. I tell this story from my vantage point, my version of vision, my fractured reality.

"She's lying. She's always been crazy and angry. What in hell is she trying to do?"

To that I say—this is my story. I earned it. I will call myself "Incested."

Disclosures

1

This story begins, strangely enough, with a wedding.

As is often the case with incest, it had gone on for years, but the unravelling began when my family gathered for my younger sister's marriage. Even before the bride began to plan the nuptials, family members muttered, mumbled, and tried to think happier thoughts. We knew it needed to come out. I liked to call it the "constipated memory syndrome."

Three months before the wedding, my brother David had decided to have his daughter christened. He suggested, since we might all be in the same city, we could gather to discuss incest. The time had come. Furtive and terrified, we freaked—we couldn't do this now—we had a wedding to plan. Besides, what would the groom's mother think?

~

ON THE PREVIOUS Christmas, the avalanche had already started. When my brother Robin dropped by for a visit, we had this strained conversation.

"Well, Shannon finally left home. He was still doing *it* to her. Did you know?"

"I'm not surprised. He did *it* to me for a long time."

"He did *it* to you? How come you never told me?"

"You never asked. I hoped he had stopped. We are so dumb."

"Who else?"

"Who knows?"

"What happens now? What can we do?"

"It's gonna be shitty, no matter what."

And then I felt a sinking feeling, like flunking a test, blowing an interview, only one hundred thousand times worse.

"Let's wait and see. Maybe it will work out. Maybe we won't have to do anything."

But we had come to a ledge, whether we wanted to or not.

And then . . . we stepped off the cliff. Notice I say "*We.*" I am mindful of pronouns, in writing and in speaking. Some of my siblings shared the same thoughts, fears, inklings of disaster. I wasn't on that precipice by myself.

First, some relevant numbers: my family of origin consisted of ten children, five sons and five daughters. I am sixth in birth order. We were raised in poverty, in a rural setting, in a small bush community called West Hawk Lake. My birth mother died of brain cancer at forty-eight, two years after her last child, Tom, was born. I was fourteen. My father remarried just as I turned eighteen, in my final year of high school. After a few years, my stepmother, Joan, adopted a daughter, Shannon, four years old.

The arrivals of my brothers and sisters spanned about twenty-five years, in intervals of roughly every two years. Most managed to get educated, get married, or get children. Some managed all three, to greater or lesser success. At the time of the wedding, I was married, with two kids.

In the months prior to the wedding, my siblings silently transmitted the following message—the ceremony must be dealt with before the incest bomb could be defused.

Not surprisingly, our family excelled at weddings. This would be our seventh. Wendy, the youngest daughter of our birth mother, deserved to have it done up right.

I gave the toast to the bride.

"Once upon a time, there was a girl with straight blonde hair, big blue eyes, and wrap-around grin. Her mother had so many children she didn't know what to do ... Whoops! Wrong story! Anyway, this girl seemed so old and so wise that everyone called her 'Little Old Lady.' When she was around six years old, her mother got sick and died, just before Christmas. The little girl became even older and wiser."

And so it went, on and on and on.

We raised our glasses, flung jackets on chairs, posed for photos, danced the polka—so boisterous and photogenic. For the moment, we could overlook the old man clutching and fondling the bridesmaids.

Wendy and her new husband Bill drove off into the darkness. Thankfully, they were far enough down the road and across the prairie before the detonation. After the honeymoon ended, they returned to a changed family, smoldering, grieving, wounded; no semblance of the happy, bright wedding crowd remained.

2

WHILE WENDY AND BILL HEADED WEST, MY SECOND-oldest sister, Belle, lingered in West Hawk Lake. She had arrived with lots of baggage, physical and other kinds. For four days, she asked questions, revealing glimpses of her own story. She pressed books about "survivors" into reluctant hands. Belle bothered people. She bothered our oldest sister, Jean, once too often.

Jean chose to enlighten Belle. But she did not talk about improprieties done to her, or any of our sisters. She told Belle about the sexual activity between Belle's adult daughter, Rena, and Belle's husband, Terry. He had been molesting her for years.

While Rena attended college, she worked as a seasonal employee for the local Parks Branch and lived in the big family home with our stepmother, Joan, and our father, Jock. During those summers, she disclosed Terry's sexual assaults to Joan and Jean. Both chose to keep quiet about these disclosures.

The day after the wedding, I returned home with my husband and children, so I was not there when Jean told

Belle about Terry abusing Rena. Belle called me later to tell me how she had lost control of every bodily function—screaming, puking, weeping, passing out, shaking, screaming some more.

Somehow, she managed to get to David's house in Winnipeg. David, one of the younger brothers, had hosted the christening in the spring. Belle spent three days with him and his wife, Sandra, vomiting and weeping, sedated at times.

In spite of her anguish, Belle phoned her husband.

"Terry, did you molest Rena?"

"Can we talk without shouting?"

"Listen carefully. Did you molest Rena?"

"Well . . . it might have been a bit foolish to treat her like that."

"Get out of the house. If I see you, I will do something we'll both regret."

"Please, can we discuss this once you get back?"

"No!" she shouted and hung up. The phone almost shattered.

On the fourth day after the wedding, Belle left for Ontario, where she now faced three separate but entwined knots: her own sexual abuse, her daughter's abuse, and her abusive husband.

Mindful of his own well-being, Terry had removed himself from their family home.

Meanwhile, back at West Hawk, Jean and the rest of us awakened to the altered map of our family. Belle's discovery of Terry's betrayal meant our father's sexual abuse of his own children could no longer be denied.

Not surprisingly, we had no idea how to confront the topic of sexual abuse.

Jean decided to visit the aged patriarch to confront him. Jock opted to play dumb but admitted he "did things" to his daughters. Some attributed this vague confession to remorse. I saw it as a bald-faced attempt to throw everyone off his trail.

Jock wanted to shift the focus to another subject— like Belle and Terry's impending divorce. Instead of talking about the real reason why they were splitting, Jock and Joan started saying things like this: "Oh, poor Terry. Belle always was crazy. Why can't she get over this? Why can't she just forgive and forget? After all, it happened so long ago."

Over the next three and a half years, I heard those same phrases over and over. They became a mantra, chanted endlessly, to convince the listener, or maybe the speaker.

To her credit, once she found out, Belle decided she could not live with the man who had molested her only daughter. Our stepmother, facing the same scenario, decided to stand by her man, who had molested not just one, but six daughters. Not only did Joan continue to live with the offender, but she faced isolation and public shame with him.

After his initial admissions, Jock reverted to his "bully-and-manipulate" tactic, which he had refined over the years. Well into our adult lives, he gave us orders on how to live.

"You don't want that (insert: husband, wife, dog, house, dishwasher . . . whatever)."

"Don't listen to those wimmen's libbers (or commies or fags)."

Our father often told anyone who cared to listen, "Since before the Riel Rebellion, my family has lived in Manitoba. We have a street in Winnipeg named in our honour. My brothers and I were war heroes. I was involved in Mulroney's campaign and dined with the Queen."

Ergo, someone with such an illustrious history could not be a child molester.

Around this time, I read about a man who worked in a foundry and stepped onto a layer of cooled steel. It cracked; he fell into the molten liquid. It burned almost all of his body, but he survived. I thought about this thin skin of "normal" we had been walking on for so long. My layers of protection were now scorched off. The only way I could surface in this shame was to start disclosing the abuse. To a person who has never experienced it, this might seem simple. All you do is open your mouth and say, "My father molested me."

As easy as falling off a sawhorse—but damned near impossible.

∼

AFTER THE WEDDING, I started to tell. One night, walking with a friend named Petchie, near the town dock in Lac du Bonnet, the community where I lived, I spoke in riddles.

"I've got something to tell you."

"I'm listening."

"I've never told anyone outside my family."

"You have cancer! Don't tell me you're going to die."

Her brother had recently died of AIDS. I felt guilty bothering her with my tiny problem.

"I'm not going to die. At least I don't plan to. It's not a big deal, but I am ashamed."

"You're having an affair. Does Warren know yet?"

Warren happened to be my husband. He now knew, but not about any affair.

"Not me."

"Warren's having an affair?"

"No, it has to do with my family."

"One of your kids is sick?"

"No, my kids are fine. It has to do with my father."

"He's going to die. Oh, Donna, I'm sorry."

My nervousness had only muddied the transmission. I needed to be direct. But first, a long thick breath, like before diving under water.

"He sexually assaulted me and all my sisters."

"Oh . . ."

The tears came. I had never cried much in front of another adult. The wetness felt strange. But I could not stop. I remember standing by the wide river, looking up at the street lights of Lac du Bonnet. They looked blurred and fuzzy. I felt wobbly and worried about falling into the water. But then it hit me. I had told someone outside my family.

Petchie listened and asked questions, and I wondered if I had done the right thing. What if she told everyone? Would anyone ever look at me the same way? Petchie encouraged me to talk, even if it meant walking and staying up all night.

Looking back, each telling was part of a progression, bringing me to a harder level, riskier and scarier. Like Mario in my son Bradley's computer games, whirling across the screen, bumping into things, hoping I wouldn't incinerate, I sought more telling.

A couple of weeks later, I told a group. In the first weeks of the summer, Petchie organized a sharing circle of a half-dozen women. She said she wanted us to converse on a meaningful level, or perhaps to gossip. I wasn't entirely sure. For each session, we picked a topic; for example, "beauty," "miracles," "body image." So far, these gatherings had stayed safe and tame.

This evening's topic was "sexual abuse." I considered skipping.

I sat on a chair, feeling detached and empty. My heart jackhammered, anxious to pop out of my chest. My pulse roared like a jet engine. My breath stopped for what seemed to be sixty seconds at a time. After twenty minutes, no one had said anything explicit. The women took turns, talking in broad terms. Their consensus: abuse = bad.

I wanted to tell them my secret. Who could I trust? We had promised the sharing would be confidential. I knew three of the five women well. The other two were acquaintances. All of them spoke calmly and did not rant. Their quiet voices unsettled me.

Finally, the sharing wand passed into my fingers. I could not make my tongue work. I shivered and broke into a cold sweat; my entire body shook. These polite women jolted awake. Petchie came to sit by my knee. She put a hand on my thigh. The trembling increased.

I said, "Don't touch me. Arrrrrrrragh!"

The rest circled around and put hands on different body parts. I recoiled but stopped shaking so hard. I wanted them to back off so I could breathe, scream, or cry, but I needed those hands to hold me still, hold me down.

I said the words, "My father sexually abused me. And now it's out in the open . . ."

3

THROUGHOUT THE NEXT THREE AND A HALF YEARS— a time of searching and telling—I wrote letters. Some I never sent, and some I sent, but wished I never wrote them. I also received some. For me, letters provided an ideal forum to deal with abuse. Words can be chosen carefully. Angry people can tear up the paper, but not the person. Letters cannot be interrupted or bullied into silence. Tears can flow onto the page, but do not stop the message. I knew I would be shunned. Part of the process of banishment involves pretending the other person does not exist. Letters convinced me I was real.

After I spoke to Petchie, and the women's circle, I sought a new level of telling—revealing the abuse to a significant adult who might provide support. My stepmother, Joan, had promised me she would visit. I assumed she planned to come alone. She had been hired as a returning officer for the upcoming election and she told me she had to attend a training session in Lac du Bonnet. It was about an hour-and-a-half drive from West Hawk Lake.

In anticipation of watching her read it or even reading it out loud to her, I wrote a letter. Over the years she often said, "Donna hates her father. I don't know why, but I know she does."

I waited all day. She did not call and never showed up. While I mused about what I could have misunderstood in our phone conversation, I recalled her words.

"Well, it's all out in the open now. But he's old, and sick."

"Yes, I know."

"You'll be able to forget, won't you? So things will get back to normal."

"I don't think things will ever be the same."

"I'll see you next week."

The election came and went; she counted voters and votes. Our relationship ended with that stumbling phone call. I lost a second mother, quickly, painfully, without explanation.

Dear Joan,

I know this past month hasn't been great. I am writing because it hurts to say certain things which need to be said. First of all, I've never felt love for my father. When he assaulted me, I felt dirty and ugly and bad. I figured somehow I deserved it.

*He started when I was six or younger. Later on,
I fought back.*

*The only physical attention from him included
an erect penis or a fist. His physical attacks and his
violence toward our mother, even when she was
dying, only increased my loathing. With no other adults to catch him, he often ended up in my
bedroom.*

*As you know, I was the oldest girl at home and
did laundry and housework. When you arrived, I
wanted to tell you to escape, but my selfishness won
out. I wanted the younger kids to have a mother.
Please accept my apologies for not warning you. You
must have had some effect, because he hasn't tried,
to my knowledge, to break any of your bones. Also,
when you came, the sexual assaults on me stopped.
The first year you lived with us meant freedom for
me. I admire your strength, courage, and faith. We're
going to need it now, more than ever. If people keep
talking, I'm convinced we can survive as a family.*

I did not send this letter. I hoped Joan would visit,
to read it in front of me and tell me she still cared about
me. Later, I learned this choice of husband over children
was common. She might not have looked at it even if I
sent it. I found it difficult to accept she had wiped her
hands of us so quickly.

∾

IN ALL THE years I could remember, Jock had never written to me. But, on September 10, I opened our mailbox and saw he had written a note.

> *Dear Donna,*
>   *I am writing to ask your forgiveness for any harm*
> *I have caused you and hope we will be able to see*
> *you and your children who we miss not seeing. I*
> *have many regrets.*
>
>   *Your father, Jock*

This new approach floored me. I perspired, I wept, I prayed. The reference to our children choked me up. But then I started to look at the words more closely. First of all, I could not recall ever being named "dear" by him. Also, he fudged on what the "harm I have caused you" could be. The last statement, "I have many regrets," could include anything. The salutation did not say "love," but "your father." He valued ownership, not caring. His short note spoke volumes.

When I told my siblings about it, they expressed amazement. Some said I should be grateful to get such an admission. I never received any more notes from him, or communication of any kind. Much later, I found out someone, possibly Joan or Jean, had insisted he write to me.

For the rest of the month, I panicked. As I said, the experience was akin to jumping off a cliff. Now that I was falling, I needed to find ways to soften the impact, needed to trust people and let them catch me. I had to learn to admit weakness and to recognize when I needed help. For some, these skills may seem elementary, but not for me. I got a copy of *The Courage to Heal* by Laura Davis and Ellen Bass, and started to read.

Some siblings suggested that we needed to talk, as a group, with help from counsellors. We found two close at hand—Karen, a United Church minister, and Esther, a social worker. At the time, they were employed by a Winnipeg church that Wendy and Bill attended. The two of them worked as a pastoral team and they had started counselling people with abuse issues. Also, Karen had ministered at West Hawk Lake as a summer student. She knew our family, and had performed wedding services for Wendy and David. I did not know Esther, but Wendy did. Because there were so many of us, they both agreed to facilitate.

Wendy offered her house for the gathering and we set a date, October 3. The first meeting included Jean, Wendy, David, Shannon, Robin in Saskatchewan, via my speakerphone, and me. Esther and Karen believed it was important to exclude Jock and Joan to allow us the freedom to react openly. I agreed.

We wept and squirmed. Regression ran rampant, especially when we talked about the beatings and other violence. Karen and Esther jumped in when conflicts threatened to scuttle the conversation. Often, I forgot to breathe, and felt strangely nervous with people who were so familiar.

Following a suggestion in *The Courage to Heal,* I had written another letter, this time to my abuser. Near the end of our session, I decided to move up to the next level—identifying the abuse in the company of more

than one sibling. The words snapped out of me, slick
with spit.

> *Fuck off. Don't ever talk about my children. They
> have nothing to do with you. I wish I had the guts
> to tell sooner. Now we find out you did the same
> stupid things to Shannon. You can deny and bull-
> shit, but I know what you did. You beat our moth-
> er. You broke her nose and her arm. You killed
> something in me and I don't feel sorry for you. You
> hate women and children. And you think none of
> this is your fault. You just have "bad" children. We
> are not bad; we are trying to live like sane people.*

I could not stop the flow of words once the torrent
gripped me. I did not look up while I read. Karen told
me later she witnessed unbelievable agony etched on my
siblings' faces. Even Robin, via speakerphone, responded
with his younger self. "We never did the right things.
He hurt us. He hurt our mother. Why? How come he
couldn't love us?"

He also got a huge phone bill from this meeting—the
first of many. The phone companies profited from our
angst. We spent many hours calling each other during
the next three years.

Despite how much the first meeting hurt, Wendy and
I arranged another one. On October 16, we gathered at
her house and Robin listened in on the speakerphone.
At this meeting, the two oldest brothers, John and Ernie,
decided to join us.

During this session, more crying and squirming ensued. Ernie's face pinched up, and his high, trembling voice grated on my ears. John barked in unintelligible grunts. Then, while we were eating delivery pizza and no longer dwelling on past emotions, John rattled off endless technical details about airplanes he liked.

After we ate, I asked if they'd like to look at my letter. While Ernie read it, I watched his trapped-rabbit persona emerge. John also read it. I could not watch him. He calmly told me I swore too much. My tornado of emotion had skipped right over him; he did not appear to share those feelings.

Their fear, or perhaps their aversion to phone bills, kept these two brothers out of my life for the following years. The next family meeting did not take place until the summer of 1995. I wrote a lot of letters in between. But I did not use my speakerphone in that context again.

4

THE PAIN FELT LIKE A DEEP-SET ABSCESS THAT I had started poking. I did not know which way to stumble. Writing things down mattered. Somehow, somewhere, some way, this had meaning.

Why was it such a secret? Why were my siblings so scared to even say the words, yet at the same time insisting it was no big deal and saying that it happened so long ago that it didn't matter? If it wasn't worth mentioning, why couldn't it be discussed without yelling? Why hadn't we dealt with it sooner? I asked these questions of myself and others very often during the next three and a half years. I still don't know the answers.

Even though we were older, and my father was older, the reminders of his harsh words and hard hands were etched onto our psyches. But the cycle needed rending. My sister Belle had married an abuser and her daughter paid the price. All of our children were harmed by Jock's violence. Did we care enough for them to confront him?

We had finally admitted the simplest, most common fact about child molesters. They repeat. Jock remained untreated and unidentified, so he did what he liked with anyone he thought wouldn't tell. But Shannon told Robin about her abuse, and Robin told me, and I told Robin about mine, and things got rolling.

To my dismay, I found out later that Shannon had told Joan before she told Robin.

Not once did anyone suggest "false memory." Our biggest problems arose from "lying perpetrator syndrome" or "multiple forgiveness tendencies" or "false recovery claims." We wanted desperately to forget, preferred to forget, and worked hard at forgiving.

∼

ON A COOL fall day, between breaking up kids' quarrels and drinking coffee, Petchie, the first woman I told, sat me down and asked me about finding anger, like it could be summoned like a wayward pup. Then she explained how she needed to find her rage after her brother died, to acknowledge she was very angry with him for leaving her. Focusing on finding anger scared me. What if I found it? I had seen glimpses and it looked huge. What if it swallowed me? My stomach already ached all day and I cried at night. I decided to avoid finding anger.

But, later that night, while watching the movie *Ghost*, it happened. During the last part, wispy phantoms rose up from the sewers. Then it hit me . . . evil did exist. As a child, I had been swimming in it. The movie ended. I stumbled into the downstairs bathroom, gurgled and vomited. I fell into the shower and started screaming. The rawness astounded me.

"You fucking son of a bitch! Why did you do this?"

I repeated these two phrases for an hour and a half, pounding the walls of the shower. The booming echoed through our quiet house. I finally slumped in a heap, croaking, exhausted, whimpering. I had found my anger.

I stumbled to bed and asked Warren why he hadn't responded. He told me he thought I needed to be alone. Maybe he was right. In some way, the brakes would have been applied. It might have scared the hell out of the kids, and Warren, to witness such pain. I know it scared the hell out of me.

Yes, I had found my rage. Now I needed to figure out what to do with it.

5

ON OCTOBER 25, MY BIRTHDAY, PETCHIE GAVE me a notebook and wrote in the front—"For all the icky thoughts you want to get rid of . . ."

Laundry, dishes, phone calls, homework, chores, messes piled up. But I started to fill the pages with icky thoughts, started to dig into myself with a pen. The way I viewed my own body was the first poison to surface.

My father's words: "Built like a brick shithouse. No man would want her."

I went barefoot often, wearing long pants to hide this fact. Once, while playing baseball, I got thrown out of a provincial finals game; an opposing coach refused to let me on the field without sneakers. Someone lent me a pair. My coach would do almost anything to keep me on the team. After games and practices, he drove me home, sixty kilometres, one way. I waited for him to make advances. But he only wanted me as a "home run queen," not a sexual partner. We did win a lot of games. I swam and canoed long distances, and slept on the ground. I rode my horse, in darkness, long into the middle of the night. One Halloween, I wore a wig, makeup, and a glittery dress to a dance—it felt like drag to me.

Despite my past, I wanted to be a mother. I thought Warren, quiet and careful, was the opposite of Jock. Many people told me, "You're such a smart and wonderful person." Funny, I never felt smart or wonderful. Not once.

I wrote about how Jock reminded me of those particularly obnoxious dogs, always male, often Labrador retrievers, who single-mindedly hump anything and everything, even a bent knee. Could he ever be held accountable?

More questions. No answers. I needed to focus on real people who loved me.

6

IN MY JOURNAL, I OUTLINED THE CHALLENGES we faced in dealing with my father's abuse. Jock defined his children by his labels. "Divide and conquer" meant sibling rivalry ran amuck. He controlled us with his fists, and his selective approval. While we were growing up, we jockeyed for the inside rail, the smallest whiff of endorsement.

But a really scary, but exciting, idea had emerged—we could change this pattern.

One of the most obvious excuses for not telling about the abuse was simple: naming it would cause what we feared. Families, children, and marriages would all suffer.

I asked myself, "How had we coped?"

Here is what I figured out.

All of us minimized. We didn't want to admit that the fondling, kissing, and masturbating on us could be sexual abuse. Looking back, it was regular and deliberate. Also, the fact it was our father doing it added to the depravity.

All of us perfected denial and rationalization. We tried to be "normal"—with university, responsible jobs, and children. Even as adults, we often trotted out the clichés of our lives:

"Well, it wasn't that bad. We all survived."

"We had a roof over our heads and got fed."

"We learned to be tough. Who likes wimps anyway?"

And all of us struggled with relationships—some of us used meaningless sex, avoided intimacy, could not find emotionally healthy partners, or divorced after short marriages. Was this lonely drifting a part of being human?

Humour helped me to cope. I looked at the absurdity of life and found laughter. Sometimes, I felt ashamed of my jokes. If I wasn't mindful, I could end up like our father. He used humour to hurt and degrade people.

I often ate beyond fullness. Slowing down to enjoy anything, including food, seemed unnatural. For me, a body was something that carried my brains. I looked out at the world, and hoped no one looked at me. I hated mirrors. My body was a tool, to be used hard.

My mother breastfed us, but did not have much time for hugging once we were out of diapers. Because I had been taught to be sexual from such an early age, I often shifted into hyperdrive. I did not know how to flirt or seduce. Sex was all or nothing.

What about lying? I liked to think I was honest. Now it seemed a lot of what we lived revolved around the myth of the large, happy family; others wanted to believe in it too. Our stepmother, Joan, invested a lot of her energy building this illusion.

"They all come home for holidays and skate, ski, and eat turkey together."

But now half of the family spun in circles, half seemed ready to self-destruct. As for me, I wanted my stomach to stop cramping. I wanted to take a real breath, so I could get on with my so-called life. I looked at my own son, a preschooler, and felt utterly, utterly sickened, thinking how small he was, how eager to please, and how easy to fool. This unsettled me the most.

All of us struggled to break away from Jock's dominance. For example: in the summer of 1987, he mobilized the family army to build an indoor swimming pool, attached to his house. Even though we were adults, Jock decreed his intentions, and coerced most of his kids to complete this concrete monument. I resisted the calls to join the work crew. I hated that pool. And I hated myself for letting my daughter swim in it.

I worried about examining all my memories too closely. Going down that path seemed to lead to insanity. I needed to believe I was not responsible for a whole lot of things—easy to write, tough to do. But a realization was being born.

"Good daddies didn't fuck kids. Mine did. Ergo, he was not a good daddy, not even if I wanted him to be."

Once again, dog images came to me. I saw my family as a litter of snarling, hungry puppies, wanting love and licking. Our mother stood amongst us, exhausted. Sagging breasts, sagging spirit. She pulled away, and we dragged her down, nipping at teats. She wanted to crawl back under the porch to sleep. So the puppies struggled on alone. Whimpering and snarling, blaming each other for being hungry and needy. Then along came the old daddy dog. He hated the puppies for being needy and greedy. He taught them to fight and snarl. Bones were scarce; love was rare. Hate the world; howl at people. But worst of all, the old dog humped and drooled, polluted the pups with his foul breath and foul thoughts.

7

ON A COLD SUNDAY IN NOVEMBER, A DIM GLOW in the eastern sky lit up my kitchen windows. I had stayed up all night writing. Memories I had pushed away roared into my brain. At the grocery store, I forgot what I needed in the produce section and stared at Brussels sprouts for ten minutes. Even though I had worn out a washing machine with over a decade of laundry, I forgot how to turn one on. But I could remember the smell of semen on my skin from when I was seven or eight. I doubted my sanity.

Fortunately, someone explained it in scientific lingo. Simply put, my mind, like a computer, was calling up too many long-term memories. It did not have room for the short-term recall. Hence, I struggled to remember how to shift gears in the middle of downtown traffic. I drove home without groceries. I locked myself out of the house. I forgot exactly who I was talking to on the phone.

Naming what happened so long ago affected my present life. Knowing something is not the same as feeling it; saying the words, even if it was only to a few people, unleashed feelings. Saying the words made the abuse real. Like trying to remember how many times I had a bologna sandwich in my lunch kit, I couldn't recall the details of every sexual encounter with my male parent. But one episode kept playing in my mind.

~

IT WAS EARLY in June, already warm, even though it was only six o'clock. Sunlight spread into the room; the big house was quiet before the morning's pandemonium. Oddly, I had a room to myself. After my mother died, we moved into a newer, much larger house across the road from the old house and the sawmill. The new house was bigger, cleaner. But it also meant fewer witnesses since we no longer all slept close together.

Jock slipped into my room like he was sneaking up on the enemy. I heard him, but was too groggy to react. Some mornings I leapt into the bathroom. It's harder to hit a moving target. But not this morning.

"Stay in bed. I need a cuddle. You need a cuddle. Don't get up. Don't get up, I told you."

He climbed under the covers behind me. After he pushed me back down on the bed, I turned my face to the wall. His erection prodded me. Maybe he wanted me to admire it. Was I supposed to feel sorry for him, now that he had no wife? I wanted to jump out the window. I imagined what he would think if I did.

"Oh shit, she's not here. I'll jerk off instead." Then he'd stand there, stupefied, with his penis in his hand.

The room stretched less than two and a half metres wide. While Jock rubbed himself, I stared at a cheap copy of "Boy Blue" on the wall. The boy had long hair and blue tights, and the background looked dark and stormy, like it was planning to rain. I could identify with this pale shepherd. I might get wet.

This memory reeked of wetness. First of all, the wetness of his mouth—slobbering, nuzzling, chewing my neck, ears, and shoulders. I enjoyed the touching, hard as that was to admit. Starting on my ears, he slid his tongue in-and-out, in-and-out, all the time wheezing with intense breathlessness. After a few minutes of slobber and chomp, he decided he had enough foreplay.

In the midst of this turmoil, I grappled with my guilt. Did I want this? I needed to remember I had lost a mother. No one seemed to care what happened to any of us. No one supported or even touched me. After school and on weekends, I supervised the army of reluctant siblings.

"Wash. Make your bed. Pick up your clothes. Help out. If you don't, I'll make you."

I needed some love, some compassion. What did I get? A tongue in the ear, a poke in the bum, a finger up my privates. Besides the usual teenage problems of acne, school, grades, clothes, I was forced to deal with this garbage. Why didn't I tell? Telling at the time, in that family, seemed impossible.

Back to the scene of the slime.

He said, "You like this. This is what women like. I'm not even fucking you."

He slid his hands around the front of my torso. I crunched up into a fetal position. He massaged my breasts. I clamped my arms to my sides, trying to stop the massaging. He pried up my arms. Eventually, after tussling and wrestling, he grabbed the nipple, pinching and rolling it in his hand.

What was wrong with this picture? A grown man attempted to grapple his nearly grown daughter into submission under a tangle of blankets.

I knew it was wrong. I should have told. But then we would have no parents. Who could take care of us? My wacky aunts? Unknown foster families? Because of the number of kids, we'd be sent in different directions. There seemed to be no way out, except submitting. And yes, he believed he was not actually fucking. I had no way of knowing that this wasn't what all fathers did to all daughters. Maybe he was right.

He settled down for a few minutes. After gaining a firm grip, he kneaded my bosom and surrounding flatter areas. I figured he might stop, so I pretended to go to sleep, as much as a person can fake it with two hands clamped onto her breasts.

"He will stop. He will go away. He has to work soon. It's hard work fighting with me. He needs his strength. I'm pretty strong. He must be tired."

I was not strong enough. He moved in for his climax.

Before I continue with this memory, I need to tell about clothes. I did not have many clothes and did not own any pajamas. I usually slept in a T-shirt and underwear. This may seem a small point, but I was infuriated to later have my "allegations" of sexual abuse dismissed as the combination of my imagination and refusal to wear a nightgown.

Back, once again, to the bedroom. After the breast-clutching, he got out his penis. Unzipped. Unbuttoned. He must have worn something into my room; long underwear made sense. He certainly did not show up naked. Long, off-white, woollen, buttons up the front, flap in the back. Maybe he wore pants, too.

I remember the smells—sweat, sawdust, pine sap, and old perspiration, the smell of working outside. And penis. They smell a certain way after being confined in a warm space.

My back was still turned to him. The thought of facing him revolted me. He wanted to kiss me on the mouth. I felt smothered by his insistence. I was tiring. We grappled, struggled, pushed. He moved his hand. I shoved his hand. He grabbed my hand. I twisted it away from him. He snatched it again and put it on his cock. I heaved him out of bed. Wasn't he worried someone could hear? Where was everyone?

His penis slid in between my legs. Clamping them tightly together, I wanted to hurt it, squish it. The pressure only seemed to increase his pleasure. More pressure, more roughness. We strained, breathed, pushed. His penis felt like a large finger jammed in my bum bone, a giant worm squiggling under two rocks. I wanted to crush that fucking worm.

"Squeeze harder, you little bitch. You're fighting, but you like it. I know what you want. It's what all women want."

Then he planted it further and harder, rubbing to increase the friction. His semen started to dribble out, making the slip-slapping easier. We both dripped sweat.

Why wasn't he afraid of the others coming in? Maybe it was because they were all younger. Maybe they heard and were afraid. That was a recurring problem in my family.

I bit my lips, punched his hands, crossed my legs, tucked my knees, and kicked his shins. He clamped his legs around mine. It became a chess game of grappling arm and leg holds. Then he slipped his hand into my underwear; then he slipped his penis into my underwear. Hand in front, penis in the back. He did not pull off the panties. If someone came in, he could slide his penis back into his long johns. He could pretend he was just waking up his lazy daughter, cuddling her.

A human body is designed to respond. I was a teenager, and human, with no mother to warn me, and no warnings before she died. Just this fool of a parent, panting hard and looking for a moment of satisfaction between my legs.

"Why keep fighting? I pull it away before I come. Relax. I'm not hurting you."

Then something broke. I started crying; I really started crying. I had never wept much in front of anyone, especially him, not even when my mother died. Except maybe when my fingertips got cut in the sawmill. Other than that, I just didn't.

I cried for my mother, who wasn't there to protect me. Huge, walloping sobs shook the bed. I never felt so alone in my whole life.

He got up quickly. This new wetness had blunted his enthusiasm. "Why are you blubbering? I never fucked you. I never got inside. Are you stupid? I don't need another mouth to feed. You'd think I'd raped you. Shut up, you little bitch. You'll wake everyone!"

I thought I must be wrong to feel this way, or cry, or fight back. I must be selfish, and stupid, and mean.

The door slammed. He was gone. As if I had done it all wrong—to make him mad like that. He did not look me in the eye again in my life. He never mentioned anything.

No one came to find out why I cried and cried and cried.

8

THE TOPIC OF SEXUAL ABUSE POPPED UP OFTEN. I turned on the television; I opened a newspaper. There it was. The media was my message, an emotional matchbook to ignite my fire.

"This week, a priest was charged with four counts of sexual assault."

"A Winnipeg teacher lost his job after ten students alleged he fondled . . ."

"A Steinbach man attempted to force two girls into his car."

"I am a child molester. You would never pick me out in a crowd. I look just like everyone else. I could be your next-door neighbour, your best friend, even your sister or brother."

A documentary on CBC told a story about six sisters in British Columbia. Two of them decided it was not worth reporting their abuse so long after it happened. The

father ran a sawmill, had ten children, had a Scottish sur-
name, and lived in a small community. Four of the sisters
reported their abuse to the police. The abuser's wife did
not support the daughters' allegations. The prosecution
went on for years and the judge took the offender's old age
and bad health into consideration when he sentenced him.

The incest went on for thirty years but finally came
out because the youngest, who was mentally and physically challenged, told an older sister. One of the daughters, an overweight woman with short hair, talked about
the abuse in choked, stumbling sentences. Her name was
the same as mine.

Vomit boiled in my throat as I watched. Because of
the similarities, this documentary unhinged me. I tried
to write down the details; my arm muscles twitched.
Soon I could not stand up. I wanted to get up and phone
my stepmother to check if she had seen it. The uncanny
parallels mesmerized me, but the three and a half years
from the date of reporting 'til actual sentencing seemed
ridiculously, painfully, long.

The Boys of St. Vincent, a CBC show about priests
molesting boys, pushed me further along the path. The
camera focused on the tears running down the youths'
cheeks while they waited their turn to talk to the police,
and I vibrated. The beating and threatening by the
priests retrieved childhood feelings I thought I had left
far behind me. I didn't want to watch, but I wanted to
know I wasn't the only person with such experiences.

These incidents also reminded me that my father
abused me as a young child so my understanding was
stuck at a child's level—primitive, superstitious thinking.

I thought of my son Bradley's reactions to my daughter Allison's proclamation.

"I am going to cast a spell on you. You are now an ugly toad."

"Mom! Make her turn me back."

"Toads can't talk. You can only croak. Keep quiet."

"Heeeeelp me. I hate being a toad."

I told him to look in a mirror, to know he was not a toad. This exchange gave me insights into a child's logic. His sister, more powerful because of intelligence and size, altered his reality. No doubt he would have soon figured out he was not a toad.

Because my subconscious perceptions had been so skewed when I was so young, I could never view Jock's potency in a factual light. If I did, maybe I wouldn't be writing any of this.

The CBC held up a mirror for me. I saw myself in those sisters from British Columbia and the boys from the orphanage.

9

EARLY IN DECEMBER, ON A MILD BUT SNOWY morning, Petchie came for a visit. She sipped her coffee and stared at me. Then she started to ask questions.

"What was your mother like?"

"I don't remember."

"You were fourteen when she died. You must be able to recall something."

"Her hands smelled like Javex. She liked clean ears."

"Anything else?"

"I don't remember much before school started."

"What about after that?"

"Not too much. Dogs, lumber, playing in the sand."

"I wonder why you don't remember."

After she left, I sat at my table and thought. Maybe the blanks held meaning. One book I read had suggested writing a letter to my six-year-old self. I got out my journal.

I don't know you well, but I need to find you. Petchie asked me to look at her daughter, a five-year-old. She's about the same size as I was when he started. I cried. You were tough, but you couldn't handle that. A five-year-old will do almost anything to find love.

I know you ended up in the hospital often. Let's see if I can remember—double pneumonia, hernia, whooping cough, appendicitis, various injuries. But you liked it there. No one bullied you, or tried to get into bed with you. You got clean sheets and attention. Maybe you think you could have stopped him, but there was no way. You could not sleep outside and you needed to eat. Besides, he would have found you.

I watch my own daughter sleeping. How could any parent violate such beauty? Like stomping on flowers, ripping and tearing and throwing them away. How come this evil hasn't eaten his heart? Oh yes, I forgot. It has. Too bad he recovered from the heart attacks. I know he wrote you a note, but his actions since then tell the story. He will not look inside himself. If some bum off the street had tried one of those tricks in a playground, he'd be thrown in jail.

You started out so beautiful, with your blonde curls and green-eyed smiles. The penetrations, the sensations could be endured, maybe even buried. But the shame was burned into your soul. Violation is violation is violation.

I need to tell you my dream. Bradley, or maybe it's Allison, toddles around Jock's home. A broken mirror sits inside a frame. Everyone knows it is broken, dangerous, hazardous for children. We ignore the glass because we don't want to get cut. My child, Allison-Bradley, touches the frame. Broken glass flies in all directions. My baby is bleeding. Others are bleeding. Finally someone shouts and picks at the pile of shards. The blaming starts. I grieve for you, little lost girl, sitting on your daddy's knee.

10

THE FIRST CHRISTMAS AFTER THE DISCLOSURE loomed.

In August, when Wendy got married, Bradley was two and a half, and Allison was eight and a half. Being so young, Bradley lacked strong memories of extended family. Seeing Mommy rage and weep upset him, but he seemed to accept that adults can have big sadness.

My kids witnessed random sobbing after phone calls and news reports. I tried to hide it in other rooms, but that didn't always work, simply because of the noise. When they found me, they huddled around like little birds, hugging, wiping my snot, running to fetch Daddy, and wrapping me in a blanket. One morning, I flung a cookie jar, a gift from Wendy, across the kitchen. That meant every time I washed the kitchen floor, the scarred vinyl bore witness to my crisis.

Perhaps Allison got a strong message about stopping violence and abuse. Perhaps she resented me for breaking contact with my extended family. She had lost many relationships and connections, all at once. Thankfully, she did not miss one that might usually exist.

I asked, "Are you upset we aren't going out to the lake?"

"Yes, I liked seeing my cousins, Heather and Tamara. I liked swimming."

Heather was Ernie's daughter and two years older. Tamara was Jean's daughter and four years older.

"What about Grandma?"

"I liked her cooking. But she used to get mad at me for not eating the right way. She said you should spank me."

"And we don't. What about Grandpa?"

"He hardly said anything to me or noticed me at all."

To me that meant he had not touched her. She would tell on that old man. At least I wanted to believe this. In retrospect, I realized how vigilant I was around Jock. Erections and ejaculations could happen in a few seconds. Hands could grab in a flash.

Other siblings argued that he was so old he would not harm anyone anymore. My brothers did not seem to want to admit that the beatings and insults they endured were abuse. Also, they forgot how he was presently damaging his family with denial and manipulation. They continued to spend time with Jock and Joan, justifying their visits by saying that he only liked to abuse girls so their sons were safe around him.

To that I responded, "Bullshit." He did not deserve to be near any kids, period.

Prior to the disclosure, usually either Warren or I hung around to watch our kids. We were criticized; children needed to learn how to get along without parents and be left with others.

Twice, we had left Allison with Joan. When we drove away from the house, I repeated to myself, "Wendy and Joan are there. They will watch her. She is four years old, and we are entitled to a weekend to ourselves."

She was not safe and I regretted it. Both weekends were to the same place, a cross-country ski resort in the States. The next time we went, we took the children. Later, I learned this hypervigilance is common with parents who have been abused.

Dealing more openly with my own abuse left little tolerance for any offenders. This sensitivity widened the gap with my in-laws. Strangely enough, or perhaps not so strange at all, Warren's father, Ben, had molested Warren's sisters. His mother and sisters had admitted it.

I didn't want to spend Christmas with him either, or let him near my children. Warren's youngest sister had told us a few years earlier. I had listened and told her that

I supported her in whatever she wanted to do. When she told me, I was too ashamed, and scared, to reveal our shared history of sexual assaults.

Now that I was allowing myself to feel the feelings, the horror of all these offences hit home. This old man resembled the other old man too much—similar stature, war history, and impulses.

In October, Jean Chrétien had campaigned to become prime minister. In the same month, my husband had run for office as a councillor in the rural municipality where we lived. Both were elected on the same day. Considering the small financial considerations, Warren's reasons for running were not clear. He said he wanted to offer something as a public persona.

Meanwhile, I resigned from every community committee I volunteered for. Warren's political obligations gave me the perfect excuse. Someone had to stay home with the kids. But his countless evening meetings added to the stress of coping. I wrote him a letter:

Dear Warren,

I do not know what to believe anymore. Certain members of my family ignore the issue. I can't connect with them. The rope between us is frayed as well. You tend to your council business. I was deeply shaken by your comment, "I've got to get on with my life." I also think you prefer I turn to Petchie for support. You say self-help and self-examination is garbage and, if I really wanted, I could fix it. Well, I can't do it on my own. And you are just as much a victim as I am. Your father is an offender. I have seen less of you than any time since we married. It feels like half my family died in a plane crash and the rest are badly injured. But people will not send Hallmark cards for this. They don't even like to talk about it.

And Warren replied:

Dear Donna,

I can't imagine a more difficult thing than what you are going through. Plus Bradley is getting more of a handful. I know council business does not help, but I think it can be managed. I detest your father for what he has done. I think we can survive the effects; it may take a long time. I'm prepared to hang in there. I don't care to see your father anymore or take our children to visit him. I love you but I have not been showing it. From what I've read, there is little I can do except stay in the background. I don't know where it will end, but I hope our relationship will be stronger. We have achieved so much and have such beautiful children.

We cried together on the couch.

Many nights, Warren found me sobbing and pounding on the floor. Often I walked long into the night, or saddled up my horse and galloped into the darkness. Every morning, I woke up, fed, organized, delivered, retrieved, fed, cleaned, washed, swept, fed, read, laundered, and then tried to sleep again. Every night I stumbled around the dark house, yard, and roads.

Within my family of origin, siblings swung back and forth from side to side on this issue. Some days it settled into roughly three camps—those who wanted to face this problem and do something about it, those who wanted to ignore it, and those who were too scared to make a decision. Some switched camps according to their insecurities of the moment.

"They been sitting on the fence so long they ain't got no balls left," I said to one of my friends, regarding my brothers' reluctance to land and stand on either side.

All through this fall, my siblings continued to visit West Hawk Lake. Now that this crime was out in the open, I wanted people to refuse to associate with the offender. Instead, it seemed that life went on as it had before, except we were no longer a part of it. Why was it such a big secret all those years? No one seemed to care anyhow. But I knew I wanted to stay away from family gatherings.

Right from the first disclosure, I saw a simple choice—either child abuse was okay or it wasn't. Where my siblings saw valleys of grey, I saw black or white mountains. Maybe my brothers and sisters wanted to hang on to the family myths. Maybe they wanted the safety and comfort of the known, the old ways. This led to a litany of excuses they recited for their right to respond as they wanted.

"You can't tell people what to do."

"People see things differently, you know."

"We all make choices about these things. Your choices are different."

Life did go on. They were right about that. Before Christmas, John's wife, Sue, gave birth to a baby girl. I did not see the baby. To this day, I still have not seen her.

Charges

11

WENDY AND BILL HAD MARRIED IN AUGUST; THE disclosure followed right after the wedding. It threw our family into crisis and we had met with Karen and Esther, twice.

My sister Belle, who had departed to Ontario to deal with the separation from her husband, her own abuse story, and her daughter's abuse story, had hit some kind of wall. Because she had not attended the two family sessions, she remained unaware of how we were dealing with the disclosure. Maybe we did not tell her enough. Maybe we were all in too much shock to realize what direction this might take.

She phoned a couple of times in such distress that I contacted the police in the town of Wasaga Beach to get them to check on her. I also compiled a list of phone numbers of friends, neighbours, ministers, and therapists. I spoke to her children, who were all teenagers and still lived with her, and tried to alert them to the dangers.

Belle wanted to see her husband charged, but when she asked her daughter, Rena, to report him to the police, Rena refused and responded with some questions.

Such as: "How can you ask me to do something you can't do? What has anyone ever done about your father?"

I can only surmise what was going through Belle's mind during all of this. I assume she decided to show Rena that she could do something about her own violation. At the end of October, she contacted the RCMP in West Hawk Lake and told them our father had sexually abused her as a child. Now, larger forces were at work. It was no longer a choice of handling things, or keeping this under control, or ignoring it.

At first, I doubted if the police out there would take her seriously. Maybe I wished they wouldn't. Second, West Hawk Lake was a small community, less than 200 full-time residents. I thought the local police might look the other way and assume, as some of us were saying, "It wasn't that bad."

To my amazement, in December the RCMP set to work on Belle's allegations. Jock's abuse of Shannon was not that long ago. They decided the years of combined transgressions were "bad enough" to lay charges.

After Belle reported her abuse, emotional distances amongst some siblings tripled, and, for some, the relationships ended. Others called and talked about the upcoming festive season as if the police investigation never existed. Joan even sent presents for our children. Although I didn't send them back, I chucked them in the garbage after Christmas.

The Mounties began interviewing members of my family before, and shortly after, the holidays. We did not know who would be called upon next, and we most certainly had no idea how each other responded.

We didn't go to West Hawk Lake for Christmas. And most people in my family stayed away from me. Except for the winter when I travelled in Greece, this was the first year that I did not elbow up to the long table at my parents' house.

But television, newspapers, and sales flyers continued to remind me about the importance of family connections, especially now, in the holiday season. I decided, right then, that this constant buttressing of the myth of "happy families" is the number one reason why more incest is not reported.

From Saskatchewan, Robin went out to West Hawk Lake. He sat down one-on-one with Jock and told him that once the police knew about his sexual activities with his daughters, they were probably going to act. Jock could expect a visit from them any day. After that, Robin drove the hour and a half to our house.

He recapped his conversation at West Hawk and told me Jock and Joan had planned to leave Manitoba. He looked so sad, so subdued, so disappointed, so empty.

Wendy and Bill had arrived about an hour and a half before Robin. While we sat on couches, digesting the turkey and the enormity of what was happening, the phone rang. I answered it. My youngest brother, Tom, had learned about Robin's visit.

Tom spoke so loudly everyone could hear him. He said, "Oh, and a Merry Christmas to you. I want to warn you, Donna, and Robin too. If you put my Dad in jail, there's going to be trouble. I'll put David in jail. You guys better watch out. You can't do this . . ."

This juxtaposition of Christmas greetings and threats and news that David might go to jail summed up the paradox of our situation. Once, we were family; now we were adversaries.

I handed the phone to Robin, who wanted to talk to Tom. He explained the facts behind his visit with Jock. Wendy also spoke to Tom. I left the living room to put Bradley to bed, so I didn't hear the whole conversation, but neither Robin nor Wendy seemed to be making much headway. Judging from their loud exchanges, he was still pissed off. He accused David of molesting him as a child. I had no prior knowledge of this but it didn't surprise me. Children with parents who do not respect sexual boundaries often abuse each other.

In Tom's mind, David's actions meant we should not be doing what we were doing. I didn't expect to hear such anger directed at us and the victims painted as villains.

We huddled together that night, afraid to even think of what would happen next. Wendy and Bill left later in the evening. Robin stayed for two more days. We had long discussions about the issue. I told Robin, "We do not *have* to forgive, or forget. Jock needs to forgive himself and look inside himself. He might die if he saw the evil inside."

New Year's came and went. My oldest sister, Jean, invited us to her place but we didn't go. She had been at West Hawk for Christmas with her husband and kids. I did not have the energy to deal with Jean pushing for a truce.

On January 3, 1993, an officer from the Lac du Bonnet RCMP phoned to invite me to visit their detachment. He called when Wendy and Bill were visiting again. We all assumed it was Robin on the line. The officer said he wanted to discuss something that could be better dealt with in person. We arranged a time to meet the next day. While I was on the phone with the cop, the thought occurred to me—Wendy probably wanted to hear it would all be forgotten.

The next day, Petchie offered to take me to the police station, but I declined. I drove into town, half crying. Every passing scene slid by in slow motion. Only my breathing sped up. I noticed every little detail along the way: snowbanks, potholes, gas stations, cars, hydro poles.

Constable Kingsbury came out to greet me. Lac du Bonnet has only around 2,500 permanent residents, in both the town and the rural municipality, so I knew the police officer and played ringette and hockey with the receptionist. I imagined she wanted to ask questions, given the expression on our faces.

I mumbled, "How's your horse?"

She replied, "He's fat."

Kingsbury escorted me into a private room. He started to talk and I started to cry, sweat, and shake. He remained quiet and composed. I was sure the receptionist could hear me. And there was no Kleenex. He jumped up to get some. The receptionist looked up again. I tried to shrink back into the chair. Her dad owned the local newspaper. I imagined the headlines.

"Local Woman Spills Childhood Secrets"

The tissues arrived. Kingsbury didn't ask much more. He quietly said, "There have been allegations made by your sister, Belle Puloski, about your father, Jock Tod, sexually assaulting you and your sisters, and physically assaulting your deceased mother. Would you like to make a statement about this?"

I said, "Yes"—loudly, quickly.

Kingsbury offered to give me time to go home and write up my statement. But he made it clear that I did not have to do this. He also made it clear he understood what a difficult thing it was. His empathy bewildered me. I had expected worse.

I drove home in a blur. On the one hand, I knew the repercussions would ripple out for years. On the other hand, I had been waiting all my life for someone to ask me this exact question. I stumbled into the house and Warren's arms.

I said, "Kingsbury wants to come by after supper to pick up my statement and go over it with me. I feel like vomiting."

Warren asked, "How will you live with yourself if you don't tell the truth now?"

Warren happened to be a lawyer. Although he was not a criminal lawyer, his logic kept me on track. I sat down and started writing, brief and factual.

Then Warren said, "I need to go to a council meeting."

"I want you here with me."

Either I didn't ask the right way or he did not see my fear. His ride showed up and he left.

Kingsbury arrived and we went into Warren's office. He looked over what I had written.

I had asked Allison to try and keep Bradley upstairs and quiet. Ten minutes into the interview, they burst into Warren's ground level law office. Bradley wanted to see the policeman. He loved shiny boots and uniforms. Kingsbury clutched my statement to his chest, as if to shield my children. Once Bradley had a good look, Allison convinced him to go back upstairs and read a book with her.

I still felt queasy, but thankful the officer had suggested doing this at home. He explained some things and then wrote down my answers to the questions he asked, at the end.

My statement began with "Name, address, phone, occupation, date and place taken."

My father sexually molested me when I was a child. He would invite me to sit on his lap while he watched television. After he pulled out his penis, and put my hand on it, he would try to make me rub it. He used a blanket to cover us. He would pull down my pants and insert his penis between my legs. It was a routine thing while watching television. Members of my family, including my mother, were present.

Because we had such a large family, three of the girls slept together. He would come into bed with us, grabbing and fondling whoever was not quick enough to get out of his way. I remember trying to peel him off my older sisters many times. We would all swear and hit at him. These incidents often took place in the morning.

My mother died when I was fourteen. He was physically and emotionally abusive to her as far back as I can remember. I saw him grab her head and break her nose on the arm of an armchair. He also broke her wrist. There were many other incidents similar to this. After my mother died, he would climb into bed when I was sleeping. Sometimes I managed to push him out of bed and get away. These assaults usually occurred in the mornings, especially on weekends.

I was physically assaulted several times and ordered out of the house several times, as a teenager. When I was younger, he would often beat me with belts and other objects. When I was seventeen years old, my father remarried, and the sexual assaults stopped (for me, at least). The physical assaults did not.

QUESTION: Can you recall what time span this occurred over?

ANSWER: Around age six or seven until I was about sixteen or seventeen years of age—from 1960 until 1970.

QUESTION: How often did these incidents occur when your dad would sit you on his knee watching television?

ANSWER: At least once a week—it happened more in the winter than in the summer months. My dad was a timber cutter and he had a sawmill and he worked while there was still sunlight in the summer months.

QUESTION: Was there any incidents of physical abuse where your dad bruised or cut you or your brothers or your sisters that you recall?

ANSWER: I have dentures and he would hit me hard enough to break them. My glasses were also broken.

QUESTION: Can you recall your dad's state at the time of these assaults?

ANSWER: Sometimes he was drinking but other times he was not.

QUESTION: Can you recall if anyone ever told the authorities about these incidents?

ANSWER: No. To my knowledge they were never reported.

QUESTION: Do you know of any incidents involving your dad having sex with animals?

ANSWER: No.

QUESTION: What are your feelings about what you would like to see happen with this investigation?

ANSWER: I don't want to see him go to jail but I don't want to see him get away with it.

We stood up. It seemed as if he was going to leave but he kept talking. I asked him if he thought I was a stool pigeon. He told me it seemed crimes were committed and Jock deserved to be punished. Everything moved in slow motion.

After the police officer left, the now familiar physical sensations threatened to shatter me—pacing, heart racing, gasping for breath. I did not sleep that night, or many after that. I began locking the door every evening.

Warren came home after I put the kids to bed. All he wanted to talk about was the business development meeting. I did not give a shit.

12

A NAMELESS FEAR FILLED ME FOR DAYS. I IMAGINED Jock and Joan were in West Hawk Lake sticking voodoo pins in me. A bolt of lightning would strike our house.

I asked myself—what if someone abused my kids? Why can't I summon the same sense of injustice for my own past?

My brother David told me Jock called him "Judas." I wanted to scream and bang my head against the fireplace. How dare he compare? Jock was no saint or saviour.

I thought about the commandment, "Honour thy mother and father." King Lear returned again and again to my mind. Were all of the sisters "unnatural hags"? Was he an old man "more sinned against than sinning"? What were the worst repercussions?

Disinheritance: Jock shed money like water, so no loss here.

Excommunication: Certain individuals wouldn't speak to me again.

Violence: Jock would probably not risk it but disgruntled siblings might.

Bad reputation: Most people seemed more interested in daily routines than old crimes.

What did I want? To tell and be believed; to see remorse and change. Was this realistic? A parent's normal reaction would be to want to kill the person who molested his or her child. Ergo, he might mouth one of his shotguns and pull the trigger.

After making the statement, I felt as if my skin was still getting peeled off layer by layer. I feared if I started crying it would never dry up.

I heard through the network of siblings that Jock and Joan had disappeared. No one admitted to knowing where they went. This departure caused panic. Our father hated to sleep in a strange bed, or eat bad food, or leave his recliner. The phone calls started up again and questions buzzed across the lines.

"What have we done? How would they live? What will they do for money?"

So . . . the offender received the sympathy. The victims received the blame, for we had "driven them out" and "made it impossible for them to live in their home."

How did I know? Joan wrote a letter to Wendy damning our behaviour. And Joan knew Wendy would relay her message to the rest.

The offended parties did not stay away too long. After spending most of January travelling in parts unknown, they returned. As expected, Jock and Joan got sympathy from certain siblings. People in the community saw it as no more than a winter jaunt for two snowbirds; they deserved a little sun.

As for myself, I did not care about the refugees fleeing from our "conspiracy." Even Bradley didn't use the tactic of "I'll run away from home" too much nowadays.

13

AFTER I MADE MY STATEMENT TO THE POLICE, life catapulted onto a huge roller coaster. I often scribbled long into the night. One of the Mounties told us there was a court order that prohibited the offender from having contact with the witnesses. He also advised us not to get together for any more family meetings with Esther and Karen, to prevent accusations of collusion and conspiracies against the offender. However, I still spoke with siblings and friends on the phone. But we did not talk about the specific physical details of our abuse.

I needed a counsellor, but finding one in a small town stumped me. I did not know where to look. On the one hand, if I used a local person, I could not be assured confidences would be honoured. On the other hand, I did not want to take a whole day and go to Winnipeg. Childcare was also a challenge. And we lived on a single income. Spending money on emotional problems felt frivolous.

Also, finding someone who knew how to deal specifically with sexual abuse proved challenging. At first, I met with the local mental health worker. He told me, "You seem to be doing the right things," but he could not suggest anything more. I assumed he had not encountered anyone who had been abused—an absurd idea, in retrospect.

Visiting the public health nurse at the Lac du Bonnet Clinic was an option, but not ideal. She held various New Age beliefs I didn't understand, involving crystals and chakras. I convinced myself it would do for now.

One night, I sat in my kitchen, writing, and weeping. Warren came in, told me he had another meeting, and he wanted supper right away. He said I needed to adjust to the facts and concentrate on the present and important things. Then he dashed out of the house. I felt abandoned, like all he wanted was to get away from me.

I also felt guilty. What about all the violence in the Middle East and the Third World? I was not starved, shot, or tortured. What right did I have to dwell on this? I saw Warren less and less because of council business. Mostly, I hung around with Fran, another friend from Lac du Bonnet, and Petchie, and kept both updated every day. Fran was a stay-at-home mom who had been present that night when I birthed my truth in the women's sharing circle.

I worried about wearing out Petchie and Fran. A few times, I made the mistake of telling people who didn't want to know. Some recoiled, some backed right out of my life, and one woman told me straight out that I was crazy. Other friends fluctuated between repulsed and frustrated. A typical telling went like this.

"I need to tell you something."

"What's the matter? If you don't want me to use your photocopier, just say it."

"My father sexually assaulted me and all my sisters. He will probably be charged."

"Ohhhhh . . ."

Finally I summoned the courage to phone up my childhood friend. One detail I noted throughout this crisis—the longer I knew the person, the harder it was to tell, and the difficulty doubled if the individual knew Jock, Joan, and my siblings.

This friend, Barb, was "best woman" at our wedding. She lived at a resort on Falcon Lake, about ten kilometres from my home. In our younger years, we spent many hours together, swimming, climbing trees, pretending we were cowboys. During university, we roomed together and even ran a painting business and did construction jobs together. Barb had become a journeyman carpenter and stayed in the area to marry and raise her three children.

We shared a special, tragic bond. When I was in grade eight, Barb's father suffered a fatal heart attack. The following year, my mother died. Barb's mother ran their family's resort on her own for a season but sold the next spring and moved her three teenagers back to Souris, her hometown. However, every summer, Barb returned to West Hawk to work in campgrounds, resorts, and contracting businesses.

Barb said, "I'm not surprised. One night, I was waiting for you to change out of your horsey clothes, sitting in the front seat of your family's station wagon. He
attacked me. I jumped into the back seat. I didn't tell my
mother. I wondered why you hadn't visited West Hawk
at Christmas."

I summarized the details, still troubled by fear and
guilt. Now people in West Hawk would know. Barb reassured me it was definitely not my fault in any way, shape,
or form, and urged me to call again.

On March 3, 1993, Wendy phoned to say the police
had officially charged John Norris Tod with sexual
assault. She sounded small, distant, and scared.

When I told Warren, he said, "You need to put all
your family's messages into perspective. I heard about a
young guy who was threatened by his relatives because
he planned to testify against them. The police charged
them for interfering with due process."

Even though I heard Warren, I could not respond.
I only stared.

He looked at me and sighed. "The police must have
enough evidence, or else they wouldn't have laid charges.
Several of your brothers and sisters must have said
something incriminating. Any lawyer with any brains
or conscience would tell Jock to plead guilty as quickly
as possible. It would be easier, financially, physically, and
emotionally, for everyone."

The next day, around 10:00 a.m., I called Petchie,
explained what had happened, and cried. At 10:30, I
cried with the health nurse at the clinic. I discovered
two things. First, I was still terrified about betraying

Jock. Second, I was inexplicably glad about what was happening.

Barb phoned after lunch to reassure me I was doing the right thing. We discussed the cross-country ski trip we had organized months earlier. Barb, her husband and children, along with several families from West Hawk, had planned to visit a cross-country ski resort in Minnesota. Because most of the folks going knew my entire family, I felt panicked. What would they think?

I picked up Allison after school and ran some more errands. At 5:00 p.m., while we ate, the phone rang. Shannon, my youngest sister, had questions about the legal process. After Shannon hung up, Petchie phoned to express concern about the morning phone call. She thought I sounded unglued. Around 10:00 p.m., my sister Jean called, scared and upset. Her kids had given her flack about the charges. I listened again.

Around 11:00 p.m., I talked to Warren about what Shannon and Jean said, and wondered aloud about organizing another family meeting. Warren said the prosecutors needed a chance to build their case. If we all got together and started trading stories, the outcome might be compromised. We were already being accused of a conspiracy and another meeting would add fuel to that theory.

I fell asleep. In total, I had spent over ten hours talking to people. I slept for two hours, woke up, could not get back to sleep. I started to write. After an hour of writing, I had decided:

1. Everyone except the offender was taking care of business and doing the dirty work.

2. He ceased to be a father the instant he laid a hand on us. He was just a sperm donor.

3. I did not own his shame.

4. Not going to Maplelag (the cross-country ski resort) would only give him power. We had planned the trip for over a year.

14

DESPITE MY MISGIVINGS, THE NEXT DAY, I packed up our swimsuits, winter outerwear, and cross-country skis. We hauled the dog to the dog hotel, piled into the four-wheel van, and headed south for five hours. When we got closer to Maplelag, both Warren and I forgot the exact route and started yelling. We arrived around six-thirty. All of the people in the group of twenty-five were out skiing. After we settled in our shared cabin, we looked around the lodge. The skiers returned; their greetings raised a lump in my throat.

Alec, a friend of over twenty years, hugged me. He said quietly, "How are you, Donna?"

"I think I'm glad to be here."

"Well, that's important. I'm glad you're here."

Barb repeated, as she squeezed me, long and hard, "His shame is not your shame. It is not your fault."

None of the others revealed if they knew; they just greeted us happily. I didn't know some of the people. However, one of them, the teacher at West Hawk Lake, had spent many hours with Jock and Joan. Now married, he did not visit them as much. I thought, what did he think of the situation? Did he even know? I lacked the courage to ask.

Alec's wife, Theresa, talked to me at length. Their construction company employed my brother Tom. I had worked as a carpenter's helper for them, before marriage and children. While we sat in the hot tub and drank weak American beer, she said, "People don't think about you and your siblings the way they see your father. I hate talking to him. He never fails to insult or put down someone."

The homestyle food was tasty and the skiing invigorated me. Often, I went out alone, early and late, stabbing the snow. Barb had hired a teenager to watch her three kids so she could ski more often. This young woman offered to watch Bradley. Unfortunately, she took her eyes off him in the hot tub. He submerged, and came up scared. Then he fell down the stairs in the cabin and almost landed on the cast iron woodstove. During my massage at the main lodge, he fell again and chipped his tooth. He had more accidents in three days than he had in his whole life. A paranoid notion reoccurred—was I being punished?

Past midnight, after skiing for hours, I sauntered down to the sauna with Barb and another woman from West Hawk. I spotted our friend Margie with her still-perky breasts standing by the hole in the ice. I shucked off my clothes. Going into the sauna and ice-cold water, naked, with the guys reassured me. Not every man was out of control and dangerous.

But one fellow in our group bothered me. I didn't know him and he told many lewd and misogynist jokes. Finally, the teacher's wife, a woman from Japan, who misunderstood his words, but understood his intent, reamed him out. I felt a shudder of relief. But I asked myself, if it upset me, why didn't I tell him?

We sang in the talent show, danced, and laughed. Soaked in the hot tub and jumped through the ice hole. Perfect weather, perfect snow, valued friends, almost a full moon, and delicious meals, not cooked by me. Allison "took the plunge" through the hole in the ice eight times. Both kids loved the group experience and the atmosphere of Maplelag restored my battered faith in humans. On Sunday, we said our farewells and headed north to Canada in a convoy of minivans.

15

ON APRIL 4, AT 10 P.M., MY OLDEST SISTER, JEAN, phoned. She kept talking, focused on how busy she was. After about ten minutes, she stopped and said, "I called Joan. She told me she was angry and depressed."

"Sounds reasonable. Joan has burned most of her emotional supports."

Jean said, "The RCMP arrived, put him in handcuffs, and took fingerprints. The local magistrate was there. She's known us for years. What would she tell everyone?"

"You're saying that like it's the worst part of this situation."

I pictured Jock shuffling into the room where they take mug shots. Did they push him around?

Jean said, "He's hired Harvey Pollock to defend him."

I cursed under my breath. Anything Pollock touched ended up in the newspapers. How would he get paid? And why was I worried? If the punishment needs to fit the crime, it was appropriate that the client fit the lawyer. This call made me question the wisdom of answering the phone at night. After dark, people panicked, unable to handle the slightest tension.

She interrupted my inner monologue. "We're going to West Hawk Lake for Easter. Joan is really happy."

"Did I ever tell you how those 'divide and conquer' tactics make me puke?"

I stopped talking and thought about West Hawk. It was no longer neutral territory.

Jean said, "Wendy is in Joan's bad books. She's very angry with her."

I asked, "What about me and you? But who's really to blame here?"

"Well, I don't know. Life goes on."

"What does that mean?"

"We have a cottage out there. We've got to get on with our lives."

Jean's silent message: "Forget, forget."

Then I remembered that Warren had repeatedly pointed out that the Crown attorneys knew Jock's age and must have weighed that factor. The legal system worked the way it did for many proven reasons.

The next day, Wendy phoned to tell me that she and Bill planned to visit his brother in Vancouver. She sounded more strained. Tom had phoned to warn her not to visit Joan or come out to "the lake" any more. He had said he wondered how we could do this to our father and she had said she wondered how our father could do this to us.

This exchange demonstrated how the communication in my family worked. Instead of Joan telling Wendy, she told Tom to tell her. That way, she didn't have to listen to Wendy's logic or anger. It was also an indirect warning from Jock—shunning, the ultimate punishment, could be used.

On April 8, 1993, I got this notice from the RCMP at Falcon Lake:

This letter is to advise you that John Norris Tod has been charged with several counts of indecent assault as well as other offences relating to the investigation on which you were interviewed. For your information, John Tod is presently prohibited from certain things under a court order. One specific prohibition is to not have any contact with you. We anticipate his first court appearance will be in mid-April, 1993. Should you have any questions or concerns regarding this matter, contact us.

When I asked Warren about the charges being called "indecent assault" instead of "sexual assault," he said Jock was being charged with the definitions that existed when he committed the crimes. Indecent assault seemed minor to me. Why all the denial?

I phoned Jean, maybe to gloat a bit. She had claimed this criminal charge wouldn't really happen. Despite multiple requests from the police, she still hadn't made a statement. Right away, she stated how surprised she was that Wendy was able to extricate herself from the family quicksand, despite the fact that Wendy had lived with Joan much longer and even called her "Mom." Then she told me she had phlebitis.

I said, "I'm sorry. But why can't you make a statement?"

"I can't do what you are doing. I'm not strong."

She hung up.

I sat and stared at the phone. All of Jean's excuses came up empty and sour for me. She was my oldest sister and I had often looked to her for support. But I could not rely on her any more. Not only that, every word was probably reported back to Joan.

Then I remembered the incident before my wedding. In 1981, the year of the national postal strike, Warren and I got married. I had just returned from six months backpacking in Europe and Israel. The wedding was planned for August, but the mail was still not moving, so I phoned people to invite them.

For a few years, before they bought their own cottage, Jean and her family spent their summers in the lower suite of Jock's lakeside cabin. Two weeks before the wedding, they invited me for supper. Joan and Jock were also there. The men relaxed after the meal; the women cleaned up. In the screened porch, Jock complained about my handling of the invitations; he insisted certain relatives had to be present.

"We'll invite who we want," I said, loud enough for him to hear.

He stood up and charged me. In my hands, I held a small frying pan. I swung it at his head. He staggered. Jean's husband pinned Jock's arms behind his back and dragged him into the porch. Joan shouted. They escorted Jock back to the big house up the hill. I stayed overnight on the small, lumpy futon. I didn't sleep much. Going up to the big house was out of the question. Instead, I reflected on my travels, my husband-to-be, my upcoming wedding, and my new job.

Next morning, Jock did not appear but Joan told me I had to move out, pronto. I phoned Warren, loaded my horse into the trailer, and piled my clothes into the back of my half-ton. None of my siblings dared help. Warren arrived and helped load the last boxes.

Just before we drove off, Jean came out of the house. "Goodbye. I hope it works out."

"I am so fucking angry with that bastard. He could go to jail a hundred times for all the things he's done."

"What do you mean? What things?"

"You know what I'm talking about."

"Shut up. And get out of here, as soon as you can."

The rain started. No one else said a word to me. Thirteen kilometres down the bumpy road, the trailer came unhitched. We stopped and hooked it up; horse and trailer were not damaged. I stayed with Warren for the two weeks before the wedding. At the last minute, Joan told me Jock would walk me down the aisle.

At that time, I was upset with Jean for telling me to shut up and leave. And she was still telling me to shut up. Over the next three and a half years, Jean fought hard to preserve the silence.

16

PETCHIE CONTINUED TO VISIT OFTEN, PHONE twice a day, and send cards filled with vows of friendship. I appreciated her support, but our relationship felt unequal. I had the problems. She had the answers. I decided I needed to find a listener who would be present to simply hear the pain, and wait, and not interject.

Although I worried about spending money on travel and fees, I had discovered there were conferences and retreats and support groups for sexually abused women. My first chance to attend one came when the health nurse signed up for a day-long workshop in Winnipeg. She decided she had chicken pox, so she offered me her spot.

It opened up a new world. I had never heard about many of the theories, treatments, and authorities. The first session was "Working Creatively with Anger," a chance to identify and understand anger, and to find unique, non-violent expressions. Although I was not used to guided meditations, they calmed me. When asked to visualize a safe place, I imagined sprawling face down on our dock in the summer sun with Bradley and Allison.

Then the facilitator asked us to visualize an angry scene and an ally who would have helped. The old, cramped house where I lived as a child appeared in my mind. Jock sat in his recliner in front of the fireplace. My mother sat on the side of the hearth, warming her back. They argued. Trying to be big and small at the same time, I jumped up from the other side of the hearth and yelled. Jock grabbed my mother's head and smashed her nose on the arm of the chair. It made a sound like watermelon dropping. Blood sprayed across her face.

A wolf with bristling ruff and bared fangs stepped into the memory and lunged at his throat. Then she dragged his body outside, leaving us to tend to our mother's broken face. Although this imagined scene scared me, it captured the fear and helplessness I often felt. A raging wolf was exactly what we needed.

In the rest of the workshop, we threw things, moved around, howling, swearing, kicking, and scribbling pictures. We wrote angry letters, similar to my first angry letter to my abuser, but shorter. Since the morning, my whole body had felt tight, with a pounding headache, but the tension eased.

The facilitator talked about the kinds of anger, hidden and expressed, and the uses of anger. She told us that expressing our feelings allowed others to take responsibility for their actions. She taught us some non-violent, creative ways to access our anger. Over the course of the day, I began to feel more relaxed, even playful. Some of the exercises resembled games I might try with my children.

During the last session, before lunch, the leader started to sing. I had stretched out on my stomach, chin resting on my hands, thinking about whether her last name "Wisechild" was real or invented.

"How could anyone ever tell you
You were anything less than beautiful
How could anyone ever tell you
You were anything less than whole?"

The next moment, I sobbed into the carpet. These words had somehow scorched my sensitivities. But I hated to cry in front of sixty strangers.

In the afternoon, the women reassembled in a large room. At the end of the session, I stood up and said, "I'm looking for people who have been sexually abused by a parent and have been involved with the court system. Has anyone had charges laid and had a trial?"

Every woman stared at me. Even though I had heard many stories of incest and assaults during the day, no one answered. After a minute or so, a single hand shot up.

"Was it your father?" I asked.

"No, my uncle. He was charged, but it was dropped."

My stomach sank. I had really wanted to connect with someone. I looked around, hoping to find another hand. The workshop leader glanced at me. She said, "Those who share this history can meet after the session ends. This is not something I'm prepared to discuss here and now."

The conference ended. Still reeling with disappointment, I turned away and prepared for the long drive home. Two questions spun around in my head. Why didn't more women view this as a crime? What else was a more appropriate expression of non-violent anger?

Throughout the following years, at workshops and conferences, I met hundreds of women who had been sexually abused but did not report. Much later, I found out that 90 percent of women do not report sexual assaults.

I had to admit, before Belle went to the police, I used to think that way.

17

THEY WERE RIGHT. LIFE WENT ON. WARREN'S sister had her first baby and Bradley decided to take an interest in peeing on his own. He talked, counted, and pretended to read.

Allison raced toward puberty. Her personality altered, with mood swings and withdrawal. The slightest upset caused both mother and daughter to weep. Her teacher told me she was concerned. I told the teacher about my crisis.

I decided to sell my horse, Chester. Too often, when I rode alone, he whinnied and pranced because he missed our other horse. I liked to ride to sort things out, but I could not relax on such a horse. At seventeen hands, he was a handsome mount and I knew I would miss him.

As the months went by, I recognized how draining and stressful it was for my siblings, at least the ones who still contacted me. Wendy sounded sad and quiet. Robin sounded depressed. David struggled with the demands of his teaching job. Shannon mourned the loss of another set of parents.

If I spent any time with a person, I felt uncomfortable until I told them about my father. Some listened and did not venture an opinion. Some stated flat out that it was not what they wanted to hear.

One friend said, "This must be hard for you. You don't have to talk about it."

I said, "Sounds as if it's hard for you to hear about it."

"I can't even watch the news. I don't like to think about things that don't affect my family."

Others listened, made Christian affirmations of sympathy. Many told me to get on with my life. Their comments felt as helpful as ambulance attendants telling a person in a car crash to stop hemorrhaging.

On the other hand, some people amazed me. The kindergarten teacher at the local school astounded me. She got infuriated when I told her and her fury uplifted my spirit.

Others, usually women, bolstered me with their support and caring. But I had to learn to stop second-guessing myself. What people did with my revelation was up to them. If nothing else, maybe it helped them to know abuse was not only found in the movie of the week or welfare cases. Real people got abused. It happened in the best of families.

18

AT THE BEGINNING OF MAY, A FRIEND VISITED and we talked, at my house, long into the night. The moon hung full and warm, the frogs croaked a loud chorus. Light rippled over the river, the ice long gone. The water slid by, a liquid sheet of glass. The friend left.

Restless and still wide awake, I decided to take the dog for a run, first riding my bike, then riding my horse. This would be my last chance for a moonlight outing with the big gelding. I briefly regretted my decision to sell him. It didn't matter; a young woman interested in a dressage horse had borrowed a trailer and was coming next week to pick him up.

I went inside and called Petchie. We talked until 3:00 a.m. It seemed weird to phone so late, but she insisted that I call any time. She had stayed up many nights with me.

I hung up and stared out at the brilliant moon, toying with ideas and actions. Should I call the RCMP in West Hawk Lake to find out what's going on? Should I write letters to all my relatives to tell them about how my father abused me, and to explain what I needed?

On May 16, after Sunday school, Allison wanted to ride Peanut, our pony. I walked alongside the two of them. When we returned, Warren met me halfway down the stairs and said he wanted to talk to me alone. For a few seconds, I wondered if one of the grandfathers had passed on. Then he explained that Barb had phoned a few minutes ago.

Jock and Joan's house had burnt to the ground. It had started while they were at church. After Jock's errant behaviours became public, he started attending a fundamentalist church. Prior to this, he regarded churchgoers as major jokes.

My friend Barb called this particular institution, "the Church of Hate."

As a small community, West Hawk Lake struggled to support its single house of worship, a United Church, year-round. A couple of years earlier, a Baptist layperson had been hired to lead services for the winter. Every week, he preached homophobic messages. The church leaders pointed out that his sermons contradicted their same-sex stance and fired him. In retaliation, he started his own church, taking his anti-gay followers with him. Jock now supported him wholeheartedly.

I phoned her for details about the fire. She told me that Tom had panicked and called an ambulance. Then she informed me that Beverley, the local postmistress, who ran the store and post office across the road from Jock and Joan's former house, said she was not surprised, but wondered why everyone waited so long. Much later, she would face a part of this dilemma herself.

Barb said, "The news of the fire spread much more quickly than the news about Jock's abuse. I don't know why. I've been telling lots of people."

I said, "Yeah, I've noticed how reluctant some are to talk about it."

This reticence baffled me. Friends refused to discuss it without my permission. For example, I'd tell a wife and assume she'd tell her spouse. I'd tell one friend, hoping I'd be spared the energy it took to tell the other. At first, it seemed Warren's family would rather have their tongues pulled out than talk to me. It remained unspeakable. Therefore, I felt unspeakable.

Barb said that people believed it was malicious to tell. I explained to her how it felt like I had been carrying a huge bag of stones all my life. Now, every person I told got a rock. If they accepted it, they could choose what they wanted to do with it—throw it at the offender, or throw it away. It made my load lighter.

Wendy phoned after I talked to Barb. The two dogs, an Irish setter and a cocker spaniel, had died in the fire. As she talked, memories of house parties, Christmas crowds, Thanksgiving meals, Easter egg hunts, and family weddings overwhelmed me. I started to choke up. But, when I thought about it, for me, the house and the people had disappeared after Wendy's wedding. The fire made it complete. Everything was wiped out, clean. The beds and the bedrooms were gone too. I liked that.

I asked, "Did Jock and Joan have insurance?"

Wendy said, "If they did, the company will inspect the remains closely. They tried to sell the house after the trip to the States. No one showed any interest—too old and too big, with a homemade pool attached."

"Barb told me people are saying he did it to get sympathy."

Wendy said, "I want to see the damage. I'll ask David to go with me."

She didn't ask me. I told her to look after herself. I think I said I loved her. I didn't want to go to West Hawk.

I phoned Robin in the afternoon. He was worried about being transferred, because of his job, and having to sell his house, so this latest loss hit him hard. He sighed frequently and repeated, "You're kidding; you're kidding."

He told me he had attended the wedding of my third-oldest sister's stepdaughter, in Alberta. Joan had been there but would not talk to or look at him. I felt responsible for this shunning. If only I hadn't. Hadn't what?

Jean called around 11:00 p.m. She talked at half-speed. One thing I learned from all these late-night calls was "the voice of trauma." The person mumbled slowly, almost inaudibly, like a shy, scared child. I dreaded that sound. It usually meant an hour or two of conversation. I felt compelled to listen, even if I burst into sobbing after I hung up. Maybe I could have shown more of my pain to them. Not just to my friends and husband and children. But I didn't. Not enough, anyway.

Jean moaned about Jock's great loss. Once again, I wondered if I was a monster for not feeling sympathetic, but I knew I did not want to be sucked back into his sphere of influence. She also informed me Belle was dating a man ten years younger. My mind drifted off. I was falling asleep on the phone.

The house fire forced me to face the issue of forgiveness.

Like Wendy and Jean, I felt torn. Unlike Wendy and Jean, I stayed away and did not rush to sort through the ashes. The image of Jock picking through the charred rubble, kicking at the ashes, pointing at the skeletons of the two dogs huddled under the stairs, twigged my deepest guilt. After all, we had food, horses, trips, educations.

Then the new voice kicked in. Did any of these things justify what he did?

A few devoted churchgoers stated to me that I would never be whole until I forgave Jock. However, when asked, they admitted they had not been sexually abused, and insisted they had happy families. They also forgot that Jock failed to show remorse. And we had forgiven him for decades and look where it landed us. He had abused Shannon because we had all "turned the other cheek" for years.

What about the damage now being inflicted? Belle had lost her marriage and her image of being able to protect her daughter. What about Shannon, physically abused in her original family, then adopted by Joan and Jock, ostensibly a "good" family, and then sexually, and physically, abused? Weren't Belle's and Shannon's pain important?

After the fire, Robin confronted me during a phone call. "I believe in the part of the Lord's Prayer which says 'as we forgive the trespasses of others.' I do this because I consider myself a Christian."

Flipping open *The Courage to Heal*, I read him the line about survivors only needing to forgive themselves. Maybe Robin didn't believe this concept because it didn't fit with his Christian compassion, but I had started to believe it. After he hung up, I reread the section on forgiveness. It gave me the courage to phone Karen, the minister who had helped us in the previous fall with the family meetings.

She said, "It's not your job. You don't have to see anybody you don't want to see. Your feelings about Jock are not 'unchristian.' Wendy will do what she needs to do."

Her next comment, about Christ on the cross, startled me. "Jesus said 'Father, forgive them' . . . not 'I forgive you.' He was, at that moment, in too much pain to forgive. You will be hurting for the next while. Jock needs to own his sins. Until he can do that, there won't be any movement, any noticeable changes in your family."

I knew I wanted to talk to her more.

19

ON MAY 19, WENDY, JEAN, AND I ATTENDED AN evening presentation, given by Laura Bass, one of the authors of *The Courage to Heal*. Over 300 people showed up; I felt reassured to see so many women who perhaps shared our history.

The next morning, I counted up the total of my disclosures; I had told forty people. Then there were the sixty or so women at the anger workshop, so that made it more like 100. I needed to tell, not only for myself, but for my children. I encouraged others to tell.

On Friday, a warm spring day with a light breeze, some long-time friends arrived for lunch. We sat outside and drank beer and talked. I told them about my father's prosecution. Petchie joined us for dessert. These women didn't ask too many questions, but somehow I felt more human. After 3:00 p.m., after everyone left, another friend showed up. Her first name was the same as mine so I called her "Donna P" to avoid confusion. She had wanted to come for lunch but she couldn't make it.

Right after I welcomed her, my brother John strode up the sidewalk. I had not seen him since the family meeting last fall at Wendy's house. I really wanted to talk to Donna P alone, but John opened the front door and entered without knocking. His presence felt like a cloud in the midst of all the absolute support. He did not offer any explanation or apology for appearing without warning.

Before her marriage, Donna P had worked with Joan, so I assumed she knew John. But she didn't. She looked at him and said, "Oh, you're the fellow I was supposed to marry. Joan always wanted to set us up together."

John asked Donna P what she did for a living.

I stifled a laugh.

"I investigate child abuse. I am a social worker for this area."

John did a double take and stared at me. But he agreed to stay for coffee. He sat down at the kitchen table, examining us like two small bugs. "Did you hear about the house?"

"Yes. What's happening?"

"I guess they will rebuild."

He didn't say anything more about that topic. Instead, he ranted about the condition of the ski trails during the past winter and the survival prospects of a West Hawk man who had suffered a heart attack. Then he began to tease and insult my son. Bradley did not like it. I did not like it. John left after twenty minutes.

After he departed, I explained the family situation to Donna P. She said she had thought I was unhappy to see her. Because of her job, she could offer unspecific insights on the legal process and her court experiences. I told her about John's position on the situation, and how he continued to leave his kids with Jock and Joan during the day.

"What? You ought to tell the social worker out there."

"I know. But a court order prohibits Jock from having any contact with me. So I'm afraid to phone Joan and ask if she's still babysitting. I really don't understand why John's wife allows it. Or maybe she doesn't know about the charges. Someone should . . ."

"What am I saying? I'm legally obligated to do that."

Donna P stayed to visit and went out for supper with us. Before she left, she promised to find out if the grandchildren were staying with Jock. Like her, I was surprised that the Falcon Lake police hadn't prohibited Jock from any contact with kids. But, in 1993, they may not have had much experience with this issue.

After she left, I faced the now-familiar waves of emotion. I felt disloyal and scared. I pictured Tom with his high-powered rifle at the front door. Warren had rushed off to a meeting. The kids were long ago in bed. Our English setter barked in her kennel and didn't stop.

I stared at the dark windows. Why did John want Joan to look after his kids? Then I remembered the second family meeting where he had grunted and barked when we talked about our abuse history. He hadn't denied any of it. When he got up to leave, Wendy, Jean, and I followed him to the door. He turned to us.

"There's just one thing I want to say . . . I'm sorry."

He had closed the door quickly and we stood and stared at each other. Jean said she thought he was sorry for punching her. Wendy thought he was sorry for not defending his sisters. I thought about the times he paid me a quarter to give him oral sex. I had wanted to run after him and punch him in the face.

At that meeting, John had kept saying how inconvenient these charges were. I agreed—doing the right thing is often inconvenient. His main concern seemed to be maintaining his image in West Hawk and maintaining his relationship with Joan. I could not count on him for anything.

Then it hit me. He had abused me. He couldn't acknowledge our father's crimes without acknowledging his own. And, as I was finding out, once the cards are on the table, we have to start dealing with them.

I'd forgotten to ask John, before he left, if he had made a statement to the police.

20

CHILDCARE AND WORK FOR WARREN KEPT ME going.

Although I knew I did not want to give in, this defiant stance took energy. I figured that I must have been the only one who had made a statement. Could I take back what I said?

Jock's reaction to the charges did not surprise me. But Joan's responses hurt.

My friend Margaret visited for coffee. She knew Joan through United Church connections. She sat down at my kitchen table and said, "Something's wrong with her. She divides people and hurts them. Why isn't she upset about what he did to Shannon? She cared for her, as a daughter, for fourteen years. How could Joan climb into bed with him?"

I explained how I was learning the hard way why more women didn't report sexual abuse. It was a "lose-lose" scenario. We would be damned if Jock went to jail and damned if he didn't.

Since the fire, David had not phoned and Wendy had not said anything. This family rupture hurt, as painful as divorce, but it was not just one person who had abandoned me; it was hordes—not only siblings, but in-laws, cousins, nieces, nephews. Relatives on the Tod side of the family owned eight cottages on West Hawk Lake, within short walking distance of Jock and Joan's place. Now that I no longer visited the enclave, I had ceased to exist.

I regretted that our plan to hold more sessions with Karen and Esther got sidetracked. This seemed the most positive path—all of us sitting together to tell what happened, how we felt about it, and what we wanted from the abuser.

On May 23, I taught Sunday school at the Lutheran church. But it was growing problematic. Constant references to "the Father" and forgiveness upset me. I almost burst out bawling when I heard the Lord's Prayer. Also, the Lutheran pastor poked fun at parents who spared the rod, lauding the "good old days." I did not feel I could approach him for any kind of support. He appeared to not recognize me when we met on the street, even though I had attended his church for five years, taught Sunday school for most of those years, and had invited his whole family over for supper.

Warren's mother called. She wanted us to come for a visit. I resented her invitation, her focus on my situation, and her refusal to acknowledge her own. She did not ask questions directly until I requested that she do so. When we visited, she treated me like an emotional volcano, ready to erupt. She watched my every move. Maybe she was scared I might do something drastic or bizarre, like crying, in front of her.

~

LATE AT NIGHT, I wrote in my journal. Since so many parts of my life seemed to be falling to pieces, I decided to list the positive bits.

I was still married. We had two healthy children. Many people cared for me. Our home was situated on a scenic riverfront. We could now go to new places, no longer stuck in the routine of always heading "to the lake." For example, on the May long weekend, we had gone to a horse show and a museum. We visited a wildlife centre where Bradley zoomed around the wide rooms, exclaiming about the fish, the snakes, the puzzles. He liked the elevator best of all. Allison examined all the exhibits carefully.

My social life no longer revolved around the West Hawk Lake cottage colony. These past months had given

me an understanding of how my family of origin oper-
ated. Most important of all, staying away from Jock felt
healthier, like I was finally an adult.

After I finished writing, I decided to go for a bike ride.
The half-moon glowed. It was bright enough to ride. The
light from the moon reflected off my helmet. When I
looked down at my shadow, it looked as if my head had
an aura shining from the top. This light reminded me of
Karen. She had talked about not lying, telling our real
stories. I wasn't so afraid any more.

Besides, I had my own halo. What else did I need?

21

IT WAS THE FIRST WEEK IN JUNE, ALMOST TEN
months since Wendy's wedding, and I still struggled
to figure out my true emotions. When I got agitated,
I ate or exercised. But I knew I needed to nourish my
"hollow soul" differently. Turned out, I was not the only
"hollow soul."

Warren and I had gone out for supper with friends
but got up early for coffee and conversation. The kids
slept late since they had not been ordered to bed at their
usual time by the teenage babysitter. About 8:00 a.m.,
a compact car drove up the lane to our house. We were
not expecting anyone. I walked out to greet the driver.

My brother David climbed out. The look on his face
spooked me. Had he slept in this tiny car for a month?
He approached and hugged me hard, shaking all over.

We talked out in the parking lot for twenty minutes. He explained how his life seemed to be falling apart and how he couldn't handle his job as a physical education teacher. His need to be alone was so strong he had snuck into a nearby picnic area and camped there for the night.

I was glad he had come, but he was so changed from his usual self I found it hard to look at him. He came inside the house. The kids were still in bed, so we had a chance to talk. David spoke for about half an hour, his voice breaking on every sentence. His opinion of Jock had fallen much further than mine. I did not love our father and he did not love me. But, because of David's dark good looks and athletic prowess, he was the favoured son.

I shared my own difficulties and told him I hoped he could hang in until the end of the school term. Teaching adolescents when suffering from trauma was like diving into a pool of piranhas.

After a while, the kids woke up. He joked and wrestled with them. They loved his playful spirit. During family gatherings, he was the uncle who tussled with nieces and nephews on the floor. He returned to the city shortly after the kids got up.

The next day, Allison and Warren attended church. My stomach churned at the thought of listening to that pastor. I stayed home and wondered—would I ever be able to go back? It took a while, but I finally managed to write a letter to David and send it.

Ever since your visit, I have been thinking about you. When you were younger, you had the most energy and optimism. I remember you bouncing up and down for hours, watching football. I got stuck with the mother role. I apologize for chasing you and making you do your chores.

I hadn't seen you since before Xmas. Your grief showed on your face. Maybe you saw the same hurt on mine. I admit I'm disappointed that more people are not as outraged as I want them to be. But this experience has forced me to figure out what really matters.

In mid-June, it started raining and did not let up. I bought another horse, a smaller mare. Although she seemed quiet, she was untrained. A colt came along with her; he had been born in a snowstorm and had a frost-damaged foot and ears. The kids adored him. Between the rain and the colt, the mare did not get much training. I halter-broke her and saddled her twice. I even rode her a bit. But the real work had to wait until next year.

Later in June, Warren's father had an operation and almost died. His cigarette addiction and poor circulation slowed his recovery. Ben decided to auction the junk from fifty years of running a garage. Warren kept leaving us to sort tools and pitch garbage. Every time he left, I cried. We shared a similar dysfunctional history; we had so much to overcome, so much shame and stigma. And our children could never trust either grandfather.

This situation underlined how uncomfortable I felt around Ben. To me, these accumulated piles of junk symbolized the coping methods of Warren's family—put stuff in corners and forget. I was not the only one who lacked sympathy; both of his daughters told me they hoped he'd die quickly.

Then I decided—I had enough family problems to worry about. Warren could deal with his own family.

On June 29, Donna P phoned to say she had contacted the social worker for West Hawk. She said he sounded surprised and asked why the police hadn't informed Child and Family Services about the charges. This was just one of the many anomalies of the system we discovered as this prosecution proceeded. The worker promised Donna P that he would inform John and his wife, Sue, right away that their children would be apprehended if they continued to leave them in the care of Jock and Joan.

I could not comprehend Sue's position.

John's laxness stemmed from years of brainwashing and his own trauma. But why was she willing to take this risk? I knew I would be blamed for his actions. As Donna P pointed out, "If you name the problem, you are the problem."

On July 1, my sister Jean visited with her daughter, Tamara. It was Tamara's birthday. Jean never mentioned the legal delays. Wendy and Bill came out for the Canada Day celebrations, parade, and dance. Wendy was not saying much either. I felt sorry for them; they hadn't had a chance to adjust to married life before this crisis.

I received a note from my cousin Sharon. She had decided to organize a family reunion. I felt an overwhelming sense of dread and frustration. Jock had eleven siblings. This meant dozens of cousins and offspring would gather for the picnic and baseball games. I wondered if Sharon knew about her uncle being charged. Sharon was also a lawyer, so surely she would recognize it as a crime.

My therapeutic relationship with the health nurse ended. Because I did not want to drive or pay, I had settled for what was local and available, and it did not work out. I applied for free counselling from the Addictions Foundation. They put me on a waiting list but advised me to look elsewhere. And the women's sharing circle organized by Petchie fell apart.

On July 8, Robin came for the Winnipeg Folk Festival, but he didn't visit us at Lac du Bonnet. I only saw him for a few hours, in a crowd. After the weekend, I wrote him a letter.

> *Too bad we didn't get more chance to visit; we spent most of our time at the children's tent. Right now I'm sitting in our gazebo, alone. I admire how you're dealing with the situation. The police wrote me a letter telling me about the charges and they said not to have contact. No matter what happens, we'll get blamed. The true test, as Wendy says, is: Would I be upset if someone did those things to my children? I want to thank you for admitting the family blight is a big deal. You were willing to confront certain people. You could have clammed up and pretended, like some brothers are doing. But you haven't.*

After I wrote this letter, I could admit the depth of this crisis. The year before, I had hoped to get it over with as quickly as possible and return to "normal." Now, I was exhausted, in mind and body. I struggled with the ideals about happy families touted in the church I attended. How could I admit I did not have a family to spend the holidays with?

I also wrestled with the impact of Jean's phone calls: the unloading and then the quick hang up. In the past summer, before Wendy's wedding, she and her husband had a major addition built on their cottage. This summer, they worked on finishing the interior. Her lists of projects fatigued me. Here I was, just managing to get up, and there she was, constructing her dream vacation home and entertaining crowds of visitors.

Up until Wendy's wedding, we visited Jean's family often and stayed at her cottage. Now I felt deeply betrayed—how could she golf with Joan? How could she visit them for Christmas and not notice the missing people? How could she invite them for dinner?

She defended her hospitality by protesting, "Well, he doesn't say much. He just sits there."

On July 20, the Addictions Foundation of Manitoba wrote and outlined the basics of their program, promising to notify me when they had a counsellor available. They also included some valuable information:

> Sexual abuse when you are a child is traumatic and leaves you with many memories, feelings and thoughts. The counselling will give you a chance to find out how abuse and addiction have affected your life, to identify and deal with the feelings related to the abuse, and to look at your

beliefs about the abuse and how you have sur-
vived. It is common to have mixed feelings. One
day you can be sure it is a serious issue, the next
day you can wonder if it was really that bad. It
is also common not to have many memories of
the abuse. Your counsellor can work with you on
these concerns.

Given their long waiting list, they advised me to find
other supports. I felt disappointed, and also wondered
about the reference to addictions. Did all abused women
drink or use drugs? But this letter reassured me I was
doing the right things. I was not crazy. Also, it emphasized that I needed to "be gentle with myself."

At night, I lit a bonfire and I sang an altered version
of one of my favourite songs:

"Summertime and the livin' ain't easy
It's been rainin', and the water's real high
My daddy's a prick
And my momma ain't livin'
So hush, inner baby, don't you die . . ."

22

ON AUGUST 7, WARREN'S PARENTS, BEN AND
Anne, celebrated their forty-fifth anniversary with
a small gathering. I did not want to go, but Warren

convinced me. No one spoke to me. The kids and I ended up wandering around the yard looking for dew worms.

The next week, Petchie's sister visited from Ottawa so we piled all the kids into our vehicles and headed out to show her a nearby picnic site where people went to slide down the rapids.

The older kids had fun, smashing into the standing waves at the bottom of the drop. I knew it was a bad idea, but Petchie convinced me to bring Bradley into the rapids, where the current was gentler. He slipped down a few times and I caught him. Then Petchie let him go from a higher spot. His momentum knocked me off my feet. If my hands had been free, I could have used them to break my fall. Instead, I landed on my forehead, on the rocks.

I staggered with Bradley in my arms to the side of the river. Allison panicked when she saw the blood pouring down my face, but Petchie shuffled her into the other car and drove my truck to the hospital. Despite all the blood, the cut only required four stitches. That evening, between my headache and a mysterious bug Bradley caught after I left the hospital, I could not sleep.

Warren was at a business development meeting in another town. When he phoned, I told him about the stitches and the puking kid. He said, "I can't come home; I feel obligated to these people."

The next day, my head swelled and my eyes blackened. Then it started raining again. The mosquitoes tormented the horses at night and the flies chomped on them during the day. Our one consolation—we were not farmers. But we were supposed to be finally taking a vacation.

Vacation: part one.

Dear Warren,

I get that you don't like vacations. In the summer, you say you're too busy, and in the winter, we never have enough money. So we usually go for weekend trips, like the one to Maplelag. But people with less money manage to take trips. Allison has not been to many places, and in a few years, she'll have a summer job. Bradley has not been anywhere. Our holiday was supposed to begin on our anniversary, August 15. When you said you needed a little time to finish up some work, I assumed you really meant a "little time." I assumed you would help pack and we could finally decide where to go.

Just so you know, Bradley went on a Ferris wheel and drove the bumper cars. He went down the water slide all by himself. He saw that big ship and pretended he was a pirate. We went to the Children's Museum and swam in a big pool. We visited Wendy and Bill, and rode on a city bus. Allison also did things she has never done. Being alone with the kids worked out okay. I made decisions without waiting for you to make up your mind. Please remember: after fifteen years of working, you can allow yourself a few days off. We will go again without you.

Warren wrote back.

I wasn't happy you left in such a big rush. I had a long discussion with Marley the night you left. He has the same problem, even though he is in a firm with twenty lawyers. No one, including spouses, can understand a lawyer's obligations. The way I run my practice is as good as it gets. I know you don't spend foolishly. But I feel pressured financially. I tried hard to be finished when I said I would be, but legal work is so unpredictable. I missed you and the kids.

Vacation: part two.

When we got home, Allison and Bradley yelped with excitement. We washed clothes and repacked. While I did this, I heard the phone ringing and Warren turning down business. We drove to Spruce Woods Provincial Park. We swam, played minigolf, hiked. We drove to Riding Mountain National Park. We swam, hiked, rode horses, toured the town. We drove to another provincial park. Camped, swam beside a lake with no other campers. Bradley got four leeches. Then we drove home.

Dear Donna,

  I must say I enjoyed the second part. Maybe I have grown as a result of the previous week. I want to spend more time with you and the kids, especially when they are younger.

The summer was almost over—time for back to school. The rain started to let up a bit and my stitches fell out.

23

ON THE MORNING OF SEPTEMBER 16, WHEN I cycled to town for the mail, I received notes from two women in West Hawk Lake. They had lived there since it was established as a tourist resort in the early 1950s.

We heard you might feel the community is siding against you and your sisters. Maybe some people are, but it's not something we can discuss with just anybody. I feel we are all part of an extended family, because we were the "early settlers" and involved with the building of the church. I'm sorry it didn't make us more sensitive and caring. I understand there is to be a trial later this fall. Would it help if we attended? We could also pass the word not to if you'd rather. I want you to know we are thinking of you, and wishing you well. We send our love.

—*Eva*

And another—shorter, more direct:

*Just a little card to let you know I am one of **your** many friends in this area who have you in our thoughts and prayers. God's strength be with you.*

—*Sincerely, Blanche*

I stared at these notes. After I reread them several times, their full implication hit me. Barb must have been telling the women of West Hawk. And now the family shame that my father had kept hidden for decades had been revealed to the whole community. Maybe they wrote because they had memories of my mother. Or maybe they had their own stories of assaults by Jock. Or maybe the split in the church had upset them.

Barb informed me about a rumour circulating in West Hawk. The Mounties had considered laying charges of manslaughter against Jock, for the death of my mother. I could not understand why, but I could understand the sentiment. This bit of gossip disappeared as quickly as it arose.

I wanted to write back to the West Hawk women as soon as possible. But I had agreed to babysit my friend Margaret's son, Matthew. Her husband phoned to ask if their daughter could come along as well.

A half hour before they arrived, a woman called to tell me it was my turn to clean the church. I hadn't attended for months but she hadn't noticed. Her only concern— when could I pick up the key?

While I was chuckling about this, a police officer from Falcon Lake phoned. I recognized his name; we had graduated from the same high school. He sounded as awkward as I felt. Turned out, he had taken over the file from a departing officer. He provided court dates and told me the name of the Crown attorney. He said the Lac du Bonnet detachment would serve me with the subpoena and command me to attend court on those dates. Although I think I answered him coherently, the instant he hung up, I choked and gasped, with tears streaming.

That moment, Margaret's car pulled up the lane. I went to the bathroom and splashed water on my face, and greeted her. She did not comment on the wait at the door or the state of my eyes. Then Petchie phoned, and asked some more probing questions. I hung up and started to sob.

Margaret kept telling me how important, how courageous, how healing it could be for others, not only me. She reminded me how her mother had shared memories of my mother—how gentle she was and how concerned for her children.

The next day, I told another friend, Claudette. We had taught together before I decided to stay at home with my children and work for Warren. She knew all my family; it meant another part of my history would be contaminated. She visited immediately, offering support. We sat and talked for hours. Because the kids were hanging around on the couches, I got through the details without crying.

On October 1, I wrote another letter:

Dear Eva,

I'm so glad you took the time to write. Many offer support, but putting it on paper means a great deal. Blanche also wrote a note. Jock has been charged with several counts of indecent assault and other offences. A court order prohibits contact with him. You were probably aware of the physical attacks on my mother. He may be charged with those. Given the times, it's not surprising nothing was ever reported. Our final straw was finding out about his behaviour with Shannon. We are all guilty for not doing something sooner.

Support from people who know our family really helps. I'm glad to hear you don't see all of us in the same light and I like to believe you are motivated by memories of my mother. Considering Jock's health, perhaps he'll use this opportunity to heal his damages before he dies. So far, he has resisted. Sorry I took so long to reply. What is coming will be difficult, as you can imagine. I can only speak for myself, but you are welcome to attend whatever court proceedings you can. I say, the more, the better.

I wrote a similar message to Blanche. Writing these letters gave me the sense I was doing something. The dates were set. Now I only needed to figure out how to last that long.

24

ON OCTOBER 4, THE CORPORAL FROM FALCON Lake sent a document advising me that Jock had entered a "not guilty" plea to all charges. The officer said he'd send the subpoena to the Lac du Bonnet detachment so I could pick it up there. The first "trial dates" were set for November 23, 24, and 25. He said the Crown attorney would contact me before then to discuss the matter. Later on, we found out these were not trial dates, but rather days allocated for the preliminary hearing.

On October 6, an officer at the Lac du Bonnet detachment phoned to ask me to pick up my subpoena. Once again, I drove blindly to the station. This officer, once again someone I knew, loudly read out the facts of the subpoena and then asked questions.

"Are you aware of this matter? Is this a surprise to you to be called as a witness? Were you expecting this subpoena?"

"I knew I would be called as a witness."

"Is the accused someone you know?"

"Yes . . . he is . . . uh, was . . . my father."

I said this in a quiet voice. He stopped dead and handed me the subpoena. Shaking, I turned and ran out of the building.

Fall meant new teachers. Since Allison had exhibited signs of distress in the previous school year, I worried about grade five. Not only that, this year she had two teachers sharing a class. One of them was the school counsellor, so I told her about my family crisis and asked her to tell the other teacher.

Wendy phoned and told me that she had attended the recent wedding of Tom's best friend. Once again, Joan did not look at Wendy or speak to her. However, the next day she called her up to invite her to see their new home.

Wendy said, "Jock asked Alec to build them a smaller house on the same site. Tom and Trevor worked on the place for most of the summer."

Trevor was Jean's oldest son. I ground my teeth when I thought about these three men, who I had known and loved, working to shelter Jock.

Wendy said, "Barb was at the wedding. She gave me a big hug and talked openly."

"Yeah, Barb's given lots of support. She's not scared to express an opinion."

"I talked to the groom. He said we could count on him to look out for Tom."

"How could you stand it?"

"I haven't done anything wrong. Why should I hide?"

Good question. I needed to keep asking myself that one. I said, "I'd throw cake at someone."

"I saw Jean. She said she's put all this stuff behind her. Hardly thinks about it."

I laughed and thought about this comment for a few seconds. How could Jean and Joan pull off these charades?

"Oh, one more thing. . . . Where was the wedding?"

"Where else? The 'Church of Hate.'"

25

OCTOBER 19—A LATE NIGHT AND I WAS UP, clawing with my pen at the junk inside.

When I phoned Wendy, she told me that Walter, Jock's oldest brother, had died on the previous weekend. In the past, when our large family visited his home, his wife asked the kids to stay outside. I had only seen the inside of his house once, as a teenager. Walter's daughter was now a minister. Going to the funeral to hear her perspective intrigued me.

Wendy said that Joan blamed me for the social worker phoning John and Sue about their childcare. It had nothing to do with Jock's actions, nothing to do with the laws the police and social worker were hired to enforce. It was simply my fault.

As Wendy and I talked, I shared my disappointment with the lack of support from Warren's sisters. Also, I explained how much Jean's refusal to make a statement hurt and how I couldn't understand her close relationship with Jock and Joan.

I continued to dream of beatings, stabbings, and blood. While awake, I could not shake the idea that the whole world would fall on my head. I decided not to attend the funeral but determined that I needed to speak to a counsellor, as soon as possible.

Karen, one of the women who had facilitated the family meeting, told me she would be available. So far, in every other counselling session I attended, I had spent hours outlining the family tree. Then the counsellor would forget names, interrupting the flow of the session. But Karen understood the family dynamics and knew all the names.

Donna P, the social worker, invited me for lunch. We talked so much I forgot to eat. She knew the Crown attorney assigned to the file—younger, and, in her opinion, reasonable. I asked her lots of questions and ignored the possible eavesdropping of the other diners. She assured me that what I described was abuse, and yes, he could go to jail for a long time, for even one incident, like punching me and breaking my teeth, lips, and glasses.

It became clear to me that I wanted the Crown to prosecute.

I reviewed the various positions. Robin, Wendy, and David were there for each other and me. Ernie and John couldn't take a stand. Tom and Valerie expressed open hostility. Belle kicked off the avalanche but hadn't bothered to see where it landed. Shannon seemed confused and lost, wavering. Jean's ambivalence overwhelmed me.

I found it difficult to endure the support and protection of Jock and Joan without naming this shit as shit. People denying it made me want to fling it around even more.

26

ON OCTOBER 21, AROUND 9:30 IN THE MORNING, Warren's mother phoned to say she wanted to visit. Anne hung up so quickly, I forgot to say Warren was at a meeting. When she arrived, Bradley and I were rolling out balls of dough for a batch of cookies. Squishing them gave me something slightly violent to do with my hands.

I sensed she was distraught. We kept making cookies. Finally, it came out of her.

"I was upset to find out you were also abused by your father."

"Well, if you talked to me, you'd have known. I've told lots of people."

"I assumed it was just Belle and the rest were supporting her."

"Abusers usually do not abuse only one child." I hated my tone, like talking to a slow learner. "I made a statement on my own behalf."

"What is going to happen?"

"There's going to be a trial. He may go to jail."

She took a long breath and launched into a description of her own childhood sexual abuse, and Ben's behaviour toward their daughters. Raped at thirteen, she had married a man she had to watch every minute. No money. No help. No place to go. Visions of my own mother's face got mixed up with her trembling features.

She was crying. I was crying.

After a few minutes, she blew into the tissue I handed her. She said, "I'm sorry. You have been an excellent wife and mother. You do not deserve this."

"What now? What do you want from Warren, our kids, and me?"

"I want a real relationship. I want to see the children; I love them. I will come on my own. I don't care what Ben thinks."

"Life with him sounds empty."

"Oh, it's not so bad. I just try to look on the good side, put on a smile."

The honesty had faded. She did not smile. The weight of the years pulled down her mouth, cheeks, and eyes.

I said, "What is so good about life with him?"

I wanted to know, not just for her reasons, but because I could not ask my mother, or my stepmother, the same question.

This conversation burned my throat. Her indifference to me, Warren, the kids, was simply years of frozen feelings. Not showing her anger meant not showing love. Burdened with the albatross of abuse, she used her energy to work around Ben's anger, waiting for him to change and mellow.

I said, "I resent him. And I resent you for using him as an excuse to retreat."

Her life had been spent as a buffer. No confidants, no support—only her daughters. Her story was my mother's story, my story. I knew all the lines, all the roles. And how the daughters deal with their anger at not being protected and mothering the mother.

Anne said that she had assumed that our life at West Hawk Lake was blissful, full of exuberant gatherings. Then she reversed her stance and told me that her family was really the happy family. I resented this all-good or all-evil dichotomy.

"Both families have deep problems and unhappiness."

"What about Brycee and her husband? What parties they have, so many friends."

"What about her denial? She says she has finished dealing with her abuse."

She deflated. "What do you want me to say?"

"I can't tell you. I only wish you knew what you feel or want or need."

She said she wanted a relationship with Bradley. I decided to let her. "I need to go shopping. Will you stay with him?"

For the first time in his life, she stayed with Bradley at our house. While I was gone, my friend Fran came over with a bottle of wine for my upcoming birthday. Later she told me she had never seen Anne's face shine like that, smiling with her eyes, practically bouncing when she saw Fran. Allison came home from school and visited with a different grandmother.

I went shopping and then stopped at Petchie's house. She exclaimed, "What courage! What a gift!"

The next day, Petchie asked me if Anne might resent me for dumping on her like that. Had I gone too far?

27

ON OCTOBER 22, IT WAS FRIDAY, BUT THERE WAS no school. We could sleep in.

I told Warren about the conversation I had with his mother, about the rape, the pornography, the voyeurism, the exhibitionism, the alcoholism. He started talking about reaching forty and searching for new sexual experiences. While rubbing my back, he revealed that he had answered an advertisement for "a like-minded couple."

In the midst of my struggles with childhood sexual abuse, awaiting a trial for my father, he had developed an interest in group sex. Not only that, he had failed to ask me. After I grilled him about the details, the safety, and the reluctance to consult me, he backtracked. He admitted he wanted to screw other people without leaving the marriage. I wept.

He said, "Oh well, it was just an idea. I didn't do anything more than phone them."

Later that night, Wendy called; she had decided she wanted to throw a party on Saturday night. The next morning, we debated whether or not to go. Then we argued about sexualized clothing, prostitution, and pornography. Warren insisted that just because a man was interested in those things it did not mean he was deviant.

I asked him, "Why don't you wear tight pants and gold chains, or unbutton your shirt to your navel?"

"I just don't dress like that."

"How do you think I feel about you springing this shit after I told you what your mother went through with your father? The line between him and you seems pretty thin right now."

"I am not going to apologize for my interests."

The day declined from there. Foolishly, I decided that going to Wendy and Bill's party might alter the mood. No such luck. That evening, on the way into the city, he went on about how much he liked blondes.

He said, "Why don't you dye your hair?"

"It's hard on hair. I used to be naturally blonde. What's the big deal?"

"Why don't you try it again? It would change your whole image."

He kept grilling me about my appearance. By the time I drove through the city core, I was vibrating with anger.

"Do you want to get out? You'll find a blonde here for sure. Just make sure you wear a condom."

The kids sat still, shocked into silence. Mommy was using the F-word every second sentence.

I yelled, "Do you want out?"

"No, keep driving. Don't be so stupid. Get a grip."

"I'd pick you up later. Are you ashamed to have Allison hear this?"

"Shut up already and drive to Wendy's."

Somehow, I did. When we parked, we recovered our company faces and went inside. The party was in full swing. In the thick of it, I approached Karen, the minister, to ask her if she would help me get through this mess. Judging from my recent anger, I needed more counselling before I crashed. She said she had been facing problems within her church and had thought about starting her own counselling business. I was relieved that she might be available.

I talked at length to Wendy and Bill, Karen and her husband, Peter, and my brother David. He looked healthier since the day he drove up to our house after camping at the picnic grounds. He gave me powerful hugs. Allison and Bradley remained quiet.

Warren sat with Bradley on his lap, feigning interest in the World Series. Even when the Blue Jays won, and everyone cheered, an expression of unutterable sadness remained fixed on his face. What possessed him? Could we survive as a couple?

On the way home, he muttered and then stopped talking. I wanted to drive home, in order to focus on something. I did not want to talk. Controlling my crying so the kids would not wake up and controlling my driving while crying kept me occupied all the way to Lac du Bonnet. When we got home, I fell apart—total regression. I talked like a six-year-old for three hours. And I cried and cried and cried.

"No one could love me. I'm dirty. I'm ugly. I'm mean. Not sexy. Not pretty. Not clean. Not worthy. I only hurt people. I want my mother. My family hates me. I'm bad."

Warren embraced me, like he was trying to scoop a puddle back together. After this outburst, I felt exhausted but relieved, reassured that he still cared.

On October 24, a Sunday, Wendy and Bill visited.

Wendy and I took the kids for a walk. I hoped that Bill and Warren would use this time to talk without distractions. They shared so many of the same problems. Wendy remembered to bring out a cake. In the midst of the turmoil, I had forgotten it was my birthday on Monday. The rest of the evening lapsed into a jumble of wine, good food, relaxation.

The next day, David phoned to offer birthday wishes, and possibly check up on me. He handed the phone to his wife, Sandra, a school psychologist. She recommended a psychiatrist to me and suggested I might consider medication. After talking to her, I felt deflated and hopeless.

Then Warren surprised me. On a work day, a week day, he invited me to go fishing. The weather was warm and calm for late October, as if we had been granted one last chance to enjoy the river. We fished until noon. Then he invited me out to lunch. After lunch, he showed me his letter. It seemed that words on the page now defined and delineated my life.

Given all you have gone through the past year, a gift did not seem right. I will try to give some of myself. This is a love letter. You really are beautiful. Your father was wrong. When I first met you in high school, you seemed vibrant, witty, full of fun. You had a special quality that attracted people. I had no idea what was going on at home for you.

You have two gorgeous children, a husband who loves you deeply, and many friends who admire you. I love your body next to me. I love the way you care for our children and treat them as if they are so special, which they are. I love your ability to laugh and communicate openly. I love your readiness to take charge and organize. I admire your talents for building and designing things, like our home. I admire your patience with me, the kids, the horses. I love your intelligence and ability to work through your feelings—something a lot of people never do. I admire the strength you have shown dealing with your father and your compassion for those affected. It doesn't help that my father is also a child molester. I never wanted to hurt you. I just wanted to enhance what we had. May our fathers rot in hell.

P.S. Here is some cash. Don't tell me how or where you spent it. You deserve it.

Now I felt weird. His kind words were mixed with a strange message about money. I couldn't help but think of the prostitutes we drove past on Main Street. I bought some winter boots for the kids with his "gift."

Petchie visited with cake and another card pledging undying affection. She also brought flowers. Someone else sent roses, anonymously. What was going on?

28

ON OCTOBER 27, I DROVE INTO THE CITY TO talk to Karen at her home office. I felt anxious but we settled in like two dogs with a long-buried bone. At first, it took some adjusting to get over the years since our last one-on-one encounters. In her time at the West Hawk United Church, she had started an informal youth group, something the kids in my small home-town had never experienced. She admitted she thought of me as a strong and competent teenager.

On October 29, a local farmer, in dirty overalls and boots, showed up at 10:00 p.m. to talk to the lawyer. He asked me to photocopy documents and then asked if he could wait for Warren. While listing his legal dilemmas, he stared at my breasts. Warren was at a council meeting. I excused myself and phoned Fran. She yanked her son out of bed and drove to our house. Warren showed up a half hour later and invited the farmer to stay for a visit. The four of us sat at the kitchen table, drinking coffee and eating cookies, while Fran's child snoozed on the couch.

The next night, Margaret hosted a Halloween party, with cake and presents to honour my birthday. We carved pumpkins, told ghost stories, howled, cackled.

The next morning, I finally went to clean the church. This last year I had struggled constantly with the "F-words"—father, forgiveness, and family. I asked Fran to help me. Two reasons: it was a big building, and I did not want to face the pastor alone.

When he approached, I assumed he'd ask why I hadn't come to church for months or why I had stopped teaching Sunday school.

He said, "Hello, how are you?"

"I'm . . . depressed."

"Oh, what happened? Did your kids blow up your house?" He guffawed and trundled off to his cubbyhole office.

Fran stood there, staring, with the vacuum hose in her hand. After a dozen pews and two toilets later, he came out of his office. "Oh, did you mention you were depressed?"

I looked at him and spoke slowly. "Yes, I am depressed."

My voice cracked, but I wanted to offer him a chance for an honest exchange.

"Well, I'm pretty depressed myself. Yesterday, I parked in the church parking lot, right where I've parked for the past fifteen years. Let's think, when did I start here? Oh well, it doesn't matter. Anyway, I parked as usual. And someone left their car right behind me. Can you believe? They should have known I don't expect any cars behind me. So I jumped in, not thinking or looking. BAM! I had to take my car to the auto body and I'm still not able to use it . . ."

He droned on for ten minutes about how much his fender-bender upset him, and how he hated damaging a new vehicle, and how much a pastor relies on his car. Fran glared at him while she wiped off the pews.

After we cleaned the church, I picked up our mail. To bring Karen up to speed, I had left all my journals with her so we could discuss them at our next meeting. She had written me a short note.

> *The writing is hard—good—beautiful. It comes from your pain. You've done an incredible amount of deep self-searching. It's painful but it does lead to healing.*
>
> *—Karen*

She had asked me to draw pictures of myself as a child before the abuse. I had only a couple of photos of my childhood self. All the family albums had burned in the fire. My drawings surprised me. First, I drew Little Donna sleeping on her stomach, stretched out in the sun. Then I drew Little Donna riding a draft horse, playing in the sandbox with a puppy, leaning against a pile of stacked lumber. When did Jock's crimes start to show? In all the drawings, the little kid had a big grin and a puffy ball of hair. I knew I wanted to make more.

I had a memory of one particular photo that had been destroyed in the fire. I tried to draw the child as she was in this picture, a fair-haired cherub, curls backlit by sun, green eyes. Unnaturally bright colours had been added later. The picture was so detailed in my mind; I could visualize every fold in the blue blankets underneath my bum. Karen's request for these drawings drove home my size and vulnerability.

Petchie decided to host a Halloween party after trick-or-treating. She hurried all the kids from house to house, and even picked Bradley up and plunked him in front of doors. It was his first time collecting treats and he had trouble trudging along in his dinosaur costume. I assumed she was rushing because she had invited people over and wasn't ready. Then she stopped at her supervisor's house and spent twenty minutes chatting. After that, she insisted she had told me to bring our guitars to her party. She hadn't.

Back at her house, she kept bossing kids and adults. At the end of the party, she ordered Allison into the washroom to scrub off her face paint. Allison did not like the vigorous washing. Petchie yelled at her. Allison cried. The yelling continued, so we left.

The next week, we had an interview with the school counsellor who was also Allison's homeroom teacher. I was relieved to hear Allison was achieving well above average and not showing signs of distress.

That same morning, Petchie had phoned me to pick up Tupperware I'd ordered. I told her I'd come after the interview. Allison saw me at school and asked for a ride home. When we got to Petchie's house, she started shouting at Allison again.

Allison hung on to my shoulder and quietly told Petchie that her feelings were hurt. Petchie kept yelling. This scene upset me, but I couldn't muster the energy to solve it right then. Also, we wanted to get to the Girl Guides registration meeting.

That night, Warren's sister Brycee visited. She talked about the weather and hockey. She didn't mention the legal situation.

On Saturday, we had planned to work on the local cross-country ski trails with other members of the ski club. Petchie had weight problems and had expressed an interest in taking up cross-country skiing. She phoned while we loaded up the axes and saws.

"Are you mad?" Petchie asked.

"Yes. Why didn't you use the communication skills you teach in your parenting classes?"

"I admit I lost it. I was angry."

"I don't think that's a real excuse."

"I know you're feeling vulnerable with all this court stuff. But I need to tell you what I think of your parenting. First, you are ineffectual and too passive . . ."

She listed the instances where she disapproved. I had shared at length with her how inadequate I felt as a parent, given my history, so I was shocked. I said, "I don't tell you every time your children irritate me. They're just kids."

"I've tolerated her behaviour long enough. Maybe I could see you without your kids?"

"What? Meet in the bar? What about all the crap about being friends forever?"

"We could draw up rules for getting along."

"She's afraid of you. You are a big person and you shout," I said.

"I wanted to tell you. I hated it when she held on to you when I yelled at her. How can she stand up for herself?"

"We don't yell like that at our kids."

"I can't accept her behaviour."

"I can't understand your behaviour."

She got quiet. "I won't be coming to work on the ski trails."

The next day, I called her, to ask what was going on. She insisted that she wanted a one-to-one friendship, no kids or husbands involved, or no relationship at all.

First Crown

29

WARREN AND I HAD ARRANGED TO MEET WITH the Crown attorney on November 10.

I had already determined I would disclose as much as possible. The Crown prosecutor's name was Lynne Kohm. According to my lawyer-cousin Sharon, who often went to court, Ms. Kohm was under forty and considered sensible.

Warren and I had ridden in silence until we got closer to the city. Then I started to ask questions. How long would Jock stay in jail? Could family members who refused to testify be summoned? What about the court order that prohibited contact with him? Would their testimony be tainted? Who was responsible for delays? Could people in West Hawk and Falcon Lake also be called to testify? How significant was it that the assaults happened years ago? Who had made statements in my family? Did he think the Crown or the defence had subpoenaed John and Ernie? Warren was able to answer some questions, but not too many. I'd have to wait.

I brought along some pictures. I had the most recent family portrait, taken at David's wedding. Also, I dug out photos I had saved from my teenage years, taken after Jock had punched me in the face for staying out too late. Barb must have taken them. They showed the bruises on my face and broken glasses in my hand. What the pictures did not show was the hole where my teeth should have been. A tobogganing accident had knocked out my two front teeth when I was nine so I wore a partial plate. Jock had socked me hard enough to break it. It was not the first time.

We found a place to park and headed upstairs. Because of his law school days, Warren remembered the interior of the Woodsworth Building. A woman escorted us into an office and asked us to wait. Ms. Kohm came down to introduce herself and then accompanied us to the secured floor where she worked. Obviously some people got pissed off enough to warrant these special locks.

Once we sat facing each other on the two couches in the library, I started to shake; my eyes filled with tears. Ms. Kohm did not hesitate. She spoke quickly, with a hint of humour. Her tone struck me as a cover, perhaps a way to hide frustrations. She was small and blonde, and had sounded much bigger on the phone.

My voice quavered when I answered her questions. I couldn't help second-guessing the process, discounting the criminal side of it. After a few exchanges, I said, "I'm worried the incidents described in my statement aren't bad enough. Are we wasting your time?"

She said, "The things he did to you and your sisters were crimes. He deserves whatever he gets. Guys like him have done jail time for much less."

Her response rolled around in my head, dizzying me. He had criminally assaulted me. He could go to jail. Then she asked about the physical aspects of the sexual acts. I started to cry but managed to describe what he had done. After I finished, I asked again if his actions were "bad enough" to prosecute him.

She said, "Look, if we didn't think this was serious, we wouldn't have charged him. We have considered this decision at length."

Throughout the rest of our conversation, Warren watched my face for signs of puzzlement and interpreted parts of her explanation by putting it in language I could understand. She seemed to defer, and turn to him for confirmation. Would she have treated me differently if I hadn't shown up with a lawyer-husband? When asked about her experience, she replied she had been prosecuting for five years in this area.

There were a total of ten charges, including indecent assaults against four daughters, physical assaults against my mother, possession of an illegal firearm, and bestiality. I wondered who had reported these last two. They seemed minor compared to the others.

Ms. Kohm explained how the laws changed in 1988 to get rid of the "indecent assault" wording. All sexual assaults were now "sexual assaults." They had charged Jock with what the crimes were called at the time they occurred.

She confirmed the Crown had summoned Ernie and John as witnesses. Apparently, both had volunteered to make statements. Their willingness to continue visiting Jock and leaving their kids with him, even while they admitted Jock's sins, confused me. And why were they so afraid to talk to me?

Ms. Kohm said the case would be committed for trial; the strength of the evidence almost guaranteed it. The trial would be held in Winnipeg and she expected it would take place in May or June of 1994. At the preliminary hearing, the contents of our statements would be scrutinized. The defending lawyer would attempt to make us doubt ourselves, make the judge question our motives. Regarding the sentencing, Ms. Kohm suggested that Jock's bad heart would not deter any judge from handing down an appropriate sentence.

She said, "I can't predict the possible length. But, given the recurring nature of the offences the strength of the testimony, and the span of years over which these crimes were committed, I suspect he might be sent to the penitentiary, meaning a sentence of more than two years. Enforced sexual counselling would, no doubt, be a part of his sentence."

A crushing terror hit me. I found it hard to breathe. I sat still and waited a couple of minutes, just staring at Ms. Kohm, until the panic subsided.

When I felt calm enough, I got out the Tod family photo, introduced her to everyone, and summarized ages, positions on the charges, emotional strengths, and weaknesses. I showed her the note of apology Jock had sent right after the disclosure. She agreed it could be about anything, but noted that the content was interesting. I told her that Jock had confessed to Jean, my oldest sister. Ms. Kohm pointed out that Jean might be a reluctant witness but she should be subpoenaed, given her knowledge of the confession and violations against her.

I gave a short version of Jock's history of sexual behaviour, not only toward his daughters, but women in general. We discussed the beatings of my mother, and siblings, and me. Ms. Kohm accepted my descriptions without clarification, so I assumed that my brothers' and sisters' statements corroborated my information. She emphasized her commitment and reiterated that the evidence was much stronger than usual, because there were so many of us.

She said, "I think Pollock hasn't handled many sexual assault defences. But that won't stop him from billing heavily. And I want to warn you, Donna. You are a very credible witness; Pollock will cross-examine you closely and thoroughly."

Warren asked if he should be present while I testified. Ms. Kohm said it might be prudent if he wasn't, in case he was called as a witness. She believed Pollock would ask for a stay, basing the request on his client's health.

She looked at me. "A 'stay' is a suspension of a case through the order of a court."

I said, "I knew what you meant."

Then she said, "Tell the staff that your calls are 'urgent' if you need to get in touch with me. Then I'll know to call back quickly."

The meeting lasted at least two hours, but her attitude gave me hope. I appreciated her thoroughness and her repeated insistence about the seriousness of the crimes.

We picked up our notes and prepared to leave; then I remembered my most important question.

"Ms. Kohm, I want to ask about one more issue. You don't have to answer. But, if you do, it will help me immensely." I paused. "Have you ever been sexually assaulted?"

She stared at me for an instant, perplexed. Then she leaned back, as if weighing the risk of replying. After a deep breath, she responded.

"Well, yes. I was."

Maybe this wouldn't be so grindingly difficult after all.

30

IT WAS REMEMBRANCE DAY. WHEN I THOUGHT about Jock and Ben, those two war heroes, I felt like puking. True to her word, Petchie stayed away and stopped calling. Now I had lots of time to think. And wonder why she had waited until a couple of weeks before my father's preliminary hearing to end our friendship.

The ringette season for the local women's team started up for another winter. I went to the first session and skated like a flailing kid for a solid hour. It reduced the stress, at least enough for me to sleep.

After the day off, I visited Karen at her home office. Driving into the city didn't bother me so much anymore, given the benefits of talking with her. We discussed Petchie dumping me. Karen suggested the relationship might have been lopsided. Then she gave pointers on surviving the hearing. Even talking about it quickened my heart rate and stalled my breathing. After our session, I struggled to gather my shattered thoughts together, to drive home. For safety's sake, I decided I'd stop at a mall and drift around for an hour or so.

The next day, David, Sandra, and their daughter, Sarah, visited. Sandra's last advice to me was to visit a psychiatrist and get medication. I had done neither.

Bradley hadn't spent much time with Sarah, who was a year younger; their fighting disrupted our visiting. Warren barely spoke to anyone and stayed out of the fray. The rest of us spent so much time sorting out the kids' tussles that we didn't get a chance to discuss prosecution until they loaded up to leave—another gut-wrenching conversation in our parking lot.

Late that night, Robin phoned, and we talked for over two hours. He told me a secret he had never revealed in all of his thirty-seven years. He was gay. And he had been afraid to disclose it because of our father's homophobia.

I said, "I'll support you in any way I can."

In the morning, I asked Margaret and her family to come for supper. She said she'd already asked a couple of friends over to share a meal, but extended the invitation for us to join them. Margaret and her husband lived on a farm. Before supper, we went skating on their dugout. Warren grumped, did not talk or skate much. Allison and Bradley scooted around the ice with the other kids. We met Margaret's friend Melanie, an actor and voice teacher, and her husband, Paul, a Lutheran minister. After we finished eating, I learned more about Lutheran theology in two hours than I had in six years of attending a Lutheran church.

The next night, I went to another ringette practice and skated wildly. After the practice, we went for beers at the local pub. Petchie's husband sat at a nearby table. Uncertain of my status, I sauntered over to inquire if Bradley's splash-pants were still at his house.

The following afternoon, Allison got off the bus, loaded with two plastic bags filled with clothes, books, and other items I had loaned Petchie. Instead of asking me to pick them up, she had dropped everything at school.

After supper, a friend's wife called to report that her husband had been phoning people to shout and swear at them. She talked of drugs, boozing, emotional and physical abuse, and calls to the Mounties. Warren decided he needed to go talk to him. He came home late, went straight to bed. I did not hear any details.

The next morning, Warren's younger sister, Shelley, phoned to ask about the hearing. After a few words, her voice shifted to the "little lost child" tones so familiar to me from the phone calls of my siblings. Eight years earlier, she had revealed that her father had sexually abused her. I assumed she had gone for counselling. But when I asked, she had said, "I only went once, and felt so overwhelmed I didn't do it again. Now I'm talking to a counsellor at work."

Right after Shelley's call, Lynne Kohm phoned. She did not waste any words. "The hearing will be delayed."

"What?"

"Two reasons. First, Pollock wants to challenge the charges on account of his client's health. He claims he needs to be fully heard on this issue before the hearing can take place. Second, we want him off the case."

"Why?"

"He's too closely known by too many of you. He may intimidate or influence responses. We'll let you know the new dates as soon as we know. Bye."

She hung up. I doubled over, collapsed, and sobbed. Waiting four or five months felt impossible to bear. After the tears slowed, I phoned Barb. Folks from West Hawk and Falcon Lake had planned to show up at the preliminary hearing. She would spread the news.

What had Pollock been doing for six months? Why did he wait until now to bring up this defence? Why was he allowed to ignore all the arrangements made by police, Crown, and witnesses? Was it a novel tactic, intended to wear us down?

Barb was so astounded she could not speak. Then she said, "Why in the hell is Jock out deer hunting? If he's too sick to go to court, he's too sick to hunt. Not only that, I heard they got a deer, right away, and hauled it out of the bush. It's not like they were just driving around looking."

31

ON NOVEMBER 18, MARGARET AND I WENT TO A sexual abuse survivors' meeting. There were only four women there, a sure sign of how hard it was to bring up the subject in a small town, let alone go to a support group. Margaret shared some of her history. While I waited to speak, it struck me that I was lucky. Although the delayed hearing had disturbed me, I had managed to find a safe place to talk about it.

More cards and letters of support from West Hawk showed up in the mail. There was one from Eva, acknowledging my letter to her.

> I struggle to put my feelings into words, and realize that is nothing compared to what you are dealing with. I feel this way because of your mom. We were young mothers together. The church brought us closer, like extended family. The last time I talked to her, she was worrying about you kids. She hoped you would remember to put on warm clothing. I like to think that she would be there for my kids. No one should have to put up with abuse, and if the parent is the abuser it makes it more horrific. We will be in court on Monday. Until then we will be thinking of you.

A letter also arrived from Theresa, who came to Maplelag and sat in the hot tub with me. She and her husband, Alec, employed my brother Tom as a carpenter.

> This letter is kind of an apology. I've been meaning to write for a long time. I think I've let you down, by building Jock and Joan a house. God, I hope I haven't made it harder for you. It just didn't seem possible not to—after the fire, especially with Tom

working for us. I feel like a hypocrite. Anyways, I think you are right. I hope you are finding support and you will still think of me as a friend. God bless you, Theresa

I wrote her back, in a Christmas card.

It seems strange to be exchanging Xmas cheer, but I wanted to reply. We appreciate your support. You do not owe anyone an apology. The people you built a house for are the same people we lived with and visited for years. It has been a massive undertaking to wrench myself away. It's funny how a relationship can change after a few pieces of paper got passed around and the right questions got asked. I can't imagine going to West Hawk yet. Plus there is a no-contact court order. Almost every single thing I thought or knew is changed. So much of what we are is what we are told we are.

During the next week, I thought about the number of books on abuse I had read since Wendy's wedding—in total, sixteen. Many focused on child sexual abuse; some dealt with family relationships and shame. Then I revealed my crisis to my next-door neighbour, after she asked a bunch of questions about what we were doing for Christmas. She seemed shocked, but offered any help she could give.

On the days when the hearing was supposed to take place, Warren, the kids, and I were felled by a bug—high fever, vomit, and the runs. Allison stayed home for three days and, when she started to recover, got Bradley revved up for the upcoming festive season. For hours, the two of them wrapped imaginary gifts. Bradley looked excited about Christmas, or maybe it was the novelty of mastering tape and scissors.

The day after I had stopped puking, Barb came to Lac du Bonnet on business. When she dropped by our house, I literally fell into her.

Fifteen minutes later, Lynne Kohm phoned for details about the hunting expedition. Once again, she got right to it. "I'm calling to find out more about the accused going deer hunting while he is supposed to be so sick that he postpones court. Do you think the person who told you about this would be willing to testify in court or make a statement?"

I smiled at the incredible coincidence. "Yes, here you go. You can ask her yourself."

Barb told Ms. Kohm all she knew and then said goodbye. We talked for a while, and she massaged and hugged me. This physical comfort reminded me of our early friendship, before kids, before marriages, before adult responsibilities, when we were so close we could almost speak for each other.

On December 3, I visited Karen again, to get hints on how to survive another Christmas. Because people's positions were now entrenched, this holiday season would be even harder. Last year, we didn't even know what we were feeling, still in shock from the disclosure.

Karen and I talked about anger. I learned:

a) Anger was not inherently evil. It helped me survive.

b) Anger can be positive. Its flip side was courage, honesty, and refusal to submit.

While talking to her, I unearthed the anger I still felt about my mother's death and the lack of dignity shown to her, right up to her final trip to the hospital. Then there was the anger with my siblings. Why weren't they more supportive? I cried—hard, wracking sobs. Maybe I was making up for lost years and my fear of crying.

Wendy had given me a gift certificate for a massage in the city. I went after my visit to Karen. During the hour on the table, the woman pummelled me back into a semblance of humanity. Non-sexual touching satisfied a deep inner longing for nurturing.

That night, despite the late ice time, our ringette team hosted a game. I skated like a slug, but it was fun and therapeutic to be aggressive in a controlled situation.

The next morning, Barb phoned. "I've just got back from giving my statement to the RCMP about the deer hunting expedition. Ron Obodzinski, the cop you know from high school, was very interested in all the details. Also, he asked me a question I couldn't answer. Why hasn't Jean told the police what she knows?"

I did not have an answer. After I hung up, I called Jean and asked her.

"I can't talk now. I've been off school for two days. My voice is gone."

I didn't respond. The irony of her voice disappearing struck me as hilarious.

She continued in fuzzy little tones. "The cop didn't ask me the right way. I didn't actually refuse. He was inexperienced, I think. It seemed like he had all the information he needed."

"You can still make a statement."

"There's not much point. This will never go to court. Besides, he'll die before anything happens."

"Sounds as if you don't want to say how it was for you. Or admit that he confessed."

"You're right. I don't want to testify. I won't deny that."

"Ron would still like to talk to you."

She released a large sob. "I can't. I'm not strong. I'm not like you." She cried some more and then hung up. Two minutes later, Ron called and talked for about half an hour. He said he might take the three-hour drive to Jean's place to talk to her in person. He believed he might convince her to support the case he was building.

Now she would definitely lose her voice.

32

ON DECEMBER 9, CORPORAL RON OBODZINSKI from the Falcon Lake detachment notified me that new trial dates had been arranged—February 28, and March 1 and 2, 1994. He told me to expect a subpoena in the near future.

On December 16, the local detachment asked me to pick up my new subpoena. After the visit to the police station, I collected our mail. Eva, my mother's friend from West Hawk, had sent a Christmas card. She included a pin with an eagle, and quoted lines from a famous Dolly Parton song.

Also, the Women's Centre at the Addictions Foundation sent a letter to let me know my name was nearing the top of their waiting list. I still wanted to meet with one of their counsellors, but felt reluctant to stop working with Karen, even if this other counselling was free.

I visited Karen again. After our session, we went for lunch, where we encountered three women from West Hawk. Eva's daughter, a year younger than me, greeted us. I felt hot with shame, knowing that she might have told her companions what was going on in my family.

That afternoon, I bumped into another neighbour. We had attended all twelve grades of school together. He knew about my family crisis because his mother had written a letter of support. We spoke briefly and he offered his sympathies. He was a Mountie; he commiserated on dealing with the justice system. Then I drove home, wondering what other surprises lay in store.

It didn't take long until the next jolt.

Warren's position on council meant we were invited, as a couple, to Christmas parties. These commitments distracted me from what I had set as my goal. I wanted to read Jock's memoir. About five or six years earlier, he had written one. Because of the house fire, I assumed all paper copies, computer records, and the computer itself had been destroyed. However, an anonymous source sent me a copy. This person believed it could be used as evidence and wanted me to send a copy to the Crown, and the police. When I finally read it, I was not surprised to know Jock had chosen to write mostly about his experiences in World War II, and not his wife and kids, other than to say, "I got married and had ten children. The end."

$\sim$

AFTER ANOTHER ELABORATE Christmas party, held in the afternoon because of the many conflicts in everyone's social calendar, we stumbled home. My overriding feeling—I was an imposter with nothing to celebrate, deprived of the typical seasonal joy.

There were two calls on the answering machine. The first was Barb checking on me and wanting me to call. The other was a call from Allison's teacher. Allison had slapped another student. I phoned the teacher right away. She was firm, but tactful. It was not the end of the world, but serious enough to warrant attention.

This evening, the small survivors group gathered for supper at a nearby restaurant. With these women, I felt more real than anywhere else. After the kids were in bed, I wrote cards to my siblings.

The events of the past eighteen months have changed all we know. You haven't been in contact for a while so I assume you're figuring out some things. Please remember we really care about you

*and your children. The truth of our family scares
me but I hope the love and support still exists.
Also, I have been remembering the spirit of our
mother. She gave us so much. Our father abused
us all and now we're all dealing with it in different
ways. Maybe we'll see you sometime, somewhere.*

Two days earlier, I had received a form letter from
Jean. She did not mention any criminal charges or family
discord. Her kids were happy, hard-working, athletic,
and high-achieving. The word "busy" or similar phrases
appeared seventeen times in the two-page newsletter.

In contrast, Belle sent out a different form letter to our
wilfully naïve relatives. She wrote about pain, divorce,
betrayal, dishonesty. Terrible things had happened;
unfortunately, she didn't state any specifics. Because she
assumed the readers knew the details, many of them
ended up confused by her muddled sentences. Also, she
signed the letter on behalf of her five children. I heard
later that some of her kids protested.

On December 18, Warren's brother, Allan, and his
wife, Leanne, appeared at our house. Since they rarely
visited, I bit my lip and waited.

After chatting about nothing for ninety minutes,
Leanne finally said, "You are coming for Christmas
dinner, aren't you?"

Warren and I stared at each other. I said, "I didn't
know we were invited."

Leanne said, "Shelley isn't coming if Ben is there. I
don't care if he's there or not. I didn't talk to my dad for

three years after his cows stampeded through our yard. I got no problems with her not talking to her dad. And I got no problems dealing with my own father either."

What I wanted to say was, "This is more significant than a herd of cows shitting on a lawn." Instead I unclamped my jaw and said, "Sounds like not talking to him for three years might indicate a problem."

She scanned my face for a hint of malice. No malice there, I was simply tired of everyone pretending. But she did not see any parallels. I knew her family's past included drunkenness, violence, arrests.

I said, "How do you both feel about this?"

She said, "I think Ben could be left out, instead of the rest not coming."

Allan said, "I'm mad at Shelley. She isn't willing to forgive and forget. I want things back to the old way. I've had enough of this crap."

I thought—how could he say that? What about my father? And would he be so "forgiving and forgetting" if some jerk raped his daughter?

For as long as I had known them, Allan and Leanne showed no indicators of Christ-worship, and they ignored our family during the other 364 days of the year. Why were they so concerned now? To my surprise, they stayed for lunch. Or rather Allan stayed to eat and Leanne stayed to watch us eat. She refused food. Allan grumped through the meal.

The next day, Warren said he planned to visit his parents with the kids. He told me he wanted to explain to them what Shelley was doing and why.

I asked, "Does Ben deserve to be near children? Can you support your sisters? Why can't you get angry at your own father? You say you're angry at mine."

He visited his parents without Allison and Bradley.

After he came home, we all went to Margaret's house to make gingerbread houses. The kids enjoyed the making, and the final results. Since it was such a mild evening, we walked outside with the kids, to get away from the oven's heat. Margaret probed gently on how I was coping, and gave me a hug when she realized I was near tears.

On December 21, we travelled to the States for a couple of days of downhill and cross-country skiing. A family of skiers from Lac du Bonnet had invited us to share a condo with them. They rose early and skied hard. Our children were smaller and slower. My bindings broke. So we were the slowpokes all weekend.

Edith, the chief cook and organizer, knew about my family situation. She was the Sunday-school supervisor for the Lutheran church and I had already told her why I stopped teaching the class. When we went for a ski, I explained how hurt I was by family members. Her response: lots of questions, then lots of advice. In summary: "Get on with your life. You have to forgive."

Her words reinforced my beliefs. People wanted to believe in happy families and resented me talking about this issue. She could not hear what I said. We came back to Canada, exhausted.

The Christmas dinner at Allan and Leanne's strained my stretched sensibilities. Clumps of decorations had been draped around their house, and hundreds of lights twinkled on hedges, fences, buildings, and trees. Everyone dressed in uncharacteristic finery. No one smiled. No one mentioned Ben. Anne arrived, ate, and went home.

Conversations stayed superficial. "Nice weather for December, isn't it?"

But it felt cleaner and healthier without him. He did not add joy to family gatherings.

On Christmas morning, the kids got up and ran around like small horses let loose on spring grass. They opened piles of presents and spent hours playing and putting things together with pages of instructions, or "constructions" as Bradley called them. We gorged on chocolates and ate a quiet meal. At night, it turned wicked cold again.

David and Sandra had invited all the siblings who cared to attend for a big Boxing Day dinner at their home in the city. The thought of seeing Jean disturbed me. She had phoned prior to our ski trip and told me that Ron Obodzinski had driven all the way from West Hawk Lake to get her statement. She told me she had refused; I asked when she might be ready.

She had said, "Maybe after Christmas. Ron said he would keep in touch, in case I change my mind."

Wendy had already told me that Jean, Valerie, and John, with their spouses and children, Ernie and his kids, and Tom all went to Jock and Joan's newly built house for Christmas dinner. Even Shannon showed up for a couple of hours, then left. It reminded me of salmon swimming back to their birthplace, battered and broken, responding to entrenched instincts.

Although the mercury had dropped to minus thirty-five, we drove to the Boxing Day meal. David greeted us and joked about the two rival gangs. I laughed and riffed on his biker-war motif. Some siblings giggled, but others stayed silent.

Jean and her husband looked glum. They had just arrived from Jock's house. Parts of the evening felt like a replay of the Christmas Eve meal at Allan and Leanne's. Everyone was in pain but no one dared say anything about it. Ernie and his kids, John and his family, Valerie and her family, and Tom did not show up, and various excuses were offered by those who cared to even maintain the pretence.

For me, this evening felt clear and strong, like diving into the lake in May. It was the first meeting of my siblings as equals. Thank God almighty. Free at last. Free at last.

33

ON DECEMBER 30, 1993, THE TEMPERATURE ROSE to minus ten; Wendy and Bill came out to cross-country ski. Robin was already visiting for part of his holiday. That night, Robin, Warren, and Bill went out to the local pub. At home, Wendy and I did not get much chance to talk, because of the kids.

On New Year's Eve, Wendy and Bill returned to the city for a party, but Robin stayed at our house. On the spur of the moment, Warren and I invited friends for drinks and snacks. Fran and her husband, Randal, arrived with their son, Malcolm. A single friend, Dave, also accepted. Others claimed it was too cold to drive. Although the temperature had dropped again, we went for a sleigh ride. After we returned to our house, Dave and Fran danced for hours.

Randal kept grumbling about how sick he was. Around 4:30 a.m., he went outside to start their car. I looked out and saw his tail lights disappear down the driveway in a cloud of ice fog. We stood around for another hour, in disbelief, trying to convince Fran that Randal did not mean anything. At 6:30 a.m., I went to bed, but Dave and Fran kept dancing.

The next morning, Malcolm woke up, wildly excited about his first sleepover at Bradley's house. He flung himself across the living room to where a bearded man lay on the couch. After he leapt onto the man's chest, his shriek of joy turned into a screech of shock. "Not Dad! Not Dad!"

That strange cry haunted me over the next few weeks.

After lunch, Fran and I went cross-country skiing. She told me how my sorrow and searching had reinforced her decision. Her marriage did not work. She met with Warren the next afternoon to discuss the legal repercussions of leaving a spouse.

The following morning, I visited her. She paced and fretted, waiting for her mother to drive her into the city. I knew I would miss her. I stared at her and then at Malcolm. I started to cry; Fran started to cry. Malcolm stood by us, his large brown eyes shining. He said, "Why is Gran coming? Why are we going to the city? When will Daddy come see us?"

Fran responded with vague reassurances and distracted him into his snowsuit. He submitted without the usual rebellion. Together, we stepped out into the blinding, chilling sunlight. It was minus thirty.

34

THE END OF FRAN'S MARRIAGE AND THE STARKNESS of January affected me. However, I started to recognize that the sharp pain of my family's betrayals had blunted. At times, I could not even visualize Jock and Joan's faces, as if they now glared at me through a fog.

I deeply grieved the banishment from West Hawk Lake.

Looking at pictures from twenty, thirty years earlier, I could look at my face and body, without flinching. Young women possess a special unfolding beauty. Older women acquire confidence in their desirability. I had experienced neither. The last two years had taken its toll on my face: furrows on my brow, lines around my mouth, dark circles under my eyes.

The indignity of my mother's death made it hard to blame her for not protecting us. After she died, Jean found letters she had written to our grandmother in England, telling her about the beatings and the shame resulting from her husband's behaviour. She never sent them. She could not go back to England. How could she afford to live in this war-shattered country? How could she uproot ten children, with no money and no relatives in Canada to help her?

On January 17, Warren's mother had surgery for breast cancer. I felt sorry for her. But she seemed unable to openly grieve the loss of this part of her anatomy.

The next day, I visited Allison's teacher. She was concerned about my daughter, but she had no pat answers. We talked for over an hour, discussing family counselling and one-on-one counselling. I promised to approach Allison about talking to someone.

When I returned home, a woman I knew from ringette, and horses, and kid connections, phoned and asked about getting together for steaks at the local pub. She said she wanted to talk about what was happening. That night, our relationship moved to a different level, and stayed there. Her clear-eyed support amazed me.

On February 1, I wrote to the anonymous "friend" who had sent my father's manuscript.

> *I'm sending this back and thanking you for it. It has been gut-wrenching to look at Jock's memoir. Now I know why I never wanted to touch it before. I felt crappy every time I tried to read it. One hundred and ten pages of shit. Also, I felt disloyal even having it. Copying for the Crown was even worse. His references to my mother sickened me. Why did they ever get married? "War bride" was right; it was a battle. Why did he pick her if he had so many who were willing? The wonder of our existence remains a miracle.*

Two days later, the Crown informed us that the preliminary hearing was rescheduled for March 21, 22, and 23.

The next day, I visited a therapist from the Women's Centre at the Addictions Foundation of Manitoba. I appreciated the therapist's attitude, but she looked so young. I realized I had come a long way; I could explain the family dynamics without sobbing.

I said, "The hearing was cancelled again. I'm feeling very disappointed."

"Uh-huh."

"But I'm not feeling so hopeless."

"Uh-huh."

"I feel betrayed by Jean. She says he's halfway dead and the court system never works."

"Let's see . . . Jean is your youngest sister."

"No, she's the oldest."

Right then I realized I needed to stick with Karen. At least she knew my sisters and their birth order. Even though this counselling was free, I could not waste any more time. Also, the Women's Centre focused on the addictive aspect of sexual abuse. I could not identify any addictions. I drank wine or beer, but only once or twice a week.

My next priority was contacting Lynne Kohm to find out what was happening. Between finding a counsellor, taking care of my physical well-being, consoling family, updating friends, and quizzing the Crown and cops, it felt like a full-time job. When would it end? When would the axe fall? Or fail? Or fail to fall?

35

IN FEBRUARY, I SKIED HARD DURING MY SPARE time, but it only lessened my anxiety for a few hours. I needed to see Karen. At the next visit, we discussed my need for mothering. Then we talked about my desire to inform people where I was going with my personal situation. We narrowed their responses into three categories. Some were scared because of their own secrets. Some wanted to believe only good things, and wanted me to shut up. Others classified me as crazy.

On February 7, I attended another sexual abuse survivors' meeting. Margaret didn't come; I felt lonely without her, but managed to participate. To my shock, one of the women asked me how I got so courageous. She said, "You're so tough I can't even talk to you."

Strange—earlier in the week, I had told Karen how scared I felt, all the time.

Around 11:30 p.m., Belle phoned.

She said, "I'm pissed off. Ryan visited Terry."

Ryan was her youngest son. Terry was her former husband, the one who had molested her daughter. I visualized her screaming at him.

I said, "Why aren't you pissed at Jean? She keeps refusing to speak to the cops!"

"She told me there was some confusion when the policeman took her statement."

"Not true. She didn't want to ruin her Christmas at the lake. A few days later, the same Mountie from

Falcon Lake drove for three hours to talk to her. She refused again."

"Oh . . . I didn't know that."

"She told Wendy she is scared to phone me. Why?"

She ignored my question. "Some relatives have responded to my Christmas letter. One of our cousins sent a hundred dollars. Others sent letters."

Belle would need more than a hundred bucks to fight Terry. Her legal struggles had just begun.

I told her about a book I had picked up at the women's treatment centre, called *Each Small Step*, edited by Marilyn MacKinnon. This author believed that twelve-step programs didn't apply to abuse survivors. Admitting powerlessness did not work. Most victims are women and already know they have little power. She also refuted the idea that alcoholism was a disease. According to her data, high percentages of female alcoholics had been abused, and used alcohol to dull their pain.

Belle mumbled something I could not understand.

I said, "Another book suggests ways to recover: get free of family traps, speak up, say goodbye to the abusive parent. Some of us are already doing this."

She agreed and told me she had to work and needed to go to bed.

After I hung up, Warren got off the couch. "I'm tired of hearing about abuse. It's all you talk about, morning and night."

I asked, "How do you suggest I stay sane?"

No answer.

On February 8, it was Allison's birthday. Warren's sister Brycee visited in the afternoon, bearing presents. She frowned when Allison complained about the makeup and powder puffs.

I thought—if she took the time to know Allison, she wouldn't buy such presents. She didn't mention the court process, or the cancellations, or even the missing breast. Then I thought about Warren's responses. He didn't appear interested in anything that was really happening—especially in his family of origin. Skating on thin ice did not appear to upset either of them.

We celebrated Allison's birthday, one day late. I worked on keeping it short and simple. Sleigh ride, games, food. Somehow, I blundered through it. This cloud of bereavement affected every corner of our lives, even my kids' birthday parties.

36

ON FEBRUARY 11, RON OBODZINSKI SENT A LETTER from the Falcon Lake detachment informing me of the new tentative dates—March 21, 22, and 23. Since I had already been told, this news did not upset me. But his letter reminded me of our lack of control.

On the following Saturday, Margaret hosted a birthday party for her daughter. At this celebration, Allison giggled with the other girls. Margaret pulled out her guitar and her dad tuned it for me. A singalong erupted with loud vocals and lots of laughter. Seeing my kids having fun lifted my spirits, but I couldn't help but think about my lost clan. I focused on the strings, hoping the vibrating wood, the taut steel, would deflect the sadness. I played 'til my fingers felt numb.

A friend of Margaret's asked about Jock and Joan.

"Well, as far as I know . . . they are still alive."

Then I thought: that must sound odd. Why not respond openly?

"My father was charged . . ." The words tumbled out.

She told about her divorce and the struggles of coping with two children on her own.

Nightmares had continued to plague my sleep. Two stuck in my brain. In the first, my brother Tom steered his four-by-four truck over Bradley. Then he backed up and drove over him again. I screamed, but he just smiled and ignored me. The revving engine, the massive grill, the knobby tires, the spraying blood, and the severed intestines horrified me. I woke in a sweat, retching, and raced to check on Bradley. In the other nightmare, I left my children with Margaret for the day. When I returned unexpectedly, she was beating them with a belt. They were naked. I pounded her face into bloody oblivion.

These visions had made me feel sick to my stomach.

To defuse my anxiety, I drove to the cross-country trails. I skied for three kilometres. Then, in a panic, I fumbled with zippers and peeled off layers of sweaty clothing, and the bottom of my long underwear, to avoid shitting my pants. I had no paper, only snow, to wipe my butt. I scuffed the feces off to the side, attempting to cover my soupy stools. Turds make lousy klister.

ON FEBRUARY 18, I talked with Karen again. When I told her about Jock's memoir, she said his narrative confirmed his sex addiction. We discussed my siblings and then discussed one older cousin Karen knew well, Eleanor, whose husband was also a United Church minister. Eleanor's family, middle-class Christians, seemed so scrubbed compared to ours. But, if they noticed what Jock was doing, why didn't they say anything? Why didn't they say anything now?

Two days later, around 10:30 p.m., Jean phoned and talked at length about superficial niceties. After repeated promptings, she mentioned the delayed hearing.

She said, "I'm a gutless wonder. I won't stand up for myself."

While listening to her, I recalled Jock's description in his memoir of his first date with our mother. He had sex with her and then took her home, hemorrhaging, back to her quiet, working-class parents. He told this incident as a joke—blood on her legs, down her dress, everywhere. They got married at the end of the war, but I had to check back, page after page, to make sure it really occurred. I know it happened. I have a picture of the wedding party. He wrote more about finding a best man than about the woman who bore him ten children—no mention of any tender feelings for her.

After their wedding, he resumed his fucking and fighting through the battlefields of Holland and Germany. He even seduced his friend's wife on the night of their marriage. Then he returned to his wife in England and pretended he couldn't understand how she got pregnant. The pregnancy became Jean. I wondered— was she conceived on that bloody night?

After that call, I decided I needed to do something; I wrote the Crown attorney.

> *Corporal Obodzinski told me about the new dates. As you can imagine, I'm disappointed. The perpetrator is being protected. Did he take our age into consideration? I'm worried this latest delay will be seen as proof of the futility of the court process. Some siblings have questioned whether he will ever face the charges. Jean has informed me, on several occasions, that she would tell the court what she could, but only if she is subpoenaed. I am aware of the risk of having so-called "hostile" witnesses. But, if she is told to do it, she will tell what she knows.*
>
> *I've enclosed a copy of Jock's memoir. You may recall this manuscript being mentioned. Although it may not be admissible, it may help you to assess his mind. I had never read any of this prior to an anonymous friend sending it to me. This person thought it would be helpful. Please phone as soon as possible. I'd like to discuss the whole mess some more.*

37

THE NEXT MORNING, WARREN ASSURED ME THAT Jean was withholding information about crimes. Then he asked what I planned to do when Bradley went to kindergarten. I was a teacher by profession. I wondered—could I stand being around children? If they rejoiced, would I envy them, remembering my stolen innocence? If they looked unhappy, would I overreact?

Barb called to ask about another trip to Maplelag. I welcomed the chance to reconnect with West Hawk friends but dreaded the exposure.

On February 22, I visited Karen. She asked me to focus on being "tough" and what it meant. I cited examples: working on the sawmill from eight years old, losing parts of my fingers, fighting older boys, building, playing sports, collecting garbage, cleaning toilets, training horses, riding in the middle of the night, bouncing down ski hills. What was I always proving?

On the weekend, we headed to Maplelag. Wendy and Bill came along this year. Many of the West Hawk people openly discussed our family's situation. On the Friday night, the women gathered in the "no-suit sauna" and jumped through the hole in the ice. The kids loved all the activities. Life did not suck at Maplelag.

We returned home, back to reality. CBC reported about a rabbi who had molested numerous children; one had died by suicide. Just like in my family, some supported the offender, some wanted to see the rabbi brought to justice, and some could not decide. Wendy mentioned that Mr. Pollock had acted on behalf of the rabbi.

At the beginning of March, I visited Karen again; we discussed my cousin Eleanor again.

One Christmas, when I was eight, Eleanor's family invited me to stay overnight. I remembered that the cleanliness of their house bothered me. Eleanor drove around the city searching for houses with Christmas light displays. I grumped and swore in the back seat.

Karen asked, "What did the lights represent? Why are you clinging to this memory?"

I cried. Karen watched me, without comment, and then told me that she and her counselling partner, Esther, planned to offer group sessions for abuse survivors. I told her I wanted to participate.

She asked, "Could we get the brothers and sisters who are still talking to each other together for another meeting?"

I explained about the no-contact order. We agreed to wait until after the hearing.

A few days later, Jean called. Because she was a teacher, the Manitoba Teachers' Society covered the costs of any therapy. From the sounds of it, her first counsellor had floated along, agreeing with Jean, not wanting to hurt anyone. But this woman had recently taken a leave of absence. Jean's new counsellor informed her that she needed to tell her story, for herself, and if she didn't, she would seriously regret it.

Jean said, "He's not as good. Maybe it's because he's male. I don't feel comfortable."

"Maybe you just don't like what he's saying."

"Maybe I have too many things to think about these days."

"Maybe you'll hurry up."

She did not visit him again.

On the next Sunday, while we attended the local winter festival, Lynne Kohm left two messages. She informed me she had phoned Shannon but did not say anything else. Wendy phoned me later that night. She had been talking to our cousin Sharon, the other lawyer in the family, who told her that some of our aunts, including her mother, had found out about Jock's antics and got upset. After that call, I looked at Belle's Christmas letter again. I guessed they gleaned something from her garbled message.

A friend suggested we visit a woman he knew for massages and then he drove me to her house. I went first. Jeanne massaged my back, my legs. Suddenly, my entire body turned freezing cold. Tears flooded the face pillow. She explained that my body had chilled in reaction to the emotions triggered by touching. She piled on blankets and tucked them around me. I felt like a child, cared for by this stranger. My mind departed, drifting to a quieter place.

While Jeanne massaged my friend, I sat in the living room with her husband. He was an engineer, like my brother John. He spoke, without noticing if I listened, like my brother John. I almost nodded off. My body felt as if it had been taken apart and reassembled. Not since before Wendy's wedding had I felt this relaxed.

38

WARREN'S MOTHER SHOWED UP AND HANDED him several one-hundred-dollar bills. I couldn't understand why. After a bit of socializing, she lifted her shirt to show her scar. The incision stood out, raw-fresh and scarlet, stretching from her navel to her armpit.

On March 9, I made another visit to the local detachment. The Crown had subpoenaed me to attend court on March 21, 22, and 23. The next day, Ron Obodzinski informed me these dates would be adjourned to some future time. I felt deflated and shaken but went to ringette. Only a few teammates showed up, so the rest of us didn't even bother to lace on our skates. We went to the bar instead. When I started a conversation with one woman who knew my family, she blurted she did not want to hear any details.

On March 11, Warren's sister Shelley visited. At first, she spoke about her job, romances, and roommates, repeatedly saying, "Everything's fine."

Finally, she asked about the latest delay. I explained how I felt. Her voice changed; the high pitch disappeared. She spoke about the hiding she had done as a child. She shared a haunting memory of Ben whipping Kerry, their handicapped brother, with an electrical cord. The image of his white, naked, deformed body being slashed revolted me. I thought of Warren. Where was he when this brutality happened?

Shelley said, "As a child, no one ever got angry for me."

I guessed she was told she could not get angry for herself. I thought of Anne. Where was she when this brutality happened? Then I thought of Allison.

Shelley said, "I'm irritated with Allan. He wants everyone to get over this. Forgive and forget." She sighed. "My mother keeps telling herself she is happy. Especially now, she wants to see the positive."

I pictured Anne's face, its traces of accumulated pain.

Shelley was losing steam. "What an image we tried to project—especially at Christmas."

I shuddered.

Near the end of March, Warren fought with his sister Brycee over their upcoming house deal. He had been working on it for a while and told her he didn't want to do the transaction.

She said, "I don't want to argue," and ended the phone call.

About a half hour later, her husband left a message. We listened to it together.

"Brycee is bawling her eyes out. I'm pissed off."

After Warren hung up, I said, "You have two choices. You can phone her. Or you can expect to be ignored for the next few years."

He chose the latter. She stopped talking to him.

On March 24 and 25, the motions court in the Justice Department heard two days of testimony regarding the motion to have the charges against Jock stayed, on account of his health. None of his victims were present.

Around 10:00 p.m., after the sessions ended, Lynne Kohm called to tell me the details. Joan had testified that

Jock was "a kind, loving father" and portrayed him as an invalid for the past decade.

Ms. Kohm said, "She lies well, but can be tripped up."

I laughed at her opinion. Joan had decided to play the conspiracy card to its full extent. Unfortunately, she forgot it wasn't real.

My brother Tom had also testified about Jock's health. In Ms. Kohm's opinion, he parroted whatever Joan wanted. Several cardiologists had given evidence regarding the condition of Jock's heart. This struck me as hilarious, all these highly paid doctors gathered to defend this particular organ.

Although she was working late, Ms. Kohm talked for a while. She told me that the justice system grinds to a halt during the summer. Although the motions court had just taken place, the preliminary hearing would probably not take place before vacations started. She mentioned a few dates, but the one that stuck in my mind was "sometime at the end of August." She asked for any photos that might be used in court and reassured me about the legal process. My head spun.

During this phone call, Warren was at a council meeting, the kids were sleeping. I was chopping celery. I thanked her for calling so late and letting me know what was happening. Then I hung up.

I hyperventilated. I stared at my wrists, stared at the celery. I examined the veins in my arms, examined the veins in the celery. The blade of the knife touched the inside of my wrist. I rubbed the flat of the cool steel blade back and forth, back and forth. The friction warmed my skin.

Unknown muscles in my legs released. I cried quietly on the kitchen floor, chanting, "Please don't do this," for over an hour.

I wrapped my arms around my torso and stared at the knife on the floor. I deliberated about knocking the phone off the counter so I could call someone from this position. Instead, I clung to myself. Allison heard me and woke. I did not want her to know what was going on so I got up and told her she should be asleep by now.

Margaret phoned about ten minutes later. She talked me through this episode. I sobbed as I repeated, "The end of August."

39

ON MARCH 26, WARREN DROVE WITH ME INTO the city. I planned to meet with Karen while he tended to business. Bradley, suffering from a high fever, had woken up twenty times during the night. Even though I felt tired and dejected, we got right into it, discussing how Wendy and I could expedite this case. The incident with the knife came up. Without hesitation, Karen told me what to do if the delays ambushed me again. She advised me: hold on to something valued, lie down, talk to someone. Through blind instinct or luck, I had done these things.

A couple of days later, Wendy visited Ms. Kohm, who had told her she wanted to examine the wedding video to determine the accused's health at that time. I felt sad to know the new associations Wendy would have with the video. It was now evidence.

The following morning, my friend Barb called. She had talked to Jock and Joan's next-door neighbour, Beverley. She retold, as closely as possible, the conversation.

Beverley had said, "Joan really changed last week. One day, she was all sweet and chipper. Next day, she was mad as hell."

Barb had said, "Do you think it was because of the court stuff?"

"She yelled at me, saying everybody knew her business better than she did."

"Does she think you talked to the police?"

Beverley got huffy. "Well, I didn't. But I'm pretty sure she thinks we told them Jock walks over to our store at least once every day."

Barb asked, "Would you be willing to talk to the RCMP about that?"

Beverley hesitated. "I don't want to. Joan would get mad. There must be someone else."

Although Beverley sympathized, she did not want to do anything. This attitude, which I was destined to encounter in different forms and intensities, mystified me.

On the morning of Good Friday, Jean phoned. Although she hadn't called since February, she launched into her recurring script, listing scholarships, championships, friendships. They'd gone skiing in Banff, and had a lovely visit with Valerie, our sister in Alberta, who still supported Jock.

During a lull, I said, "I have a hard time listening to you."

She ignored me. "Are you invited to Edie's wedding shower?"

Edie was our cousin Robert's daughter.

"No. Please, I need to talk real."

"Well, it's hard to discuss, with kids around."

"My kids hear it all the time." My voice cracked. "Does anyone in your family know what's going on?"

"This is a bad time."

"Listen to me, Jean. I can't sleep. I have nightmares. How are you coping?"

"I talk to Robin, and friends."

I snorted.

"I'm planning on talking to my counsellor again. But he is so busy."

"Not as busy as you."

"I need to go. The kids need help with the computer."

Seconds after the phone hit the cradle, the emotions hit. I collapsed on the couch and cried for ten minutes. Bradley and Allison appeared and smothered me with hugs and blankets. Bradley made faces and tickled me; I started to laugh.

We decided to go for a hike and a wiener roast in the forest. As we drove out to the hiking trails, we noticed five or six extra vehicles parked at a friend's house.

Warren said, "It looks as if they're having a big dinner party."

I felt a sharp pang of guilt and loss. While others entertained families, the four of us headed into the bush. Despite these reminders, we enjoyed our campfire.

The next day, Margaret invited us over to colour eggs. After decorating a few dozen, we walked outside, kicked at the scarce bits of snow, howled and laughed. On Easter Sunday, Warren invited his brother Kerry over for supper. Kerry had suffered brain damage as a child, but I enjoyed his visits.

The first thing he said was, "Hello, Fatso."

I said, "Hey, in this house, we don't like name-calling. I am hurt."

He apologized. Then he spilled all the recent happenings in Warren's family.

After he drove Kerry home, Warren called up his sister Shelley and chatted for at least a half an hour. Compared with Kerry's revelations, he didn't share much.

I asked, "How come you didn't tell her about Brycee's boycott? Or the court stuff?"

"It's too complicated."

"And why didn't you tell Allan when you saw him? Or your mother?"

"I didn't have time."

This exchange reminded me of my conversations with Jean. I missed Kerry already.

Later in the evening, the phone rang. I hoped it was Jean, ready to discuss the reality of our family. Instead, it was my brother Ernie. I had not spoken to him since our second family meeting, two months after Wendy's wedding.

He said, "I was wondering where everyone was this weekend."

"Oh . . . why is that?"

"No one else showed up at Joan's dinner." He seemed genuinely confused, as if he could not understand where the missing bodies went.

"It sounds like you go to the lake often."

"Yeah, Joan helped me during my divorce. I want to be there for her."

A few years earlier, Ernie's marriage had ended, but he never made any connections between his divorce, his relationship with our father, and the way he handled problems in general. Things just happened.

He said, "I'd have come to visit you this past year, but I didn't want to get blacklisted. Joan and Jock wouldn't have liked it much."

I did not reply.

He continued, "I know I'm not supposed to leave Heather with Jock. The other day, I planned to drop her off, but Joan was gone. I swear I didn't leave her there."

Heather was his daughter, two years older than Allison. I said, "Do you know why Joan went to Winnipeg? She testified about Jock's health in motions court."

"He's so old. He probably wouldn't do much to Heather."

"It never stopped him. Are you willing to take that risk?"

"Well, he's going to die soon."

When I asked if he believed our father perpetrated these crimes, he admitted Jock was guilty. When I asked about the physical abuse he reported in his statement, he shifted his focus to our birth mother.

"She deserved to be hit like that. If only she had learned to shut up, she wouldn't have gotten beat up like that."

"I can't believe you actually believe that. Bye."

40

FRAN, HER MOTHER, AND MALCOLM VISITED. We went for lunch. Malcolm poured a can of coke over Bradley's head. Fran whisked him outside so fast we didn't get a chance to discuss what was happening in her life, or mine. Before she left, Fran handed me an article she had photocopied, from the March *Saturday Night* issue. In this piece, Sylvia Fraser wrote about "false memory syndrome," a theory that had originated in the United States and crept into Canada. She drew a parallel to Freud's flip-flop on reports of incest among his patients. Freud could not believe so many children were molested so he renounced his own theories.

Fraser outlined common tactics and rationalizations:

1. The molester believed he had the right because he fed or supported the molested.

2. He was only doing what was done to him.

3. The molester rewarded the child.

4. He was drunk.

5. He never ejaculated inside the child.

6. He believed the child seduced him.

7. He never beat them to do it. No, he beat us for other reasons.

Number 2 really hit home. Jock had admitted to Jean that his older brothers had sexually abused him. Overall, this article clarified many issues about childhood sexual abuse. Things I knew but did not know. Myths we now confronted in this aborted legal snafu.

Even though I had not attended church for a year, a Lutheran parishioner asked me to work at their annual soup supper. I agreed. When I arrived, Randal sat near the door, telling his table mates about Fran's betrayal. The men listened, nodded, and patted him on the shoulder.

I felt a quick surge of jealousy. In this small town, gossip about divorce, surgery, affairs, and pregnancy circulated quickly. The facts about incest did not.

The next day, I saw Randal outside the post office. He glared at me.

I said, "Hello, Randal."

He got on his bike and rode off. By the time I drove home, he called.

"What's happening with your court case?"

"Not much. I'm surprised you're asking. You never mentioned it before."

"I'm more aware of personal crisis now."

After a long silence, he asked, "How much money are you asking for?"

"This is a criminal case. The Crown laid the charges. We do not get money."

I suspected he wanted details to discredit, or punish, me for supporting his former wife.

The next day, I received a card from my cousin Eleanor. She said her thoughts and prayers were with me. I appreciated the gesture, but resented the cliché. I craved outrage. I wrote her a long letter, outlining the abuse, the charges, and the damage. And, because she asked if she could help, I explained what I needed.

Tell! Tell about our family and our father. Tell your children and your friends. Tell people with daughters and all the women you know. Tell all our relatives. Tell any time, any person, any place you can. If you feel squeamish, please remember the pain he caused and continues to inflict.

That night, my cousin Robert called to ask if I wanted to buy tickets to Edie's wedding social. He said, "Marge told me you might not want to come, but I decided to ask anyway. Did you know Edie is getting married?"

"Jean told me. Do you know what's going on in our family?"

"I know the basics. It must be hard to talk about this."

I had heard that line before. "It sounds as if it is hard for you to hear."

"Well . . ."

An hour later, we were still discussing our family's past and his adopted daughter's sexual abuse and suicide. To my surprise, Robert, a social worker, admitted that Shannon had disclosed Jock's assaults to him and his wife, Marge, a schoolteacher. Shannon had boarded with them during her first year of university. Shannon was seventeen. Because of their jobs, they were obligated to report sexual abuse, but neglected to do so.

~

ON APRIL 22, Lynne Kohm called. I mentioned Robert's admission that Shannon had disclosed to him while she was a minor. She said, "Can you ask if he's willing to testify?"

That night, I phoned Robert to inquire if he'd speak to the Crown. He said, "Well, it was only one month before Shannon's eighteenth birthday, when she disclosed."

He admitted that he knew about the violence in our family. He also admitted that Jock had always treated his nieces and nephews better than he treated his own children, a confirmation of my lifelong belief. Finally, he consented to speaking with Lynne Kohm. I felt irritated by his reluctance but reminded myself how long it took some of my siblings to confront the abuse.

I called Ms. Kohm and gave her Robert's number. Once again, I was shaken with doubts and feelings of intense disloyalty. I questioned my motives and my sanity.

41

I STARTED TO SHOVEL A YEAR'S WORTH OF MANURE from a shed in our horse pasture. It felt therapeutic and, as I worked, I saw a metaphor. The top layers, loose and fluffy, came out easily. The deeper layers, hard-packed and still frozen, required strenuous prying.

I continued to train the mare, but wore a hockey helmet with full face mask. Although she never bucked hard enough to fling me off, she reared, bolted, and sat down once or twice. Training her reminded me I knew how to do at least one thing. And I preferred dealing with a large and dangerous animal to dealing with my family.

On the afternoon of April 24, Marley, a friend of Warren's and a former Crown attorney, visited with his wife and family. I assumed Warren had told him about my dealings with the Justice Department, but this had not happened. I wanted to ask Marley questions about the justice system, and how it worked, or didn't work. Instead, we discussed weather, children, and health.

Somehow, I found the time to get massaged regularly. When Jeanne worked on me, I felt safer than I had ever felt in my life. However, during one massage, Jeanne brought up the subject of forgiveness. My head snapped up, out of the cushioned hole where I placed my face, and my shoulders tensed.

I said, "It would not mean anything if I said I forgive Jock."

I could not relax for the rest of the massage.

The next week, I accompanied Allison to an allergy doctor. It turned out that she was allergic to dust, mites, dogs, horses, and other irritants. To help her breathe easier, I moved our dog outside, eliminated contact with horse dander, cleaned more often, and changed her bedding regularly.

During this same week, Warren attended meetings every night, and then left for a weekend conference in Brandon, a city on the other side of the province. The morning after Warren returned, I woke up and touched my chest. When I inhaled, it felt like a large hoof ground into my upper body. I wanted to cry, but hesitated because it meant taking larger breaths. The pressure lasted all day.

The following morning, Warren drove me to the Pinawa Hospital. The doctor listened, thumped, informed me I had inflamed ribs, and prescribed pain-killers. He didn't tell me how ribs got inflamed. I didn't care. All I wanted to know was that I was not dying. The next day, seven giant pimples and three cold sores appeared.

I visited Jeanne, and asked about the chest pains and skin eruptions. To her, it meant the emotions were moving out of my body. I gave her the chapter on forgiveness from *The Courage to Heal.* She promised to read it before our next time together.

42

ON MAY 2, WENDY, MARGARET, AND I ATTENDED THE first in a series of weekly group sessions, facilitated by Karen and Esther. Margaret and I drove into the city together. The first meeting covered the importance of confidentiality and established guidelines. At the end, Margaret brought out a cake for everyone.

That night, I argued with Warren about a women's retreat, starting on Thursday night, at a resort on Hecla Island. He said we could not afford it.

On May 5, Wendy and I drove to the retreat together, and shared a room. The resort faced a large lawn with a small pond, and the vast expanse of Lake Winnipeg stretched in the distance. After we unpacked, I talked to a few women, as well as Karen and Esther, who were presenting the next morning. I appreciated having Wendy there, but knew we needed to allow each other space to step outside the family roles.

In the opening session, the leader asked us to sign up with an animal group. I picked the Wolf. When asked to explain our choice, some women gave long, poetic answers.

I panicked. "I like to sniff and piss. And I like to howl."

The women laughed. The next task was choosing a "sister" from our group. A woman named Jan picked me. She said she selected the Wolf because she was a loner. Of all the women there, I was the only one with a sister and a "sister."

The next morning, Wendy slept in, but after so many years with young children, I had forgotten how. Food at the retreat was all about healthy choices, so granola and fruit abounded. It appealed to me, but mostly I loved not cooking.

Wendy and I went to Karen's workshop on abuses within the church. She showed us a book cover with a picture of a crucified woman. Some of the women revealed how they had been told they were dirty and had been forced to kneel and pray for hours. After the session ended, we rushed to the second half of another one. It included playful and fun activities, meant to get us in touch with our bodies. I wrote a dialogue to my sore back.

After a fibrous lunch, Wendy and I decided to go for a bike ride. Karen and another woman came with us. We had brought our mountain bikes; they borrowed street bikes from the resort. We returned for our small group gatherings. But Jan did not show up. She had been in the session on religious abuse and she slept right through the rest of the day. I wasn't surprised; she came from a family of Jehovah's Witnesses.

Before supper, everyone assembled for a kundalini meditation. In the first fifteen minutes, we shook to throbbing music. During the second quarter of the hour, we stretched and swooped to quieter music. In the third quarter, we sat on the floor and listened to low chanting. Then we reclined for the last fifteen minutes, with no sound. The meditation left me drained but exhilarated. For the rest of my time at Hecla Island, I retained this tired-but-stimulated state.

After the meal, the women gathered in a circle, read poems, and told stories. An older woman told an anecdote about Karen. Another woman told a long story about "the last time I had sex in the big city." After the talking ended, we sang. One song was called "Dona Nobis Pacem," which means "give us peace" in Latin.

We left the big meeting space and went to relax in the pool and hot tub. Karen, Esther, Jan, and a couple of others came back to our room for conversation and wine. Jan told us about her memories of the television program with the kung fu monk. We laughed about all of us being "grasshoppers" reaching for the stone that kept disappearing. Around 3:35 a.m., I went to sleep.

The next morning, Wendy went for a massage, and I rode my bike along a mushy trail that led out to a long point. I dripped sweat. The lake lay around me on three sides, still and quiet. It reminded me of my home by the water. I thought about my children. The morning sun warmed my back and shoulders. I was startled when two men appeared, but they just said "Good morning," and vanished. Their presence reminded me that the retreat had cushioned me in a dreamlike cocoon.

My body felt both hot and cold, because of the exertion and the chill from the vast lake. The sun reflected off a large pile of ice at the end of the point and drew me toward it. I sat on a flat rock and stared at the floes that had collided so violently with the shore. I was still in an altered state, stirred-up emotions combined with exertion and fatigue.

The water's surface remained unbroken. Without the refraction of waves, I could look into its depths; stones rubbed smooth by waves sat on the lake bottom, waiting for me to examine them. The ice had already candled, breaking up slowly, hissing and popping as pieces dropped into the lake. The morning light blazed through the ice, imparting a turquoise glow. The groaning mass moved slowly, eaten by sun and water. I stared into the water and the pile of ice transformed into a metaphor. Quietly, slowly, it was changing.

A pounding of wings broke the silence and water birds shared their morning songs: ducks quacking, coots hooting, loons yodeling. This last lonesome sound tugged at my soul. I looked around the three sides of the point. I wanted to absorb this scene, to be still and solid, and slowly drop off pieces that didn't fit any more. In this setting, "Dona Nobis Pacem" made sense.

43

WENDY, JAN, AND I SIGNED UP FOR THE NEXT morning workshop, "Universal Healing Principles," facilitated by three women. They asked participants to tell why they had come, but my throat felt suddenly constricted by silent sobs. When I could breathe, I asked Wendy to explain and she summarized our family crisis.

One of the facilitators sang a "healing" song with a microphone. With only three participants, it seemed odd. In the middle of the session, the other facilitator pulled out a princess crown and a glittery wand. She asked us to put it on and share whatever came. Wendy took the crown, gritting her teeth and crying. I felt sick watching tears stream over her clenched grimace.

When my turn came, I clowned around, putting the tiara around my neck like a dog collar, swinging the wand like a baton. Then the shaking and sniffling started; I blurted out how I could not stand to touch such things—I was never someone's precious little princess.

After the session ended, I apologized to a facilitator. "I'm not sure why that happened."

She said, "Thanks for your honesty. I admire you both for being present."

The next session pulled me back together with its combination of ritual and symbolism. Karen and Esther presented "Seasons of a Woman's Soul," which included poetry and songs written by both of them. No one spoke during the program, and at the end, Esther sang alone, "Woman, woman, healer, sisters healing for change" in a low voice.

After the evening meal, the women gathered, sitting in a circle. The leaders asked each woman to speak about their day, or their life. I wanted to tell these women about the pain of the last two years and the pain of the first part of our lives. I felt like I was standing on the top of a high tower, the wind rushing by, the turret rattling in a hurricane. All I had to do was let go, let myself drop. I remembered the morning session and how I had been unable to speak. My body vibrated. I stretched out on the carpet. I wanted to stop shaking long enough for the sounds to come out. The speaking stone passed from hand to hand, drawing closer. A First Nations woman talked about her broken childhood. Her lilting voice mesmerized me—unwavering, full of haunting images. The speaking stone passed to me.

Sprawled on my stomach, shaking like a jackhammer, I spat phrases out. I wanted to convey how hard it was, but it still could be done. As I finished each sentence, the words evaporated from my memory. The only part I recalled—my two questions.

"Has anyone here reported her abuse to police? Has anyone gone through the court system?"

One woman raised her hand. She told about going to court with her abused child. I shook harder. In my peripheral consciousness, I sensed women reacting around me, a pinball of energy. I stopped talking. Three women rushed to comfort me. I waved them away.

After three more women spoke, the sharing circle ended. A dozen women approached and lined up to give me hugs. Their comments barely penetrated my rattled brain. One woman thrust a drumstick into my hand. She wanted me to lead the drumming, perhaps as a sign of respect. I struck the hard skin a few times and gave the stick back. I walked into a corner and studied the wallpaper. Karen put her hand on my shoulder.

I said, "Why did they respond like that?"

I saw Wendy. "I'm sorry. Maybe you didn't want me to tell so much."

More women appeared. They hugged Wendy. The drums pounded louder and harder. During a lull in the chanting, a woman yelled, "We're going outside, to the bonfire."

The crowd exited through the doors facing the lake and marched toward a large blaze. Karen stuck beside me. "What are you feeling?"

I drew a blank. I could not name it.

"Watch out for the backlash."

"Watch out? Why?"

"You revealed your abuse publically. There's bound to be a reaction."

Right after she finished speaking, a wave of emotion hit me. The surge almost knocked me sideways. Karen clutched my arm. My legs wobbled. I bent over to retch, but nothing came out. I noticed a creek leading to the big lake. I walked to its bank. Sitting under the water appealed to me—a solitude where I could look up at the night sky. I didn't want to die; I just wanted the water wrapped around me. I stumbled; Karen pulled me back on the path. Wendy and Esther had caught up with us. They helped her steer me away from the water.

In the distance, the bonfire crackled and drums boomed. Karen kept asking me to identify the feeling. I tried to focus. Then the word came to me—shame—in my mouth, behind my eyes, up my nose, all over my body. And I was terrified. I had told too many people. What would happen?

The wave subsided. I started to feel almost normal, still fuzzy, but normal. We arrived at the fire; the noise swallowed our conversation. I wanted to build the fire higher, to match the noise, and my feelings. Karen and Wendy dragged me back from my search for wood.

Then the scene assumed dream qualities, with the chanting, the smoke and flames, and the drumming. The waves returned, in five intervals. Each time, I'd crumple and mumble about getting into the water. I wanted to smother the feelings, like a child wanting to hide under blankets.

Karen said, "We need to go back. It's too dark. We can't keep dragging you out of the bush and away from the water."

"No! I like the fire and the noise."

"I like it too, but I'm freezing."

I needed to sit down. "Yeah, we could get a hot drink at the bar."

Wendy, Karen, and Esther clamped their arms on mine and didn't let go until we were seated around a small round table. They examined me, as if they had unearthed a land mine—no sudden movements.

The drinks arrived. Jan and some other women walked by and I yelled at them to join us.

Satisfied I was safe, Karen and Esther left. But the feeling of wanting to submerge my body had not gone away. To the remaining few, I yapped about going for a swim in the indoor pool. Jan told me to fuck off and left. Then Wendy said she wanted to go back to our room.

While we undressed, I ranted. She climbed into bed, rolled over, turned out the lights. I sat on the toilet lid and thought about swimming, by myself. But I didn't want to scare Wendy, or anyone else. I lay down, but did not sleep for hours.

The next morning, Wendy and I ended up in the same session again. The facilitator, one of the women who stayed up late with us, talked about "The Authentic Self." During the guided meditation, Wendy's eyes and face collapsed into a rictus of deep sadness. After it ended, she went to sleep and I rushed to a presentation on "Mother-Daughter Relationships." I shared details about my mother and got upset, again. The facilitators asked us to write a letter to our mothers. I read my letter to the group.

> *I regret I was not kinder to you when you were leaving. I laughed as I dressed you. The image of a teenager tying on shoes and buttoning up clothes on a grown woman seemed funny at the time; now it haunts me. I didn't know you were dying. I should not have been allowed to treat you like that. I apologize, although that kind of callousness was encouraged in our family. I never saw you alive again. The next time you were in a casket. I touched your face.*

After the letter, we did another guided meditation.

A vision of a dragonfly emerging from its nymph stage appeared to me. During my sharing, I described the aquatic larva splitting out of its brittle shell to reveal the iridescent vulnerability of the adult insect. I told about the thread-like strands lacing the back of the discarded husk, the wings unfurling slowly. I focused on a dark spot on the floor as details tumbled out. Once again, women reacted; I was only aware of their charged responses in a peripheral sense.

Before we left the room, Karen spoke to me. "You finally finished the story."

"Huh? What story?"

"When we first met, you showed me some water bugs. I thought you were pulling a city girl's leg. How could those ugly things ever become a dragonfly? Now you told me. Twenty years later."

We gathered for the final sharing. All the women lingered, hugging and laughing, exchanging phone numbers. I knew we'd probably not keep in touch, back in the real world, but I recognized the connections.

Jan wanted to ride back to the city with us. I asked her why she preferred talking to Wendy; she laughed and told me I was in her face too often. When I dropped them off at Wendy's house, Jan hugged me for ten minutes and whispered, "You'll never know how much you have helped me."

I drove home in a contented stupor. A whole night's sleep did not make the fatigue disappear. It lasted for three days. The weekend was intense and difficult; I felt pierced and exposed and opened.

44

ON MOTHER'S DAY, JAN VISITED LAC DU BONNET with her husband and three children. I felt nervous. We had established an intimacy, but the shared history of a usual friendship was missing. She reassured me that she loved me anyway. We watched the fathers handle the chicken on the barbecue and the squabbling children. When they left, Jan hugged me, long and hard.

Several times, after the retreat, Warren complained about me being gone so much.

When I told Karen about his protests, she said, "You'll be different after looking at this stuff. He'll be different, too; it might open up some things for him. But it's up to him to decide if he needs to work on them."

On May 21, Wendy phoned to say that Lynne Kohm had informed her that the defence testimony was not finished and the judgment on the motion to have the charges stayed on account of Jock's health might be rendered in July. I had grown more conditioned to these delays but still felt sad and desperate. In August, it would be two years since we disclosed the incest.

In the next support session, Wendy shared how hurt and exhausted she felt. She pointed out she had lost two mothers. Then Margaret revealed she'd decided to leave her marriage. When she told about her abuse, slowly and detached, she looked as if she had separated from her body, describing a far-off picture. I held on to her foot. Then she curled up in a fetal ball.

After a short break, I read an account of my abuse to the group. Wendy and I were still worried about the no-contact order, so she went for a walk with Karen. Since I still doubted anyone else would care to hear my description, I rushed through it. I twitched violently and stopped often to literally push my chest into motion. Once again, faces and bodies around me fuzzed and disappeared.

"Oh God, he was some bastard."

"How did you stand it?"

All my life, I had been told "it wasn't so bad."

On the Victoria Day weekend, Warren hiked a sixty kilometre trail with two other men, and came home with a blister the size of an apple. Allison went on a camp-out with the Girl Guides. I felt scared all weekend long.

During the following week, Lynne Kohm called. She said, "If your siblings contacted me and told me to stop, I would."

"You would?"

"Well, there would simply be no point in it."

She hung up. The shock of her new strategy over-whelmed me. Since when did the victims of crime control the outcome?

On the first weekend in June, we decided to install wooden siding on our garage. We'd be using power tools so we invited Anne to watch Bradley. When she arrived, she asked, "Can I take him in the car? I want to go for coffee."

I panicked. "Where do you want to take him?"

"Oh, just to Brycee's place."

I panicked some more. "I don't feel comfortable with that. I don't know where you will take him. And I can't rely on you to protect him."

"Ben wouldn't hurt anyone these days."

"I don't believe he's harmless. How has he learned to control his behaviour? Child molesters do not cure themselves."

"Oh, he's old now."

It was the same line spouted by my sisters. She stayed, but looked unhappy.

Although we got a few boards nailed on, the price was high. I envied friends with parents willing to enjoy grandchildren. My son did not have grandparents I could trust. The hard part was accepting it would not change.

45

ON THE THIRD WEEKEND OF JUNE, BARB CONVINCED me, despite my twinges and hyperventilation, to visit her.

"You have every right to be here. They don't own the whole place."

"I know that in my head. It's the feelings in my body I have trouble with."

The closer I got to West Hawk, the harder it got to control the car. Every granite outcrop and clump of trees brought up childhood memories. Every approaching vehicle caused me to duck low behind the dash, with only my eyes peering over the steering wheel.

We met at a small bistro in Falcon Lake. After supper, we went to the golf course for a beer. We discussed our relationship, and "the case." Then she drove me around to reacquaint me with my home community. I was petrified, and ashamed of being petrified.

She parked in front of the fundamentalist "Church of Hate." Like me, she was surprised that Jock had chosen this new structure as his religious sanctuary. I tried to imagine him praying for his daughters to abandon their conspiracy in this hallowed space. It looked unremarkable with its white stucco, and dark eaves.

We wrote a note in block letters and stuck it under the door. "PEDOPHILES AND ADULTERERS WELCOMED. NO HOMOSEXUALS ALLOWED."

In the twilight, Barb drove me up the driveway of Jock and Joan's new home, built on the same site as the burned house. For ten minutes, we stared in silence at the glowing windows. No one came out.

Back at Barb's, Theresa joined us. We drank and talked until 3:00 a.m. Theresa told me about Tom's marriage plans. Jean's kids also worked for her construction company so she talked about them as well. She said she admired me and cared for me. I cried a bit, but not much.

I told some stories about Jock's violent behaviour. She agreed he was faking. Then I pointed out his methods of control: beating, lying, yelling, intimidating, shunning, fondling, and threatening heart failure. I said, "The first six tactics won't be allowed in court, so he's relying on the seventh."

Their laughter lifted my spirits. Barb knew the facts, and she appreciated Theresa getting some insights into Jock's background. When we finally went to bed, Barb tucked me in. As I waited for sleep to come, I thought about her mothering, and how I appreciated it. I thought about my children at home, and Warren's fathering—willing, and a bit scared of the responsibility. I thought about Craig, Barb's husband, and how he fathered, bemused and gentle, and slightly detached. Then I reflected on Ben and Jock's "anti-fathering."

I lay in a warm bed, seven kilometres away from where I grew up. I pulled up the comforter and fell asleep.

It was Father's Day.

46

DURING THE LAST WEEK OF SCHOOL, WARREN and I visited Allison's principal. He told us about the teacher she'd have in the fall. We had both gone through high school with the principal so I mentioned how long my father's prosecution had been delayed. He didn't know anything about it. None of Allison's teachers had told him.

After talking to him, I had an idea. All of my siblings, from Ernie down to Shannon, had been taught by the same high school English teacher. In the past, this woman had alluded to Shannon writing about abuse. When I called her, she agreed to look through the letters from Shannon she had saved.

At 9:00 p.m., she phoned back.

"I found a letter written in 1989 with specific details about Jock abusing Shannon. In her letter, she referred to him as 'Mr. Tod' and Joan as 'Mother.' She told me about mutilating herself and thinking about suicide. After she left university and was working as a teacher's aide at Falcon Beach School, she wrote me again but the tone was quite different."

"What an asshole!" I said. "Oops! Excuse me."

"You have every right to be angry. I remember how many times you asked about the best way to commit suicide."

"I don't recall that." I squeaked out the words.

"I also remember how the staff cherished the story of the brave widower raising his ten children. All of you must be feeling emotions you weren't allowed to feel so long ago."

We talked for over an hour. At the end, I told her, "I appreciate this. Would you be willing to bring this letter to court?"

"Yes, but I need to ask Shannon first."

"Okay, thank you."

"I'll keep in touch. Remember, none of this is your fault."

∽

SCHOOL WAS NOW out for summer. Margaret and her estranged husband, Don, arrived with their two kids for a barbecue. After we ate, we climbed into our sixteen-foot fishing boat to watch the Canada Day fireworks shot off the town dock. With eight people in this small boat, Margaret could not help but sit near Don. They all stayed overnight and Margaret left for work early the next morning. Don hung around but didn't say much; then he left to take his children on the midway rides.

On July 2, the phone jolted me awake. My former English teacher wanted me to know, before she left on her vacation, that she was willing to speak before the court.

Three days later, I sat, staring at the phone, listening to the rain on the windows and musing about my latest interaction with the Crown prosecutor.

I had called her and said, "Hello, I'd like to speak with Lynne Kohm."

"This is Lynne."

"What?"

"Hello."

"Sorry . . . I'm just surprised to hear you in person."

"I have to scoot. I have a meeting. I'll phone you back right away."

"What does 'right away' mean?"

"Within an hour. I'm meeting with this Crown and . . ."

She ended the call.

I wanted to tell her about my English teacher. I wanted to know if she believed Jock would ever end up in court. I wanted to go outside and watch the rain fall onto my tomatoes.

The ring startled me. I snatched up the phone.

Her offhand tone had disappeared. "I'll give you the bad news right away. The date for the judgment has been put back. It should be given in the middle of October. Pollock delayed things too long again. The doctors for the Crown did not have a chance to look at the medical charts and other evidence. I tried to have his motion disallowed. But that meant I would have had to give evidence, and be cross-examined, and then I couldn't continue as Crown. And that would delay things even more. By the way, the judge, named Hanssen, was ticked off and yelling at Pollock."

The phrase "middle of October" spun around in my mind. Despite this swirling, I noted Ms. Kohm seemed all fired up. Not once did she suggest dropping the charges.

"Hanssen is going to Ottawa in September. He'll write his judgment there and present it when he comes back."

My voice rasped, caught by the lump in my throat. "Do you think the judge is aware of the effects on the family?"

"He's aware. He wants to end this as much as anyone."

At that moment, I hated Jock for hiring Pollock, I hated my aunt for coughing up the retainer to hire Pollock, and most of all, I hated Pollock. The thought of another summer of waiting stalled my brain.

"Well, goodbye now. I have to scoot."

Tears of rage and regret splashed into the holes in the phone's mouthpiece.

47

ON JULY 6, MY SISTER BELLE CALLED AT 9:00 A.M. and talked for two hours in her "little girl" voice. Her daughter, Rena, had accepted a large sum of money from her ex-husband. I suspected she might have been drinking or using pills. She mentioned the unbearable pain and alluded to suicide. By the end of the call she spoke more firmly and louder, but I was drained.

Allison and I drove to the Folk Festival and Wendy, Robin, and Jan met us there. Under a huge tent, with about 500 people surrounding us, we watched The Wyrd Sisters perform. Robin sat to my left, Jan sprawled by my right leg, and Allison leaned up against my knees. The air, sweltering and humid, barely circulated in the crowded space. After their comic song about using a water faucet for sexual pleasure, the trio shifted the mood, weaving harmonies in a haunting tempo.

I caught fragments of lyrics. "The sins of the father" . . . "A truth never told."

I started to cry. The profound power of the music could not be denied. This sudden weeping struck me as funny, right after the water faucet song. Robin grabbed my hand; Jan leaned her face into my right shoulder. Soon all three of us had tears dripping down our cheeks.

Allison sensed we were upset. "What's wrong? What's going on, Mom?"

I couldn't answer.

After the Folk Fest, Robin travelled to Lac du Bonnet for a short stay. In the morning, before he drove out from Winnipeg, he had visited the aunt who was bank-rolling Jock's defence. My sister Jean had been named after this aunt.

He said, "I tried to talk to her about this stuff. She just blathers on and on about Monty, who broke her heart when he left her at the altar. Then she cries."

"That happened sixty years ago. What does Monty have to do with us?"

"I don't know. She says she knows betrayal. We must forgive and forget."

"It doesn't sound as if she forgot and forgave Monty. She's still crying."

Two days later, Robin was still at our house. I asked if he planned to visit West Hawk.

He said, "Don't you like having me for a visitor?"

"I can't say much. You're an adult."

It was the first time he'd driven from Saskatchewan and did not visit Jock and Joan.

∾

WENDY, MARGARET, AND I continued to attend the abuse group. After one session, Wendy even phoned Jean to tell her how angry she felt about the latest delay. I had been labelled the mastermind behind the conspiracy; now I could see the roles were shifting and spreading.

I phoned my youngest sister, Shannon. Her stories saddened me, especially when she told how often Joan slapped her. I knew our stepmother was strict, but the physical battering surprised me. Shannon said she didn't have any confidence in the court process. Before Joan had adopted her, at four years old, she had suffered extreme physical abuse and starvation; she had no reason to trust anyone. I told her about talking to our English teacher. She sounded glad to know about this unearthed evidence.

On August 2, Barb phoned and said someone in the Crown attorney's department, who didn't want his or her name known, had told her the case was going to be dropped. Shortly after this call, Margaret and I left for our support group session. I didn't realize how upset I was until I attempted to explain the latest news to the women and broke into sobs. Karen and Esther asked me to stay after the session ended, to examine the feelings brought up by this rumour.

For ten minutes, I cried and swore. Hot and tired, I repeated, "I'm scared."

"What are you afraid of?"

"I can't last any longer."

Wendy convinced Margaret and me to stay at her house. I was tired, but the three of us talked long into the morning. We finally went to bed, but I could not stop the swirling agitation or fall asleep. On the one hand, I felt cared for by many people and the legal situation had forced me to grow. Yet I felt exhausted, and betrayed.

The next night, I wrote a detailed summary of all the delays, events, and effects. I had decided I'd send copies to Lynne Kohm, her supervisor, the Deputy Attorney General, people in West Hawk Lake, family, friends, and anyone else who might be interested.

"The sins of the father" had landed.

48

AFTER SUPPER ON AUGUST 15, ANNE ARRIVED AT our house. We'd asked her to look after Allison and Bradley during the next day, while Warren and I attended a business seminar. She had agreed to stay overnight, even though she rarely slept anywhere other than her own bed. We planned to leave at around six in the morning.

The sun set across the wide river and she drank coffee at the oak table in our kitchen, exhaling large breaths and examining the knobs on the cupboards.

"What's happening?" I asked, after the tenth sigh.

"I need to talk to someone. I don't know what to do."

"Do you need counselling?"

"I guess so. Are you still seeing Karen?"

"Yes." I was surprised she thought that I could get over trauma so easily. "Do you want to talk to her?"

"Yes."

She began to tell stories of her past and present life. Warren fiddled with his cup.

"I'm tired," he said and walked into the bedroom.

I looked at his mother. "You can call Karen. I'll drive you there, if you want. I know you don't like city driving."

Anne talked for a while longer; the sighs diminished.

The next morning, when Warren and I drove into the city, I said, "I'm mystified by your lack of empathy for your mother."

"I've heard her stories."

"At least she's admitting some problems. It's not easy, for her generation."

The next day, I picked up another subpoena at the local police station. This routine had become routine; the extreme panic of the first experience seemed irrational.

In the afternoon, I found out that both David and his wife Sandra, and Shannon and her husband Shaun, planned to move to the west coast. Since they might not be in Manitoba again for months, or even years, Wendy and I organized another meeting. We agreed we would make sure that we did not discuss any of the specifics of our abuse.

On August 20, when I pulled up to Wendy's house, Karen and Esther were climbing out of Esther's Honda Civic.

"You look stressed," Karen said to me.

"Stressed, and scared. They are calling me the hard-hearted ringleader."

I went inside. Shannon, David, Jean, and Wendy sat on Wendy's sectional couch. John hadn't bothered to respond. Ernie had promised he'd come but didn't show. Tom was in the city but declined. I fumbled with the speakerphone, got Robin on the line, and sat down. The tension felt thick, almost palpable. Karen and Esther laid out the ground rules and we jumped right into the crisis.

David spoke first. "I admit this is hard. I've been up all night packing. But we've got to do something before Shannon and I move."

He turned to Jean, "As a teacher, you're obligated to report. How can you say the court system doesn't work? It doesn't, when people withhold evidence."

Robin's voice squawked. "Why do you care so much about Jock and Joan?"

David said, "I'm looking forward to a fresh start. I've had enough of this shit."

His face was a mask of pain, furrows carved along his eyes and mouth. He turned to Jean. "How can you do this? You're the oldest. When you started working, you bought us toys, and took us to the circus and plays. Why can't you stand with us now?"

Between sobs, Jean muttered. "I am gutless. I know I'll live with this for the rest of my life. But cases get dismissed and everyone who comes forward ends up losing."

I didn't say much while they cried and talked. After they stopped, I read my three-page summary of the situation. They started to cry again. I showed them the letter about Jock's prosecution that I planned to send out, with the list of delays and dates. They passed it around and asked for copies. Everyone present, except Jean, agreed to send similar letters, or at least phone the Justice Department, and encourage others to do the same.

When Karen and Esther left, I accepted an invitation to stay for chili with Wendy, Bill, and Jean. After seeing her doubt and terror revealed, I felt uncomfortable looking at her.

I left at about 8:00 p.m. Halfway home, I realized my car's headlights did not work. I turned on the four-way flashers and drove at about twenty kilometres per hour. Every time lights approached, I pulled off to the side. It took four hours. At 2:00 a.m., I turned up our driveway, an emotional, physical, and mental wreck.

49

AT THE END OF THE MONTH, THE SURVIVORS' support group ended. To commemorate our sessions together, I organized an overnight canoe trip with Wendy, Margaret, and Irene from the city, in the provincial park where we grew up. For two days, we ate tasty fire-cooked meals, slept in a rain-soaked tent, and skinny-dipped off the rocks. Paddling with these women reminded me, just as the visit with Barb did, that I had a right to be present in the boreal forest I loved.

When Irene and I sat drinking wine by the campfire, she pointed out a rip in my pants.

In mock horror, I said, "Oh no, I have a hole in my crotch!"

Irene deadpanned. "I believe that's normal for women of all ages."

We rolled on the ground, hooting with laughter. The next day, we loaded up and headed home. Karen, Esther, another woman from the group, Hettie, and her husband, and Margaret's husband and kids greeted us at our house.

"You missed a heck of a trip. And some marvellous weather," I said.

"If you edited out the rain and all the exercise," said Irene.

Karen laughed and pointed at my torn pants. "You look like you were dragged behind the car. No one else is dirty like you."

We celebrated our pain, strength, and connections. The wine flowed; the barbecue sizzled.

On September 9, I wrote furiously into the night, hunched over the kitchen table. Bugs flew around the light above me; some landed on the paper. I squished them, wondering if my life had more worth than those smears on the loose-leaf. Wendy had phoned earlier to say she had contacted Lynne Kohm's supervisor. He reassured her that the case was by no means "forgotten." When I phoned him, he gave me a similar line.

The next morning, during my weekly massage, Jeanne told me she'd heard the local priest, a convicted pedophile, had done time for his crimes. I wanted to go and punch him in the face.

I was still determined to take control of events. I sent out the letters, asking people to phone or write the

Justice Department. I applied for remuneration from the Criminal Injuries Compensation Board. I also arranged for Allison and me to take voice lessons from Margaret's friend, Melanie. I wanted to "find my voice."

Warren finally agreed to visit Esther for counselling. Right after the session, he phoned to say he was "okay" and to tell me how Esther praised him for coping. I could not help thinking either he lied to me or he lied to her.

On September 14, at 11:30 p.m., my brother Ernie, who lived in Kenora, called.

Right away, he said, "Hello, I got your letter. I couldn't come to the meeting you had at Wendy's. I had a big job to finish . . ."

I said, "We run a business. If you wanted to come, you could have come."

He muttered a few excuses and then spoke in a louder voice. "What's happening with the court dates? How come I haven't been subpoenaed?"

"That's strange. You see Jock so often; you could give a fine report on his state of health."

"If you wanted, you could go and look at him."

"There's a court order for him not to have contact with witnesses. And I am a witness."

"I take my kids to see Joan. I hate to do it, but I make sure she's watching them."

"You say you hate it. But you have choices."

"Choices? People call Jock to line up work for me. I go there to collect rent from the old house. I need the business. And my supplies are stored in the old garage."

"You could ask people to call *you* about jobs and get your renters to mail *you* their cheques. And you don't have to go into Jock's house to pick up stuff from the garage."

He sighed. "Why does Lynne Kohm only phone you and Wendy?"

"Why do you think?"

"I guess . . . you make an effort to contact her."

"Have you tried?"

"I hate phoning people who don't return calls."

"Has she done that to you?"

"Well . . . I haven't called her. I hate lawyers anyway."

He sighed again. "My ex-wife took me to the cleaners with help from those slime balls. Look at Pollock. He's dragging out this crap to make money. And then there's Warren, defending low-lifes he knows are guilty."

"Warren doesn't do criminal work."

"I paid my lawyer thousands to collect money from a bankrupt company. We never saw a cent."

"Does he deserve to be paid for work he did?"

"He should have known they were going bankrupt."

"Did you, when you wired the building?"

He repeated six of his previous statements, getting louder and squeakier. "I'm taking a neutral stance. I don't want to testify. But I don't know how John and his wife stand it. Everyone in West Hawk knows. Shit, half the people where I live know. I'm only doing it for Joan."

"Do you think Jock has his children's best interests at heart?"

"Not really."

"How would you feel if his delaying tactics work?"

His voice fell to near whisper. "I'd be glad. At least all this crap would be over."

"Do you think if he dies, things will get back to normal?"

"No. But maybe something . . . like it was. I hope he dies soon. It would be best for all of us. Would you go to the funeral?"

"No. Why do you support and protect him?"

He didn't answer.

Instead, he said, "Is there really a Crown prosecutor working on this case? Is it a man or a woman? Who is the Crown attorney? Who can I contact about this?"

His response confused me. At the beginning of our conversation, he knew the answers to these questions.

I felt a wave of pity. "It's all in my letter, if you care to look."

He didn't want to tell his children, in case his ex-wife found out. If she did, she wouldn't let him dump their kids with Joan. He had no friends, and Joan was probably the only adult he spoke with at any length, outside of his job.

After a long silence, he said, "I've got to hang up. This is costing me a bundle."

"You're an adult. You know what you need to do."

He gulped, and hung up. I felt like throwing the phone on the floor, or throwing up, but I didn't do either. It might wake the children. It was 1:30 a.m.

I tried to talk to Warren about Ernie's phone call. He pretended to be asleep. Only when I told him about the lawyer-bashing did he get riled up.

50

THE NEXT DAY, BY MID-AFTERNOON, IT WAS twenty-four Celsius, mild for September. When Allison came home from school, we swam and sat on the dock until twilight. After our late supper, Jean called. I had fallen asleep on the couch and the ring startled me. She rattled on about job, school, children, home, coaching. Then she told me she was making plum jam, while helping her daughter, Tamara, write a speech.

I shook my head to wake up.

I said, "What do your kids think of this? How will you feel if his charges get stayed? How will you feel if his defence about being too old and sick is used by other pedophiles?"

She didn't answer. Instead she told me the jam needed stirring and Tamara needed help spelling. Then, speaking slowly, she said, "I've made my choice. But I really care about you."

"Is that true?" My voice broke.

"But I guess I don't care enough."

"I guess not."

A jar crashed to the floor.

She said, "Got to go now. And clean up the mess."

After she hung up, I flung myself on the couch and sobbed into the pillows, wondering who would clean up my mess. Her "caring" stance hurt more than the open hostility of those who supported and protected Jock.

I went outside. There was a full moon, no mosquitoes. After I went skinny-dipping, I sat on the picnic table by our dock, pounding on my guitar, yowling at the sky. I was thankful for the lack of neighbours. And I marvelled at how quickly life could shift, from the edges of despair to a sweeping wonder at the beauty of this warm night.

I phoned Karen in the morning and she helped me figure out why Jean and Ernie sounded so confused, vacillating between wanting approval and wanting clear consciences.

∼

THE LETTER TO the Justice Department that I had distributed motivated people to write to the Crown's office. Barb shared part of a letter she had sent to Lynne Kohm.

> *You mentioned that you thought that the community did not want a scandal and would prefer to sweep this case under a carpet. I understand how you might get this impression from the lack of willingness of some neighbours to come forward with statements regarding Jock's health. All the more reason that a message gets sent that his behaviour will not be tolerated. These people are obviously confused. Many in the community are outraged and angry, and do not want to see Jock get away with this. I believe you are trying hard to win this case. The purpose of this letter is only to urge you to keep trying. Please do not give up on these victims.*

Other women from West Hawk and Falcon Lake sent letters.

He should be brought to court and convicted immediately. The stall tactics used by the defence are sickening. He goes without punishment while his daughters are punished every day.

My masseuse, Jeanne, invited me for a meal at a nearby restaurant. Since Warren was at a council meeting, I hired a babysitter. I figured I deserved the break. Halfway through the meal, Anne and Ben walked in and sat at an adjoining table. My first impulse was to bolt but Jeanne whispered, "You are the healthy person. Sit down. You do not need to be ashamed of anything. Sit down. Keep eating."

The next day, I picked up Anne. Karen had agreed to see me at 11:00 a.m. and then meet with Anne after lunch. During the drive into Winnipeg, I gave Anne my summary letter to read. She wept. While I talked to Karen, Anne visited a nearby relative. During lunch, she shook and sighed, but after her session, her mood had lightened.

Right after I dropped her off, I rushed home to pick up Allison for the half-hour drive to our singing lessons. The sounds coming from my mouth surprised me; my fingers slipped and clanged on the guitar strings.

Melanie acted as if all of her students asked her to turn around and not look at them. She stayed an extra hour listening to me. Allison emerged from the church loft, where she had been playing during my lesson, and announced she was hungry. We agreed to go for ice cream. When we walked outside, the unusual warmth and the light from the waning moon amazed me.

I said, "Can you believe this? It's almost the end of September!"

Melanie said, "It *is* a gorgeous night."

"Did I tell you I like to swim in moonlight, as often as possible? This year I'm trying for a record. Would you care to join me?"

"I'll think about it while we drive to the dairy bar," she said.

Melanie decided to come for a swim and followed us back to our house. We walked down to the dock and shucked our clothes. Once the jolt of the cool water wore off, we floated on the gleaming surface for half an hour. The resident beaver swam by and slapped his tail and Melanie yelped. After our swim, we drank tea and munched on homemade oatmeal cookies.

I said, "I can't believe you drove so far to do this. Not many people would."

"I'm glad you asked. I like doing things like this."

"I'm glad you're teaching me to find my voice."

If all humanity could be divided into "the quick" and "the dead," Melanie certainly fit into the "quick" category. I knew I could learn from her.

51

ONE MORNING, LATE IN SEPTEMBER, WARREN LEFT for a conference on the other side of the province. I

shovelled the garden and picked the last of the tomatoes. Then I drove into town for the mail and opened an
important-looking letter. The Assistant Deputy Attorney General advised me he was "having senior officials
look into this matter" and they would be in touch with
me in the near future.

After lunch, the local florist delivered a single yellow
rose. I felt rattled by this gesture and asked her who paid
for it, but she'd only say it was a woman and it was sent
in friendship. During the past two years, on dozens of
occasions, I'd pick up the phone, and the caller would
hang up after a few seconds. I asked friends about the
flower, but they all denied sending it. I could not even
phone Wendy for reassurances. Two weeks prior, they
had left for Greece, on a month-long holiday.

Allison broke out in chicken pox blisters.

Three days later, Warren returned from the conference and I left to visit Jan. We attended a women's
event organized by the women responsible for the Hecla
Island weekend. After the gathering, we went to a bar
and danced until 3:00 a.m. I wanted to release the tensions from five days of coping with two children, and
a vicious case of chicken pox, alone. In the city where
they held the conference, Warren had bought a set of
weights and a small bench. I embarked on a weight-lift-
ing program.

On September 26, a constable from Falcon Lake
called to get David's new phone number and tell me
the motion would be heard on October 11, 12, and 13.
A judgment would be handed down at that time. He
said Jock appeared well enough to attend church, and

then mentioned that he thought the judge would be impressed because it showed Jock was not a sinner.

Wendy and Bill returned from Greece. Other than being disappointed with the commercialism, and amused by the giant penis statues everywhere, they reported a relaxing break from the family situation.

I went to see *Forrest Gump* and cried when his true love threw rocks at her family's shabby house. She had told Forrest her father was always "lovin' and kissin'" her. I wanted to hire a backhoe to flatten our dilapidated family home, just like Forrest did.

Two days later, I visited Karen again. She said she had no faith in the justice system and wanted me to focus my energies on myself, rather than the legal morass. Cramps, headaches, and loose bowels had afflicted me all the past week.

On Thanksgiving, Wendy and Bill visited. Bradley stopped eating, grew irritable and blossomed with chicken pox. The next day, Lynne Kohm informed me the court had met and was still waiting for written summations from both sides. She told me the judgment "might" be finished before Christmas. Because court dates had to be booked at least three months in advance, the pretrial hearing "might" be heard in March. As usual, Ms. Kohm spewed facts and dates, and as usual, I hung up, devastated, sobbing.

Later, when I felt a bit revived, I phoned Wendy to let her know. She reacted with a silent acquiescence, which unnerved me more than anything. After talking to Wendy, I phoned Barb. She was also stupefied, but promised to tell all her neighbours who were following this case. She had other news to report.

She said, "Beverley told me Pollock was crowing about winning the case, getting Jock off the hook."

Warren was at a meeting. I put the kids to bed and sat alone in the dark.

Then I remembered Karen's words about holding on to something important. Shaking and choking, I slid into Bradley's bed and cuddled him. In the dim light from the hallway, I stared at his serene face, still spotted with red marks. Clenching my jaws to suppress the noise, I wept into his pillow.

The next day, the bridge over the Winnipeg River closed for repairs. Various crews were slated to work on it for the next month. It now took almost an hour in the car to get to town, instead of a twenty-minute bike ride. Between the chicken pox quarantine, the court delays, and the bridge closure, I felt trapped and lonely.

That night, I woke up at 4:30 a.m., shaken by a vivid dream. In it, I stood with my five brothers and five sisters in a dark, wooded valley, near a high rock wall. I could not make out their faces but I knew we were all there. The wall stood at least five metres in height, old and covered with moss, razor wire and broken glass on the top. We were afraid to climb over, but someone found a ladder. A few of us scrambled over and tumbled to the ground on the other side, bleeding, looking back at the top. Some had straddled the wall, entangled in the wire. They screamed, but were too scared to jump, or fall, on either side. Some insisted the wall was too painful to scale so they refused. We could not see them anymore. I got up and wrote about the dream.

At 7:00 a.m., Bill phoned to announce that Wendy was pregnant, a result of their Greek holiday. I yelped in delight; she was growing a new life, a sign of hope in the midst of all the senseless pain. I decided I needed to celebrate. My fortieth birthday was on October 25. We'd have a Halloween costume party. I just had to figure out how to get everyone to our house.

52

I WAS ALONE AGAIN, WRITING. A SLOPPY RAIN HAD started and stuck around. The temporary detour into town turned into a quagmire, full of potholes, often impassable. I missed my friends on the other side of the river, especially Fran and Margaret.

Despite the rain, I visited Karen. At the end of our session, I read a poem I had written for her. Her eyes misted up and she said, "I think you need to write more."

On October 20, Warren and I drove into the city, with both kids, for Allison's orthodontist appointment. On the way home, she complained about the wire-tightening and then yelled at me,

"Who have you invited to the party? Have you phoned Wendy and Bill?"

I mumbled, "I don't want to talk to you when you speak like that."

She continued to grill me about guests and decorations. "What about me? What about my friends? It's always about you and what you want!"

She pounded on my shoulder and wailed. I tried to grasp both of her hands. "Stop hitting. Would you like it if I walloped you?"

Warren shouted, "Shut up! I can't drive. I'm stopping the car!"

He slowed to a halt and parked on the shoulder.

"She never listens. We always have to do what she wants!" Allison screamed at me.

Warren turned and grabbed Allison. "I feel like whacking you myself. Stop flailing!"

I jumped out of the car and stomped along the gravel shoulder. After pacing back and forth and cursing for ten minutes, I returned to the car, stiff with cold. Allison cried, insulted, and called me names for another ten minutes. After we got home, she went right to bed. I wrote her a note. In the morning, she apologized.

That weekend, Allison slept over at a friend's and I took an extra-long ride on my horse. It felt good to be alone, especially since I did not get dumped. After supper, Warren met long-time friends at the local pub, and then invited Bruce and his wife, Lorna, for a visit. We sat around the kitchen table, drinking wine, and the conversation turned to the latest delays.

I said, "Yeah, it's difficult dealing with this shit, and the reactions of my family. The parallels in Warren's family make it even harder. We can't count on their support."

Lorna stared at me and then spoke slowly. "What's happening in Warren's family?"

I looked at him. He examined a smudge on the window behind me.

I said, "His father molested his sisters."

Lorna opened her mouth wide. "Oh . . ."

For the rest of the visit, Warren wore a pinched mask. I had seen that expression before, on David, on Wendy, on my other siblings. I knew I had not caused it, but it was hard to think I had unearthed it at that moment.

After they left, I said, "What's going on? Whenever I ask how you're coping with your shit, you say you talk to Bruce."

"Well, I did talk to him, a few times. I told him you're struggling."

"I am. But please don't focus on me. Why can't you include yourself in this process?"

"That was then. This is now. I don't know exactly what went on with my sisters."

I showed him the poem for Karen. He did not say a word. I went to bed, but did not sleep.

The next day, I asked Warren to respond to questions that had been tumbling around in my brain. I wrote:

What is the difference between Jock and Ben? How do you feel when you talk about the sexual abuse in your family?

He wrote back.

There is no difference. The rage is still there when I talk to my sisters, or think of them. I do not have any trouble talking about it when asked, but I'm reluctant to tell people directly. My parents mean less and less to me. I feel disappointed with my mother for protecting him in the past and protecting him now.

I responded.

I saw the look on your face when Lorna and Bruce came over. You are suffering and your family is suffering; only it is not as public as mine. By the way, no one's ever going to ask you directly about this crap. They would rather eat glass. You say you admire me, but you can't seem to disclose your own stuff.

It was October 25—my fortieth birthday. In the morning, Barb phoned to tell me to stay put. The kids handed me homemade cards; Warren handed me a bottle of wine. Just before lunch, Barb arrived with two carloads of women from West Hawk and Falcon Lake. I hadn't seen many of them much during the past few years. They hauled out soup and sandwiches, cards and presents. We drank wine. Tentative at first, the conversation shifted to an animated discussion about Jock's actions. They shared stories of being assaulted by him and gave big hugs when they left.

I called Karen. She exclaimed, "Your 'mothers' really came through. And remember, they weren't doing it just for you. God only knows what might have been done to them. Not just by your father, but by others as well."

It was October 30—the day I had chosen to celebrate my fortieth birthday with a costume party. I had my period and my emotions were up and down, but I figured it was appropriate for blood to flow fast and furious during a Halloween party. While we were decorating and cleaning, some folks phoned to send regrets.

"It's just too far with the bridge out. We're afraid to get stuck."

It started snowing. More people called to say they could not come. Wendy and Bill decided to stay home, to reduce the risk of exposure to chicken pox. But, despite the snow and the mud, almost thirty people ended up at our house. Karen and Esther came dressed as matching clowns. Margaret came with her children and a new boyfriend. Fran came with her son, Malcolm, and her new partner, "Dave-in-Drag." Jan dressed as a police officer with her husband in handcuffs. She brought me a book called *Motherless Daughters* by Hope Edelman. Every guest, except Margaret's friend, was dressed in costume.

Jan's gift explored the experiences of women who grew up without mothers. The author described how a person could be angry with the lost parent for not being there. The book felt like a signpost steering me to an unexamined part of my life, telling me to look at the feelings arising from being a motherless daughter. My mother had proved to be unreliable by dying, and my other parent could not be trusted. In the next month, this issue would come swinging at me from more than one direction.

53

ON NOVEMBER 22, MY FRIEND THERESA CALLED and told me her husband saw Jock in their lumber store in Falcon Lake. She also mentioned Tom was going around telling people that Jock "got off the hook."

That night, Warren and I argued.

I said, "I feel crazy when you deny your feelings. You were angry for the past week."

"I was not. Why do you feel crazy?"

"I see the anger. Then you say it does not exist. So I doubt my sanity."

My words didn't appear to make sense to him.

"By the way, Brycee and Shelley plan to confront Ben," he said.

"Are they doing this alone?"

"No, Brycee's husband will be there."

"Why don't they get a professional to help, to keep things from getting ugly?"

"And another thing—they don't want you to get involved. They said you were interfering, trying to 'fix' our mother when you took her to see Karen."

"Your mom decided. I drove her there."

The conversation deteriorated into a skirmish over whose family was more screwed-up.

I shouted, "I'm frustrated. You refuse to look at parts of your life that really matter."

"Men aren't like that," he mumbled.

"Bullshit!" I shouted louder.

I had signed up for a weekend retreat, facilitated by Esther and Karen, held at a United Church facility in Saskatchewan. The retreat would focus on second-stage naming of abuse, aimed at women who had been dealing with the trauma for a while. On November 25, I caught a ride with Karen, Esther, and another woman from Winnipeg. For six hours, I stared at the stretches of brown prairie grass alternating with skiffs of snow. Then we dropped into the Qu'Appelle Valley and caught sight of the retreat.

After supper and introductions, participants talked about how we handled being long-term survivors. I told the women how the more openly I spoke about my abuse, the more it activated people—reactions varied from negative to positive, but they were always intense. For example, Warren's sisters decided to confront their father on their own but directed their extreme responses at me.

The next morning, Karen handed each woman a clump of clay and asked us to form something that told about our grieving. I thought—give me that clay. I'll make something and get to the next activity. Warren was right. I've spent too long on this. I can do it without thinking or feeling. I tore the hunk in two and made a smaller human, then a larger figure with breasts. Chatting mindlessly, I smoothed and stroked the forms. I moved the two shapes back and forth, pretending to be a child playing with action figures.

I said, "I do this with my kids, mashing up Play-Doh."

Esther looked at me. "Since you're finished, would you tell us about your work?"

My jokes vanished. I sputtered, "I'll pass."

The women gazed at my clay people.

Esther asked, "Do you want to do something with the smaller form?"

"I want it sitting on the larger one. But it seems too big."

"Yes, it looks like an infant, next to the other shape."

I closed my eyes and mashed the "baby" into the lap of the larger piece.

She said, "Do it slowly. Is that where you want the baby to be? How do you feel?"

Tears streamed from my scrunched-up eyes. "I don't know."

"Do it slower."

I lifted the small form off the "mother" figure in a gradual motion. My hands trembled. Tears splattered onto the clay and softened it. My eyes stayed closed. I cupped the "baby" into the larger form. Stroking and crying, I nestled the two pieces together. I opened my eyes; the joined pieces struck me as achingly beautiful.

The other women took turns talking about their forms. I clamped my teeth together and tried to listen. When they finished speaking, it was lunch break. They headed to the dining room.

Karen and Esther stayed back to clean up. With a stretch and a groan, I stood up. Before I knew what hit me, I collapsed, sobbing on the floor. They offered to cradle me. Sniffling and incoherent, I flopped onto their knees as they leaned against the wall. Just like the clay figure, I proved to be "an awfully big baby."

During lunch, I didn't speak. Other women stole glances and looked away. I excused myself to go back to my room and fell into a deep sleep. Supper had already started when Karen came to wake me, four hours later.

After the evening meal, we wrote up covenants with ourselves. I wrote the following promises:

> *I will draw more and explore the lines of my life. I will quit trying to change anyone, and concentrate on me. I will play more, and remember how good it feels. I will allow the tears to come. I will celebrate my children, my horses, the outdoors. I will fight and sing.*

Then Karen and Esther talked about self-care, asking us to write down things we could do to celebrate life. I listed dancing in the rain, howling at the moon, and skinny-dipping. We ended the day's sessions with singing in the main lounge. Esther, a classically trained vocalist, said to me, "You have a good voice for blues or spirituals. Try breathing through your diaphragm."

She attempted to show us how important a diaphragm was and where to find it. Someone stood on mine as I sprawled on the floor; I was convinced I must have a strong one. The laughing and goofing around relieved the tensions from the sessions and the inertia of sitting in a car or a room for three days. I wanted to go outside and run up the banks of the river valley.

Late on Sunday evening, Karen dropped me off at Wendy and Bill's house. Wendy was still awake, throwing up. I kept my visit brief, remembering the first trimester of my own pregnancies. When I got home and unpacked,

I lifted the clay figures out of the bottom of my bag. The two clay pieces had hardened, fused together by my tears. Only a blow could split them apart and they would crack into a hundred bits if that happened.

Karen phoned to inform me the Criminal Injuries Compensation Board offered to reimburse me for my past counselling with her, and would pay for further sessions up to a certain date.

The weekend retreat prompted me to think about self-care; I arranged for a complete physical. I had been avoiding this since before Wendy's wedding. When I went to the doctor, I explained about the abuse and the court case. I expressed my fear of dying, and my fear that I deserved to die. The doctor listened to me for longer than the usual five minutes; I felt oddly proud I might have disrupted his schedule. He arranged for a mammogram and a complete workup.

On December 4, I attended a vigil for the fourteen women murdered in Montreal. Melanie, her husband Paul, and Margaret were there. During coffee break, I talked to Paul, a Lutheran minister, about the spiritual challenges I'd encountered dealing with the abuse and the legal system. His insights lifted my mood; we talked about their big news. I was happy about Melanie's pregnancy but sad that my voice lessons would end at Christmas.

The following evening, Warren called his brother Allan about the impending holidays. Allan spoke loudly enough for me to hear, even though I was not on the phone. "Why don't these girls shut up? Things will never be the same."

After their conversation, I asked, "If Allan feels that way about his own sisters, what does he say about my family? He must think we're all nuts."

Warren had no answer. "They want Christmas dinner at their place, without Ben."

"Why? They ignore us all year long. Other people provide much more emotional care. For example, Jeanne, my masseuse, wants us to have Christmas dinner with her family."

On December 6, I visited Karen. She read an assessment letter she'd written for the Criminal Injuries Compensation Board. It was hard to listen. She stressed how important it was for me to not feel ashamed about needing care. She reminded me how difficult Christmas was for me, even at the best of times, given that it would always be an anniversary of my mother's death.

That night, inspired by Karen, I wrote a letter to my Aunt Iris in England, my mother's only sister. I had wanted to do this for a long time but had procrastinated.

I'm writing when good wishes are usually sent, because I need to tell. And need to ask. I don't know how much you know so I've enclosed a letter I wrote in the summer. It details most of what has happened. You can imagine the effects on our family. Jock is being protected by the legal system, Joan, some of my siblings, and all of his own siblings. The judge has still not given a decision to say if he is fit to stand trial. The physical, sexual, and emotional abuses were a part of my life as far back as I can remember. Jock continues to intimidate, even though he is supposedly very sick.

Lately, I have been thinking more and more about our mother. A woman from West Hawk told me she often fell asleep on the organ bench, between playing hymns. Maybe it was quiet, and safe enough for her to relax. The woman told the story with sadness, but I treasure it. I did not really know her. Babies and work took up most of her energy. Who was she? What did she like? Why did she marry him? Why did she stay? We knew his anger, and witnessed the broken bones. Your daughters may have some incidents to relate, from their visits to Canada. I know our mother tried to protect us and we tried to protect her. I'd appreciate anything you could tell me about her. But I wonder if I have a right to bother you with all this pain. Can you help me? Any memories, good or bad, would fill in the holes in my childhood.

54

ON DECEMBER 10, I MADE PLANS TO MEET JAN at a restaurant in downtown Winnipeg. Wendy planned to join us, after work. After Jan breezed in, she said, "I'm famished. I haven't eaten all day."

Forty minutes later, Wendy arrived, and insisted we move to a non-smoking table. None were available. Finally, we got our meals. We discussed going to a concert, but since it had taken so long to get a table, we decided to try the dance floor. Wendy and Jan got up for one song, sat down, and started to argue about making judgments.

Wendy yelled above the noise of the DJ. "As a nurse, I make judgments every day. If a patient looks pasty and has trouble breathing, I judge him or her to be ill."

Thirty minutes later, I called to them, "Come and dance. This will not get resolved tonight."

"We're just having a discussion," Jan smiled at me. As we all walked back to the dance floor, she turned to Wendy, "Did you enjoy the Stones concert? Was it any good?"

I laughed. "Sounds like you're asking her to judge. Are you sure that's okay?"

"Mind your own business. And get out of my face! You don't listen to me or Wendy or anyone."

I took a deep breath. "I'm hurt when you talk to me like that."

"I need a smoke."

When she came back, she had cooled, in more ways than one. I wondered why she got mad at me so quickly, after arguing with Wendy for half an hour.

After much discussion, Warren and I opted out of Allan and Leanne's Christmas dinner. In the same spirit as the previous year, I sent out cards to siblings, with messages similar to the one I sent to Valerie, on her Alberta dairy farm.

You haven't contacted me since I sent the letter in
August. I assume you're sorting out how you want

to respond. I feel isolated because of the way you and other siblings are handling this. I still care about you and your children but I am furious one person is able to control how we, as adults, relate and connect to each other. Our lives are worth it.

To my surprise, Valerie sent us a cartoon cow card and reported about school, the weather, horses, and hockey—no mention of my letter or my Christmas card. Jean sent her usual cheery form newsletter, containing the word "busy" or its synonyms, at least twenty times. John's wife, Sue, sent a longer letter:

John refuses to talk about it and I respect his wishes. In some sense I would say he's keeping his head in the sand and hoping it will go away. He doesn't know what to say to you and would rather not discuss it. I'm sorry I can't be of more support. You can't change the past. If I were you, I'd concentrate on what the future holds instead of destroying yourself on the past. Don't throw away your life. Chin up, Donna. There is a bright future yours for the taking.

For me, the most admirable thing about the letter was the fact she even wrote it. But her "get-on-with-your-life" message infuriated me. Once again, it focused on the victim as unstable. I could "get better" if only I tried harder. The criminal's actions weren't discussed. I contemplated phoning her to ask how much her husband was affected. Or why he refused to talk to her—or me.

Two cousins wrote letters of encouragement; one enclosed a book on "spiritual resources for healing from childhood sexual assault." I appreciated these gestures but, in my responses, I wanted to be clear about the shared responsibility of confronting sexual abuse. I wrote back, saying things like "it takes two people to tell a truth, one to say it and another to listen."

On December 22, Anne visited briefly. Although she was all hunched over from pain in her lower back, she dropped off gifts. She talked about Ben, waiting for her in the car.

She said, "I was paranoid. Shelley was paranoid. I had to be on the lookout, so I exaggerated. He really didn't do much."

I gawked in astonishment and checked the impulse to pound my head on the wall.

Shelley and her boyfriend visited on Christmas Eve. Nothing of any importance got discussed.

The next morning, the kids woke up early, and seemed to enjoy their presents. Wendy and Bill arrived with Robin. On Boxing Day, Margaret, her children, and her new boyfriend visited for supper. David phoned from the West Coast. He had heard through the family grapevine that some cousins were considering getting together to discuss incest, despite the protestations of Aunt Jean.

We skated on the river and skied out to the warm-up shack for wiener roasts. Then we travelled with Robin to visit Barb and Craig. While we soaked in the hot tub, Barb revealed another snippet of hearsay.

"The woman who married Tom's best friend told me she was willing to testify. She heard Jock tell Joan that he had to pretend he was sick; otherwise he would not let her drive the car. He said he was perfectly able. She said she was outraged by such blatant faking."

After the holidays ended, I lifted a twenty-five-kilogram bag of salt after skiing for two hours, and my back went into spasms, forcing a cancellation of an appointment with Karen. I ended up staying in bed for a week, getting up only to pee and eat.

While I recuperated, I noticed how often Warren nagged and blamed Allison, whenever the kids fought. And they fought often without me to referee. How much of this conflict could be attributed to being caught in the midst of two dysfunctional families sorting out years of crap and how much was adolescent rebellion?

I had more reasons to get stronger, and more reasons to stay away from Jock and Ben.

55

ON JANUARY 5, 1995, THE PROVINCE ISSUED ANOTHER subpoena, which commanded me to attend court on March 15, 16, and 17.

A couple of days later, Belle's daughter, Rena, phoned to let me know she had stopped therapy and she talked to Joan frequently. This last revelation hurt. Rena loved hanging around with her step-grandmother, yet still blamed her mother for not protecting her. She forgot that Belle threw her child-molesting husband out, right after she found out. Unlike Joan, who still supported and protected Jock. After I talked to Rena, I wished I could get over my situation so easily. I continued to dream, almost every night, about dismemberment.

The next weekend, Bradley helped me dismantle the Christmas tree, unscrewing light bulbs and winding up garlands. I paused in amazement; he was so coordinated and helpful. Every day he invented numerous projects, drew funny pictures, and created things. He appeared to cope, despite the turmoil around him.

When I started to vacuum pine needles, Warren called me to the phone. I was surprised to hear Jan's voice after her angry tirade at the restaurant.

Two friends arrived to visit Allison. Bradley and Allison fought about who deserved to have friends over and who had more friends over. The three of them excluded Bradley for a while. Then all the kids went outside to skate. Jan was still listing what she didn't like about me. After an hour of verbal jousting, I hung up. Could I make money off this knack I had for pissing people off?

After dinner, Warren and I discussed "loving confrontation." I asked rhetorical questions. "Why can't I tell my truth and expect people to do the same? Where is the line between doing the right thing and allowing people to make their own choices?"

Just when I was getting all heated up about choices and actions, he said quietly, "Lorna and Bruce do not want to come over any more. Bruce said he's tired of hearing about abuse."

"I am a little tired of it myself. Some people are damned lucky. Everything just rolls out of their brains."

I thought of Jan, Jean, Brycee, Shelley, and Anne—they said they admired my courage, but they also seemed to hate me for it. Maybe it reminded them of what they were avoiding.

The Serenity Prayer echoed endlessly in my mind. "The courage to change what I can . . . the serenity to accept what I can't . . . ." I could not figure out the last part—"the wisdom to know the difference." Where could I get this wisdom?

I phoned Wendy. She described her day at my aunt's funeral. Even without a sore back, I doubted if I would have gone. She said many of the cousins made a fuss over her, circling around, offering congratulations on her pregnancy. Joan was present but ignored her. This cold-hearted wounding incensed me.

On January 27, I received a letter and pictures from Aunt Iris. Nine of the photos showed my mother as a girl, a teenager, a woman in her early twenties, and a mother holding babies, including me. In all of these, even in the most recent, where she cuddled my brother Tom, her last child before she died, she looked incredibly young. The tenth picture showed me, about seven years old, sitting on a draft horse. The words in Iris's letter hypnotized me.

Although I had heard the previous year from Belle and subsequently Jean, the disclosures in your letter shocked us. It seems almost impossible to believe it of the Jock I knew and liked. I can never forgive him for all that he did to my sister and her children. It is difficult to write this letter to express how I feel and all I would like to say to you. One thing I fail to understand is why it caused a split in the family. I can understand Joan standing by Jock, but why do some of your brothers and sisters feel they must protect him? Dare I ask which ones they are? I would have expected them to be unanimous in their condemnation of their father. When I first received Belle's letter telling us that Terry abused Rena, I found it difficult to believe and wrote to Jean for confirmation. What I fail to understand is why it took the trauma in Belle's family for this all to be revealed. I asked my daughters if they suspected. They said Uncle Jock was always cheeky and liked the girls, but they had no idea.

I thought these pictures would help answer some of your questions. It is almost fifty years since a happy young mother with a three-month-old baby left for her new life in Canada. Little did we know her future would be hell on earth. We were an ordinary working-class family, living in the country. Our father was fairly strict. Your mother, Violet, was, of course, four years older, so there were the inevitable arguments.

Violet was very bright and had many friends. She became a telephone operator after she finished school. Your grandma was very hospitable, so we were quite happy in spite of the war. Being a very intelligent, attractive young lady, she had many boyfriends. There were soldiers, sailors, and airmen around, since we lived so near to the coast.

Unfortunately, at a camp dance, she met your fa-
ther. I must admit he was fun and quite handsome.
After that, there was no one else for her. We were
concerned she would be living so far away, but they
seemed happy. As to why she stayed, I can only
guess. She would have had little money. Also, she
would not have deserted her children. As far as I
know, she never told our mother what was going
on. Maybe it was her pride. Or maybe in spite of
everything she still loved Jock.

We find it unbelievable the difficulties you are
having bringing him to court. Please let us know if
the judge ever does write his decision and what even-
tually happens. I do hope this letter has helped you.
Your cousins send their love. Please do not allow
this to spoil your life. You still have so much to live
for. Maybe one day you will come to England again.

I put the letter aside and started to decorate Warren's
birthday cake and make him a special meal. He looked
preoccupied during supper. Then he left for a meeting. I
helped the children paint a piñata for Bradley's birthday,
which was two days after Warren's. After finishing the
piñata, cleaning up, and putting the children to sleep, I
flopped on the couch and thought about my aunt's letter.

Warren came home, eager to describe all the person-
alities at the meeting, oblivious to my mood. He said, "I
can't believe that guy. He is such a tyrant, wants everything his way . . ."

My eyes blurred and a bizarre keening slid out of me.
This was no mere crying. I howled, mourning for the

child-teenager-woman in the pictures, in the letter. Ever since she left England, she had no one to tell.

"Don't touch me . . ." I said. I did not want to be thwarted as I was letting the sounds come out. Melanie would have been proud. I opened my mouth wide. I hit all the right notes.

56

I WOKE UP FEELING CRAPPY, EYES BURNING LIKE two gritty marbles. While Warren and I drank morning coffee, I explained my dilemma. "I need support. I feel so vulnerable right now, and it doesn't look as if it's going to get any better soon."

He said, "Maybe I can't give what you need, and you can't accept that."

The conversation shifted to the upcoming party. As usual, when conflict surfaced, the day-to-day logistics of family and household forced it back down. I told him what I had planned for Bradley's birthday. Then I collapsed on the couch and sucked back a beer to calm the ragged edges. The beer was down to the foam when the phone rang.

Warren answered it and turned to me. "Brace yourself. It's Lynne Kohm."

I took the receiver and took a long breath. "Hello," I said, quietly.

"You don't have to brace yourself. The judgment turned out better than expected. I am thrilled. I just received a copy this morning."

Her voice exuded competence. She explained the process, commented on the highlights of the document, and told us what to expect now that it was submitted to the Justice Department.

"I suspect Pollock will appeal, but he'll probably be denied. It's a very solid judgment."

After she hung up, I rinsed the foam out of the empty bottle. I wanted to drink the rest of the case. It was a quirky victory—comparable to knowing your malignant tumour was finally scheduled for removal. Instead of gulping more beer, I opted to make pizzas for Bradley's party. Chopping at a long hunk of pepperoni appealed to me right then. After I finished baking the pizzas and cake, I phoned Belle.

She said, "Good news! But I just started a new job. It's going to be a pain to get off work and get there for a trial."

I was puzzled by her offhand response. After all, she was the one who went to the police. Maybe her focus had shifted to battles with Terry. While I talked to Belle, the business phone rang. It was Wendy. After switching phones, I retold what I had just explained, a brief outline of the judge's ruling. She agreed it was an empty victory.

After Wendy's call, I contacted Barb and reiterated the news. She promised to pass the word around West Hawk. I called Karen, but she was not home, so I ended up talking to her husband for a while. He kept telling me how important it was to tell our history. I phoned Esther and left a message.

Five minutes later, Karen phoned back. "I wish you could see Esther and me dancing around the room and whooping."

"Part of me wants to whoop and dance. But the other part feels kind of scooped out when I think what happens next."

Barb called again, to talk at length. I explained more of the details and told her about my aunt's letter.

She said, "I'm so glad you hung in there. I know everyone out here in West Hawk will be applauding. I want to tell you something else, before I forget. When you guys came here at Christmas, I was really touched by something Allison did. She took me aside and thanked me for being such a good friend. She said she knew I talked to you often. She's worried about you. You have quite a kid, you know, to do something like that, to be so aware."

For the birthday celebrations, Bradley's buddies met at the local sliding hill. At 4:30 p.m., we came back to the house for food and drinks. Bradley had never had a major party, so I wanted it to be positive. He was very excited the whole afternoon, and the children seemed to enjoy themselves. The snowman piñata proved to be a "big hit."

Bill and Wendy lingered, and we discussed the judgment. An appeal would be costly and futile given the contents of the decision. I showed Wendy a booklet called "Sexual Assault and the Legal System," put out by a family violence committee in Toronto. It gave an overview of all the difficulties and procedures involved in reporting sexual abuse. It reassured victims they were not failures if they withdrew from the legal process at any point.

Pollock and Jock had relied on grinding down the witnesses. Even Lynne Kohm had wanted to end it a few months ago. I wished someone had given us a pamphlet like this at the beginning of this ordeal.

The next day, Warren drove to the city for business and visited his friend Marley, who had worked as a Crown attorney.

He told Warren, "You could push for direct indictment, because of the delays. The preliminary hearing would be waived. Hanssen's judgments are well written and thorough. Pollock has thirty days to file an appeal."

That night, I reread the document sent by the Crown. In it, Hanssen stated that he was not satisfied that prosecution violated the accused's rights under the Charter. There was no reason why he could not instruct his counsel, and modern technology could accommodate the trial process. Jock did not have to be present. Hanssen said he believed the psychiatrist retained by the Crown, who had stated that Jock was "attempting to manoeuver his way out of his legal predicament through malingering and manipulating." Hanssen emphasized the charges were very serious and requiring Jock to stand trial would not shock the community. He also suggested several practical procedures that could be implemented.

～

JEANNE, THE MASSEUSE, and I went out for lunch. I showed her my aunt's letter. She cried as she read it. "This must have been hard for her. There is so much sadness here."

"But I'm glad she did. I'd like to send copies to all my brothers and sisters."

The more I reflected on the contents of my aunt's letter, the more I wanted to talk to Karen. But I hesitated. During an argument, Warren had said I was addicted to counselling. Now that my back had stabilized, I lifted weights again. Jeanne offered to give as many massages as it took to get through the preliminary hearing.

I resigned myself to waiting for March 15, 16, and 17, and focused on two newfound truths. First of all, as Karen said, I needed caring and support. Where it came from was often not where I expected it to come from, but, nevertheless, I needed it. Second, Jock had ceased to exist as a person. I felt no sense of loyalty or concern.

57

ON FEBRUARY 3, THE SENIOR CROWN ATTORNEY acknowledged receipt of various pieces of correspondence sent to his department, concerning the ongoing prosecution of Jock Tod. Four days later, I still hadn't heard from Ms. Kohm. I assumed it meant no appeal had been launched.

Despite Warren's objections, I visited Karen. It helped me; I always came away feeling cleaner and whole. When

I asked her about Jan's anger, she said, "Sometimes people who have their own stuff to deal with are intrigued by others' efforts. Because you're willing to go to great lengths, you matter a lot to her."

"Because I confront her?"

"People get mad at others when they're doing what *they* need or want to do."

"It sure explains the way people respond to me, especially in my family."

"What is your role in your family?"

"The wrestler."

"How does that help you? Hurt you? What do you want? Fighting takes energy. You can't extend yourself for everyone, every time."

We talked about the judgment and a possible reunion of the women in the support group.

THE DAY AFTER Allison's birthday party, I got up early and met Wendy, Karen, Esther, and Irene in the city, and we headed 60 kilometres south to visit Hettie, from our support group. We skied on the nearby cross-country trails, ate hearty soup, and talked all day. After supper, I pulled out my guitar for a singalong. Wendy seemed quiet and did not ski; the women clucked and cooed over her swollen belly, sharing parts of their labour stories. Driving home, I felt exhausted, but I was very happy I got a chance to reconnect. Every once in a while I'd stop and stick my head in a snowbank.

On Valentine's Day, Warren and the children were gone. I sat down and plunked on my guitar.

"I needed your love, I needed your love," I sang in a slow, mournful voice.

At first, I thought it might be about Warren, but as I fiddled around with words and made verses, it came to me. I was writing a song, my first attempt. It was a song about someone else who was supposed to matter. A father. Once that sunk in, hot tears rolled out and my voice cracked.

The following day, CBC radio mentioned the judgment and our situation. Bill had heard it early in the morning. I listened until noon but did not catch the report. The impact of widespread publicity unnerved me. I called Barb. Although she hadn't been listening to the radio, she said her neighbour had told her about it.

After an hour of fretting, I phoned the radio station.

"You ran a story this morning about an elderly man who is avoiding facing charges because of his health, and the judgment written on this situation. Where did you get this information?"

"It was taken from the wire service," the woman answered. She read a report from the largest city paper. As she spoke, the familiar, sickening disorientation engulfed me.

"Is this story accurate?"

I stammered, "Yes . . . it is correct."

"Did you know about the judgment beforehand?"

"Yes, but I didn't know these documents could be accessed so easily."

After that call, I tried to contact Lynne Kohm. When we had discussed the judgment before, I understood it was not supposed to be publicized. Barb had encouraged me, at various times, to go to the media. Lynne Kohm had insisted, and Warren agreed with her, that judges did not look favourably on witnesses who attempted to convict the accused in a public forum, in the middle of a court case. But the middle of this case was so painfully long, public interference might speed things along.

That night, a full moon radiated off the snowdrifts. Although the temperature approached minus twenty-eight Celsius, I felt as if I might explode if I did not get rid of the tension growing inside my guts all day. I went for a moonlight ski. When the endorphins kicked in, my vibrating body settled down. At least I could sleep.

Since my aunt in England had asked me to inform her about the judgment as soon as it was given, on February 19, I wrote her another letter:

I really appreciated your response. I hope you don't mind if I show it to others in the family. Some have not been very supportive. A couple of cousins have come forward. Nobody, yet, to my knowledge, has ever denied anything. They all know he was capable. Like you, I am puzzled why my siblings are split on this issue. Robin, Wendy, Belle, David, and Shannon are in favour of speaking out. Valerie, Ernie, John, Jean, and Tom are resisting. These positions have wavered a bit over the past two and a half years, but basically that is where they sit. We have had three counselling sessions. Jean comes to them. John and Ernie came to one. Although the family is not unanimous in condemning Jock, the people out in West Hawk generally are.

I felt sad after reading your letter, but I also felt stronger because of your unequivocal condemnation of Jock's actions. I've enclosed an article that appeared in the paper. The judgment, given at the end of January, stated the arrangements, such as having doctors present or holding it in a hospital, that could be made to give him a fair trial. But it was a judgment only on a motion; the actual case has not even started. We are scheduled to appear at a preliminary hearing in the middle of March.

The pictures you sent mean a lot. As you know, all family pictures were destroyed in the fire. As for this spoiling my life, I feel stronger and more adult, although it scares me some days, like when the story came out in the paper. The sexual abuse happened for years. It will take years to unwind the knots and the pain. Thank you for your letter and your love.

58

IT WAS NOW MARCH. WE WERE BOOKED FOR OUR annual weekend at Maplelag, even though it was so close to the court dates.

I felt anxious and overwhelmed but decided to focus on two main points. First, I'd focus on how I'd react if someone sexually assaulted Allison or Bradley, and nourish that same anger for myself. Second, Jock assaulted us frequently; if each act was worth a specific term in prison, he deserved whatever sentence he got.

After Jock's prosecution went public, the kids and I caught a bad flu, with hot and cold sweats, aches, and lots of sleeping. While I recovered, Warren's mother gave me a book, *Strong at the Broken Places* by Linda T. Sanford. The author believed survivors were not that much different from others, not likely to inflict trauma on others, but actually strengthened.

On March 6, I visited Karen again. I had often felt like I wanted her to hold me but felt too embarrassed to ask. The solution finally occurred—a blindfold. Not seeing her face allowed me to accept the embrace. As she sat on the floor and held me from behind, I talked about my mother and how she regularly cleaned our ears, holding our heads. Her hands smelled of Javex.

Then I talked about oral sex with my brother and cousins, and how I felt so dirty then, and now, just saying the words. I remembered the odours, the choking sensations, the quarters they gave me. How they all knew it was okay to do that to me. Then I talked about my children and how easily they could be manipulated. I soaked the blindfold, sobbing in Karen's arms.

She asked me to visualize the courtroom. "What feelings can you anticipate?"

"I will be feeling traitorous—unworthy of life—crazy!"

"You'll need to stay present. You'll be feeling and showing strong emotions, but you do not have to take care of anyone. Concentrate on what you need to say."

At 10:30 p.m., Fran's estranged husband phoned me. Randal said, "What's happening with your court case?"

"I don't want to talk to you. When you were married, you never asked once."

"Well, I was . . . not sure if you wanted to talk about it."

"I talked to people who asked, and cared."

"I know you were afflicted with a great evil. It is still present in you. I know about evil. But my prayer helps people. Did you hear about that guy who smacked into a tree with his snowmobile? Well, I prayed for his mangled body when he was in intensive care. He's home now. I phoned his mother to let her know my prayers healed her son."

I interrupted. "If you're so Christian all of a sudden, why don't you show some mercy and stop bugging me? Or, better yet, why don't you settle with Fran?"

"I'm glad the anger is coming. The evil will release its hold when you let out the anger. I am praying for you!"

"Fuck off, Randal! Get a real life, not this quasi-divine evangelical bullshit which adds to your mammoth superiority complex!"

"Go ahead, yell some more . . ."

I hung up. A minute later, he called again.

"I am praying for you. I know I can help you get rid of the evil that invaded you."

I slammed down the receiver. He redialled. I slammed it down again and took the phone off the hook. I looked at the clock. It was past 11:00 p.m.

In the morning, Randal called Warren at work and said he felt a "huge release" when I shouted at him. He phoned me again in the afternoon.

"You know, I was deeply affected by our conversation last night. After our call, I felt the evil pass through my body. I was shaking."

"Were you speaking in tongues? Did you faint?"

"I prayed for the evil to be channelled through me. Did you feel anything? I felt it."

"The only thing I felt was anger. The only release was hollering at you," I yelled. "Maybe it was your own little devil you were passing. You're so anal retentive the horns probably got stuck. Don't call me."

I hung up and stood there, baffled. After a few minutes, I devised a solution to stop his harassment.

"Hello, Pastor, I'm phoning about a member of your congregation who has . . ."

The pastor interjected, "Do you accept Jesus Christ as your own personal saviour?"

"What?"

"Do you accept Jesus Christ as your personal saviour and believe he died for your sins?"

"I believe that a prophet named Jesus lived and died. Is that good enough? If you don't talk to me, my next call is to the police. I am calling about Randal. I believe you've been counselling him."

Before he could ask if I was born again (again), I briefly explained the circumstances.

"I may be wrong, but I'm fairly certain your church does not condone abuse in any of those forms."

"Oh no, we do not. I'll talk to Randal. He's new to our church; he gets carried away."

"I'm counting on you. If he bugs me again, I'll call the police."

"I'm sure he won't do it again."

The next morning, we headed south to Maplelag and arrived in time to go for a ski before supper. After that, we enjoyed the familiar whirlwind of skiing, hot-tubbing, drinking weak American beer, guitar-playing, dancing, singing, changing clothes, going nude in the sauna, and repeated them as often as possible. On the way home, Warren threw up a few times, so I drove. Two of the cars from our convoy had mechanical problems so we were delayed driving back.

Randal did not phone again. Silently, I thanked my own personal saviour for rescuing me. If only the Jock-plague could be so easily quarantined.

59

I FELT NUMB ALL WEEK. MY ARMS TINGLED AND I dropped objects. I went to see Jeanne for a massage. While she worked, she reminded me, "You'll feel free and whole soon. Just don't take any drugs. You need to feel it all."

"I know. I've cried so much I know it won't destroy me."

After supper, Barb called. "You're a fantastic person. You have a lot of guts."

"Thanks."

"I talked to Ernie last week. I told him his sisters are doing the right thing. Before I knew it, he broke down and sobbed."

"Wow. He really needed to hear what you said to him."

"I told him he's not helping Joan. It allows her to ignore reality."

"This sounds corny, but I sense urgent little angels lifting me. You're one of the angels."

"I love you."

David phoned right after Barb. We joked about the upcoming hearing.

"Will it be a touching reunion after all these years? Will we smile and wave across the courtroom?" I said.

"It will be a real heart-warming scene. I heard you're the lead-in hitter, the home run queen. Remember, you've only to get on base. I hope you write about this. I want Michael J. Fox to play me in the movie."

"He has too much hair."

"Ouch!"

"Sorry. It's funny how some of us are communicating better than ever. It only takes a criminal trial to bring our family together. We don't take a lot of pushing."

"We're quite well adjusted."

"Seriously, I need to know you won't hate us if Jock dies on the stand."

"No. I promise."

Margaret called after David.

"I want to come for the hearing."

"Who wouldn't want to witness this courtroom drama? Ambulance attendants will rush in with defibrillators, slap on the pads, shout 'All clear!' and zap the defendant. Then the learned judge will pull down his spectacles and ask, 'How do you plead, Mr. Tod?' Are you prepared for such electrifying testimony?"

"I'm glad you see the humour."

"Do you know the difference between pathos and bathos? When something is beyond pathetic, so ridiculous it makes you laugh instead of cry. Bathetic. I think that's the word."

"I want you to know I love you."

"Thanks for telling me."

The same day, I received a note from a friend I hadn't seen since we travelled together across Europe in the fall of 1980. Linda had taught elementary school in West Hawk. The blazing intensity of her words surprised me.

> *I'm behind you one hundred percent. I'm sorry I didn't recognize any signs when I taught Shannon and spent so much time with you. It fully explains things I didn't understand but never questioned. The cycle ends with you. If there is anything I can do, like offer a place to stay, a friend to attend court, a shoulder to cry on, or faith in yourself renewed, I'll be there for you.*

On March 14, in the afternoon, Wendy, Shannon, and I were scheduled to meet with Lynne Kohm to review our statements and discuss what we could expect at the preliminary hearing. Warren's mother agreed to stay with Bradley. Belle did not fly in for this meeting. Perhaps Ms. Kohm suspected what would happen and decided it was not worth it. Whatever the reason, Belle was still in Ontario, but Shannon had already arrived.

When Warren and I came off the elevator in the justice building, Wendy was seated in the waiting area. She said, "The whole thing might fold. It's confusing to me. I'll let Lynne explain it to you."

Warren and I sat down. He chatted with a colleague from law school who was also waiting for someone. I regretted we had skipped lunch to get there. Just after Warren went downstairs to get chocolate bars, Ms. Kohm bustled into the room. After only talking to her on the phone for two years, her sudden appearance startled me. She looked bigger and blonder than I remembered, and very confident.

For the first hour, Wendy, Warren, and I met with Ms. Kohm, in the secured area, in the same library as the first time. We sat on couches, facing her. She didn't waste a moment. Pollock had almost agreed to a guilty plea, but had changed his mind after he called West Hawk. She overheard him talking to a woman; she suspected it was Joan.

She spoke quickly. "He's been running around all week trying to get the prelim cancelled, because his appeal hasn't been heard. Every venue possible has bounced him back and forth. He gets refused again and again. It sounds as if he's not ready. Your father is supposed to appear in person to waive his right to a preliminary hearing, face the charges, and do this 'commit to stand trial' thing. It might take five, or ten minutes, tops. I doubt he'll show.

If he doesn't, the judge can issue a warrant for his arrest. I don't know what this judge will do."

"You mean he might send police cars screaming out to West Hawk?" I asked.

"He could, but it's unlikely. I'll go over what to expect if this really happens. First and foremost, Donna, I want you to curb your tendency to run amuck."

"What? Me?"

She laughed and explained the procedure while warning us what tactics Pollock might employ. "He might suggest you are vengeful, or out for a big settlement."

Wendy said, "I'll tell Pollock that Jock has no money. Not even enough to pay off his leech of a lawyer."

We all laughed. I asked who could attend, what the judge was like, and how long Jock would be in the room. Since the meeting was taking much longer than expected, Warren left for an appointment with a client in the city.

In order to talk to Wendy alone, Ms. Kohm sent me out in the hall. I squatted on the floor for twenty minutes. Workers walked by and looked askance at me, but I felt surprisingly calm, thinking about what Wendy might be saying. Ms. Kohm called me back into the library to discuss my statement. I shook, especially when describing gritty specifics of the assaults.

"Don't say 'maybe.' It implies you aren't sure," she said.

"You're quizzing me about details, and I'm still thinking it's not bad enough. I almost want to tell you worse things, but I can't lie."

"Listen to me. What he did was bad enough. We would not be here right now if it wasn't."

"Maybe Pollock will construct a 'false memory' defence."

"Seeing as how there are four of you, even he would be stretching it a bit."

At 5:30 p.m., we exited the secured area. Shannon was alone, sitting on a chair. She looked deflated, but it could have been the flight, and the wait. I gave her a hug. She would be with the Crown attorney well after closing time. Ms. Kohm offered to drive Shannon back to where she was staying. Wendy, Bill, Warren, and I went for a meal. Then we drove home to Lac du Bonnet. I called Fran and Margaret, and left a message for Barb. Barb responded within half an hour. I told her about the uncertainty.

"We don't know if anyone else even needs to be there, because he might not show."

"I'll tell all the other women. They'll be disappointed. They're raring to make their presence known. I might come in anyway. I have to see a client who wants some building done."

March 15, court day. Bradley cried because Mommy was leaving again. Although we were in a hurry, I sat with him for a few minutes. He calmed down and said, "I'll handle things here and look after Grandma. If you get sad when you're in that rotten court, put your arms around your body. You can give yourself a hug."

"Thanks, and you can do the same if you miss me."

I drove into the city, speeding all the way; Warren didn't say anything about tickets. We picked up Wendy and Robin, and rushed to the courthouse. Lynne Kohm met us and directed Warren, Robin, and Barb to the courtroom.

Ms. Kohm watched them go and then turned to us. "I told Shannon to stay put until this afternoon, in case we don't need her."

She escorted us to the Victim Assistance area. I assumed it would be a private lounge, but it seemed to be a congregating spot for police officers and lawyers waiting for court appearances, making calls, grabbing coffee, exchanging gossip, hiding out.

FROM THE MOMENT we stepped past the massive doors of the Victim Assistance area, its bizarre atmosphere confounded me. Harried employees spent large chunks of time explaining why some guy was not where he was supposed to be, or directing disgruntled cops to the right courtroom with the wrong judge or vice versa. Several times, Wendy and I looked at each other and burst out laughing, when we overheard conversations between the ever-changing cast of characters who wandered in and out. Lawyers swooped in, dressed in tailored suits, dragging wheeled cases stuffed with files. Police officers sauntered in, hands jammed in pockets. Victims schlepped in, cloaked in visible indicators of low income and low self-esteem.

At 10:00 a.m., Warren, Robin, and Barb returned from the courtroom, walking in a line. To my surprise, my old friend Linda followed them. She was blonder and shorter than I remembered, but I could see by her face it mattered a great deal to be with us. Her unexpected presence melded perfectly with the overall weirdness of the scene.

She asked, "Are you certain this Lynne is tough enough to stand up to Pollock?"

We all reassured her Ms. Kohm was committed to fighting stupidity.

Throughout the morning, the four of them left and returned to the Victim Assistance area, sometimes with Ms. Kohm, sometimes without, to explain and recap the proceedings. During this time, my emotions swung between fear, sadness, anger, and laughter at the wasted hours and bureaucratic confusion we witnessed.

First, the lawyers argued about whether Jock had to be physically present to commit to stand trial and make his election of judge or jury. Although he wasn't there, Jock had already chosen to have his case decided by a judge, the common choice of sexual offenders. Juries tend to react with horror to stories of sexual escapades between adults and children, simply because they have usually not heard so many versions as a judge.

Next, Pollock handed the judge some medical reports and Hanssen's judgment. The judge called a break so he could read them. Then the court considered how Jock could get around being present, and argued about whether the court party could travel out to West Hawk Lake and hear Jock in his living room.

The judge was baffled, questioning everyone in sight, "So why can't he come into the court? Is he bedridden? Has he really gone shopping?"

My entourage told me Pollock pulled long faces and predicted tragedy at every opportunity. Finally, after we came back from a two-hour lunch break, he announced a recent three-line amendment to the *Criminal Code*. Neither the Crown nor the judge knew about it, but apparently it allowed the accused to be absent. I guessed his secretary had stumbled upon this new twist during the noon-hour; otherwise, it seemed logical he would have presented it when they started, and saved everyone time and energy and money.

I could not believe it. The preliminary hearing, which had been delayed, and dreaded, for years, ended abruptly. Shannon, who had been flown from British Columbia at taxpayers' expense, never saw the inside of the courtroom. All the work and emotion expended to get to this point, by police, lawyers, victims, friends, and counsellors, counted for nothing.

Barb and Linda returned to the Victim Assistance area, roaring with laughter, but also galvanized by outrage. Linda could not believe the delays and manipulations that the rest of us by now took for granted. We sat in the lounge, waiting for Ms. Kohm to debrief us, and I felt a weight shifting. Others were taking up the fight, talking about justice and anger.

Ms. Kohm arrived and spent another hour or so with us, explaining what happened, and what would happen, answering questions. Her eyes showed exhaustion, and strain. Spending a day sparring with Pollock must have worn on her. She could have gone home right after it ended. The other harried employees had long ago departed. I liked to think she gathered strength from our collective energy. We shared the same sense of purpose. No one needed to explain why he or she was there.

Ms. Kohm said, "Pollock forfeited his chance to feel out the witnesses, so he'll be less prepared when it comes to trial."

While the rest chattered about the antics in the courtroom, I reflected on scenes from our day. In the morning, Wendy had mentioned she didn't want to run into someone she knew. But, while we were in the law courts building, we saw several people we knew: Wendy's lawyer neighbour, Bill's high-school lawyer friend, Wendy's massage therapist, a friend from West Hawk, and various lawyers from Warren's years at university.

The most unsettling incident happened right after Warren and Robin left us to watch the courtroom mischief. Two police officers walked into the Victim Assistance area. I recognized the burly guy as a former biker from our high school. Wendy recognized his slender partner as one of David's best friends.

Startled, he asked her, "What are you doing here?"

"It's a personal matter," Wendy said.

The burly one sneered at her. "All we have to do is go look in the computer."

His comment captured the lack of sympathy we had faced during our first day in the court. It would prove to be one of many. As we gathered up our coats and notes to leave, I thought of Bradley "handling things" at home. I slipped into my jacket, reached around my shoulders, and gave myself a big hug.

60

ROBIN HAD TRAVELLED TEN HOURS FROM A northern Saskatchewan community to attend the erstwhile hearing, so he decided to drive out to our house. The children greeted him at the door, but I heard another voice. It was not Warren; he was at a meeting. Shannon walked into the kitchen.

Bradley and Allison bounced with excitement, ecstatic. Allison asked, "Why can't you be like Auntie Shannon? She's so much fun."

After they ate, Allison and Shannon plunked on the piano together. Robin and I hunched over the dirty dishes on the table and talked. Then Shannon returned to the dining room and flopped onto a chair.

"By the way, I want you guys to hear it from me. I'm pregnant," she said, without taking a breath.

I was speechless. She stood up, and returned to the piano.

In a barely audible voice, Robin said, "You know, you could have been . . ."

"I know, more tactful, more excited." I went to the piano, and hugged her from behind the bench. "This is big news. You sound very happy!"

It explained why she looked so wilted in the Justice Department waiting room. After a couple more songs with Allison, she stood up. "I'm very tired. I'm going to bed."

"You can sleep in Allison's room."

After they left, Robin and I stayed up talking until 4:00 a.m.

The next morning, Bradley woke me up around 6:30. Shannon came into the kitchen. I tried again.

"I'm sorry about last night. How are you doing financially?"

"We don't need much for a baby."

She did not need my advice. I dropped the subject. At 3:00 p.m., Shannon and Robin drove back to the city.

During midterm break, Allison, Bradley, and I visited Wendy for a couple of days. While in the city, I called Linda. She invited us for lunch. Our children's ages roughly corresponded, although they were different genders. They played for a few hours, while we caught up on the past fifteen years.

Linda said, "I phoned Shannon before she flew back to B.C. She needs to hear how bad it was for all of you, not just her. I told her she could look to you for the truth, and support."

I shrugged, mindful of how I had attempted, and blown, my chance a couple of days earlier. As we sat drinking herbal tea, Linda shared some of her past. I did not know how to respond, except to listen and nod.

On the way home from the city, we went to a magic show with Fran, Dave, and Malcolm, and Margaret and her children. All of them had moved from the Lac du Bonnet area. When we parted, I felt sad to think I would not be seeing either one of these women much in the near future.

But, to my surprise, I saw Margaret the next week. We attended a gathering of about twenty people at a church in Winnipeg. The event started off with a film featuring interviews with sexual abuse survivors. I decided to tell the group about my father's prosecution. Although it was not as dramatic, or, as in our case, anti-climactic, as telling in a courtroom, I summarized my family's story for people who were not survivors, not therapists, and not all women. One of the organizers had been instrumental in planning the conference at Hecla Island. She thanked me and informed me we added an element of reality to the presentation.

The following weekend, I went to a baby shower for my friend, and voice teacher, Melanie. She looked happy with her newborn, a girl named Emma. I brought the women at the shower up to date on the court process. They laughed at the multitude of inanities.

Warren was still away on council business, as he had been for the past week. As usual, Jean called and listed achievements. As usual, I asked hard-nosed questions, like why she decided to be a hostile witness. She could not answer me.

I cried on the couch after talking to her. When Warren arrived at 11:30, he tried to placate me. Then he announced he needed some sleep. I continued crying.

On the Saturday of the Easter weekend, we visited Wendy for her birthday. Ernie and his son, Scott, were there, but nobody talked much during supper. After the meal, other people came over for cake and ice cream. One of them, a long-time family friend, sat beside me and informed me she still visited Joan.

On Easter Sunday, Robin called. He said, "I planned to visit Valerie this long weekend. When I phoned her,

I told her a bit about the court thing. She got very angry and hung up."

"That must have hurt."

"Well, I called again and her husband answered. Bruce talked for a while. He said we're cruel, dangerous fools, jumping on a dangerous bandwagon, and we want to kill our father. Let me think. What else? Oh yeah, he said his father wasn't nice, but he doesn't hate him. I asked him what he'd do if his father sexually assaulted his kids. No answer."

"Sounds like he said all the things Valerie wanted to say."

"Valerie told me it didn't happen much. She's gotten over it, dealt with it."

"So . . . how many times is too often?"

Robin sounded disgusted. "Bruce can't get his head around the criminal angle. Family members do not commit felonies. But he may be right. It may never go to trial."

Hearing Robin's voice buoyed my spirits, but Valerie's third-hand messages upset me. I sat down and thought about the random pain and joy of the past month: the courthouse antics, the reunion with Linda, the ache of diminished family celebrations, the disclosures at the church event, the ambush of Jean's calls, the news of Shannon's pregnancy, the disconnect from friends, and the delight of seeing Melanie with her new baby.

In the thick of this chaos, a notice arrived, announcing another spring retreat for women at Hecla Island. For days, I weighed the pros and cons. I still had trouble justifying spending so much. Then I remembered Warren's casual acquisitions and trips in the past months, and remembered how the previous conference had affected me. Six days before the weekend, I sent my cheque.

61

ON THE MORNING OF APRIL 28, WARREN ASKED me to run a bunch of errands for him, so I did not get on the road until 2:00 p.m. Because of the rush, I forgot essentials like pen, paper, toothbrush, and even shoes. I bought a pair of cheap sneakers on the way up. Wendy, in the last eight weeks before baby, decided not to accompany me.

I drove up the winding approach to the resort, feeling relaxed and happy to be on my own, released from day-to-day living and prosecution delays. In the lobby, the first person I saw was Jan. She asked me to go for a walk and told me she was involved with organizing the retreat. Irene, from my abuse support group, was taking registration.

While waiting for supper, I met another woman I knew. She grew up a half-mile away from Warren's home. Without prompting, she described her childhood abuse by a family member and also Warren's father. She said he masturbated and exposed himself when she walked over to his garage to buy chocolate bars. I nearly choked on my outrage.

The opening circle emphasized the theme of the conference, "Weaving the Web." I sat down between Irene and Jan, along with about eighty women who rolled a ball of yarn back and forth across the room to form a huge web.

After the circle ended, I fetched my guitar. Another woman saw this and rushed to get hers. Soon a small group of music makers were belting out golden oldies until almost midnight. After most of them shuffled off to bed, Irene joined me for a dip and a soak. While Irene relaxed in the hot tub, I dove and splashed in the pool.

Pretending to be a little kid, I shouted at her, "Watch me! Watch me!" and flipped into the deep end.

She recognized the game and laughed. I swam end-to-end a few times, then slipped off my suit. Irene had come on our canoe trip so she knew I liked to swim naked. When I resurfaced, I yelled, "Don't watch me! Watch the door! Someone might come in!"

She laughed again. We dried off and went to the bar; I retrieved my guitar and tried to incite another singa-long. The bartender said the liquor laws prohibited guitar playing in there. So I went to bed. Before sleep arrived, I recalled the traumatic scenes from the last retreat. I was amazed at how different I felt.

This retreat focused on using creativity to recover from abuse, and featured poets, authors, visual artists, potters, dancers, singers, musicians, mimes, actors, and photographers. Many of the presenters had multiple talents. Because of my late registration, I ended up on a foldout couch in the suite next to Jan and Irene. I loved being there. The large room had a fireplace and three massage tables. It was designated "the massage salon" and proved to be a popular place for women to gather.

In a workshop called "Women Writing and Healing," the facilitator read some of her poetry and asked us to write for twenty minutes. She suggested a few literary devices to help us get started. I chose allegory and began writing. When the break came, I had seven pages filled.

I named my story "Slaying the Horny Dragon"; it was about a princess called Lady Cadaver, who "lived half-dead these many years" and had many brothers and sisters. A dragon inhabited the dungeon in her castle. He had a large, hairy lance used to poke the princess when she climbed onto his lap. After the princess took up the unwieldy sword of justice to slash the monster, he exploded in a blaze of fire and shit. The ashes contaminated everyone nearby.

After the break, the facilitator asked us to read our writing. My euphoria vanished; I gagged and bumbled through the words. Karen, who happened to be in the same session, told me later how it affected everyone. Once again, I had disassociated; people's reactions had not registered. But, at that moment, the reason for being there became clear. I had an important story to tell, and not only that, I had the ability and resources to tell it.

During a break, I met a friend's mother. I told her about the legal quagmire and its effects. At first, she sounded sympathetic, but then she said, "You'll never get over it until you forgive."

I had heard this line dozens of times, and had practised my response. "That's the problem. We forgave him for forty years. Look where it got us. I've done enough forgiving for ten lifetimes. He hasn't shown remorse. He needs to figure out his pain and forgive himself!"

She looked unconvinced. After she left, I invented an even more compelling rejoinder. The next time someone spouted forgiveness advice, I'd ask, "Have you forgiven the person who sexually abused you?"

If the person said, "Yes," my next question would be, "How? I haven't. Please tell me your method."

If the person said, "No," I'd say, "Don't ask me to do it. You don't know shit about this."

In the afternoon workshop, the artist-facilitator showed us how to use our peripheral vision. My eyes dripped and burned from the strain, until the person we were staring at developed an aura. The artist crammed the session with metaphors for examining life, seeing the real picture, no matter how long or hard you had to look. She talked about stretching our vision outside the narrow focus, daring to capture what we perceived, and finding the importance of courage and choices.

That night, they held another drumming circle and bonfire near the lake. I strolled down the path, flashbacks of last year's wild emotions whizzing through my brain. I bounced along, laughing, singing, and lifting people in the air.

After the fire, we went inside for a warm drink. The "lesbian caucus," as someone had labelled them, sat apart from the rest. The division between us bothered me. I figured we had all been hurt; I tried to bridge the two conversation clusters. It didn't work. I asked the bartender to turn up the music, and encouraged everyone to dance.

The dancing lost momentum and the two groups split. Some came back to the massage salon. Irene started to rub my back. I started to weep. It was easy crying, not my usual clenched choking and gasping.

The next day, the tension arising from the lesbian caucus came up again. I said to one woman. "I'm sure we can connect. You are a partner and a mother."

She responded quietly. "You're right. I was torn between the two sides last night. I didn't feel a part of the militant group in the lounge. I came out to the fire. I appreciated you talking to me when I was sitting on the rock."

I didn't remember what I said. The only thing I remembered was showing Irene my loon call imitation.

At the closing, more dissension surfaced. An Indigenous leader addressed her comments to women in the drum-making workshop. She said people were handling drums with disrespect, and left. Several women voiced concerns about not enough workshops for minorities, of colour or sexual orientation. I preferred to focus on the obstacles I had overcome. Karen encouraged me to mention this transformation in some form.

When it came my turn to speak, I recited a poem. "I was here, just last year. I must confess; I was a mess. When I left, felt so bereft. It don't take long to get this strong."

I flexed my arms and pretended to pump iron with a big rain stick I had grabbed from the centre of the circle. I felt silly, amongst the celebrated poets and authors, but I wanted to express what a difference a year could make.

We prepared to leave and I asked my guitar-playing buddy, "What was that sound you made at the end?"

She said, "I thought you might recognize that howl. Like the one you made last year. Please give me a hug." Then she broke into tears.

I said, "I'll hold you for as long as you need." I felt calm and centred, able to offer solace. I hugged her for twenty minutes while she sobbed into my shoulder. Nothing else registered. It felt like being submerged, with the distant sounds of women bidding each other farewell swirling around me.

After a final skinny dip and a cup of coffee, I helped people load up their stuff. I waited around to say good-bye to Jan, but she was busy. One of the presenters, a poet, had joined me for the coffee and the last swim. She mentioned riding back to the city with me, but I ended up driving home alone, giddy, exhausted, and peaceful.

62

ON THE MOTHER'S DAY WEEKEND, WARREN WENT fishing with some friends. I felt lonely and introspective, so I wrote to Shannon.

We lacked mothering in our family. I ended up assuming that job when I was fourteen. I was not good at it, and I still struggle to do it right. When Joan came, we were all so grateful. But her theories of parenting coincided with Jock's. Obedience was valued more than affection. And we never questioned her. When I had children, I had to learn, or unlearn, how to parent. I found mothering in friends like Barb and Linda. I'm glad you spoke to Linda. Allison enjoyed talking to you. If you came more often, you could take her aside and gab, or teach her to do her hair or paint fingernails.

It looks as if the dates picked for the trial will not work for you. Isn't your baby due right in the middle of October? I hear Tom is getting married then. How will he explain the omission of five or six siblings at his wedding to his new wife? Maybe he'll tell her we don't like getting dressed up. Or live too far away. Or can't drive.

I plan to get our mare bred so the kids can have a foal. They are so cute when they are small. Too bad they grow up to be pushy, large animals. (Horses, of course, not kids—Ha! Ha!)

I still see Karen once or twice a month. This spring, I went to a conference. It looked at ways to change our lives through creativity. Not just our individual selves, but our whole environment. Maybe we'll see you in the summer.

In middle of the next week, the mother of my best friend in high school, Mrs. Jenson, visited Warren to resolve certain legal matters. Although I hadn't seen her for years, she greeted me warmly, and agreed to stay for lunch. I told her about my father's charges.

She got agitated when she spoke about Jock's harassment of women. "Every dance he came to, he grabbed every woman's bum and breasts all night. To get away, we all hid in the kitchen, pretending to help out. Your stepmother often got mad at me. She told me I encouraged him. That hurt and surprised me."

Speaking in her elegant Danish accent, she reminisced about the times I stayed with her family. She expressed concern for me and my sisters, and encouraged me to visit when we came to West Hawk.

THROUGHOUT THE PAST month, Allison had experienced difficulties getting to school. Almost every morning, she missed the bus or claimed to be sick. I arranged an examination by a pediatrician in the city. Aside from her allergies, he could not find any physical ailments. He suggested she might be depressed. In desperation, I picked up a book called *Reviving Ophelia: Saving the Selves of Adolescent Girls* by Mary Pipher. The author stated many young girls suffered from varying degrees of depression, dealing with the changes and transitions of their age. The book helped, but I worried about whether I should be backing off or getting more help for her. Again, I consulted with the principal and the school counsellor.

At my next session with Karen, I asked if she would talk to Allison and me together. She agreed. Then she described a scene at a mutual friend's wedding.

She said, "Your cousins Cliff and Eleanor sat with me. Cliff wept as he told me how he had approached Jock during his last visit to West Hawk. He wanted to stir Jock's soul or sympathy. After talking for a while, he realized neither existed. Cliff could not fathom that, as a father, or as a man. Meanwhile, Eleanor took Joan for a walk to the beach, and tried to reach her, but she also met stony resistance and bitter finger-pointing."

I said, "That must have been difficult for Cliff to stare into such a heart of darkness, being a minister and all. And Joan has nailed her fate to a corpse. She'll never get the stench off."

"Why don't you get in touch with Eleanor?"

I imagined talking to Eleanor, and cried. I couldn't shake the feeling of being the poor, dirty little girl. But Karen had planted a seed. Maybe it would help to face the shame, in the person of my older cousin.

On May 19, Belle called. "In an examination for discovery, Terry admitted he molested Rena. My lawyer was shocked, I was astonished, and Rena was horrified. But he minimized his actions, right after the confession came out of his mouth."

"Too bad he can't own it."

"Terry believes it was no big deal. I called up Jock right after leaving the court; I wanted to confront him. I asked why he hadn't pleaded guilty yet. He pretended he was deaf. Then Joan got on the line and screamed at me. She called me a crazy bitch and said I ruined the whole family. I told her she was sleeping with the guy who did that."

"I doubt he could have heard you, even if you used a megaphone."

Right after Belle's call, my friend Claudette phoned to describe the progression of her mother's cancer. She spoke of how she dreaded and treasured the recent Mother's Day, knowing her mother was leaving her. I told some of the things I had learned at Hecla Island and thanked her for the mothering she gave me.

In my mind, I tried to weave all these mothering themes together. I wanted to be a good mother. I lost a good mother and a near-mother to a bad father. Losing a mother hurt like nothing else in the world. The near-mother now hated us. Warren's mother tried, but lacked courage. I thought about Wendy and how mothering must be weighing heavily on her these days.

I called her and asked, "Could I come to your delivery?"

"Yeah, I could use the help."

"I was afraid to ask. You might have chosen someone else. Or not want me."

I knew it was very, very important to be there.

63

DURING THE FIRST WEEK OF JUNE, I DECIDED to submit my story from Hecla Island, "Slaying the Horny Dragon," for possible publication. I called Wendy often, to check how she was doing. Jean got upset because she was subpoenaed in front of her colleagues. Bradley came with me to the school for his pre-kindergarten orientation. He approved of the teacher and the classroom.

Then Allison and I visited Karen together. Karen, impressed with the trust and openness in our relationship, reassured me I was doing the right things but needed to recognize Allison's differences and listen to her. On the weekend, we travelled to Winnipeg, to get our mare bred, in a borrowed truck pulling a borrowed trailer.

On June 11, Lynne Kohm left a message on my answering machine.

"Four days ago, we applied to dismiss Pollock's appeal. It succeeded. The trial will definitely proceed in October. Since I will be out of the province, I won't be handling the case. Neil Cutler will take over. Take care. Bye."

Her news stunned me, in a jumble of regret and triumph. On the one hand, the dismissed appeals moved the case forward. On the other, I wanted Lynne Kohm to finish it, to see it through. She knew the family. She knew the stories. Most important of all, we trusted her, and she was committed to the process.

This switch in Crown attorneys was not unlikely, given the years it had taken to get it into court. Pollock had used a common tactic—stall, stall, stall, until no one remembers why the prosecution started. Ms. Kohm had admitted, during one of our interviews, it was one of her most challenging files, and the paper pile kept growing. Replaying her message over and over, I decided I needed some closure with her, to clear up the unanswered questions. I left a message for her to call me.

The next evening, Lynne Kohm returned my call. I noted it was again long after normal office hours. She described, at length, how the case had evolved and what Pollock might do next.

Then she said, "When his appeal was dismissed, he vowed he would take it to the Supreme Court."

"Don't all lawyers love to say that?'

"Whether he would, in reality, take on such a costly and labour-intensive project, is another question. I wanted to tell you. I've decided to subpoena all your siblings, except for Valerie and Tom, as you have suggested."

Then the conversation shifted, or rather, I shifted it.

"Maybe I imagined this, but did you tell me at our first meeting you were sexually abused?"

"You didn't imagine it."

"Was it your father?"

"No."

"How does that affect what you do?"

"I feel angry about these men getting away with this shit. When I see them sitting there, glaring at the girl or woman who is bringing this stuff forward, at such great personal cost, I see the pain, the damage done. It pushes me to do something, whatever I can, about these assholes."

"Who is Neil Cutler?"

"Donna, Donna . . . Donna. I mean this in all seriousness, even though he does have a penis, he might be able to handle this."

"I wanted you to finish. You started this."

"Thanks. I'm touched. Before we part ways, I want to tell you something. I found your husband to be very supportive. I wish I could find someone like him. In fact, I was impressed with the lot of you. Your sister Wendy is something else; she doesn't swallow any crap from anyone. And your friend Barb is a strong woman and a wonderful friend. You are lucky to have people like them in your life. Bye. And I really do mean this. Take care."

I knew it was not just another case for her. Every day, she dealt with the wounded, both victim and perpetrators, and I had no doubt it affected her. Maybe she got courage from us. At first, her flippant tone scared me, but we soon learned to recognize the determination underneath. She laughed at my grim jokes and seemed to understand, without too much explanation, what we needed to say.

When I visited Karen the next week, we sorted out why I got so unhinged when someone from the Justice Department called. The legal process was not designed to make anyone "happy." I knew that, but it sucked me back into the original feelings—the lack of control, and the absence of power to influence the outcome.

On Father's Day it was hot, so we decided to go on a picnic. As we drove out of the yard, Bradley flung open the car door and vomited. Warren and Allison went without us. Bradley and I spent the day camped on the floor of Warren's air-conditioned office, reading and playing cards.

Wendy called to tell me that Jean's second-oldest son got drunk with some friends and pulled out the newspaper clipping about his grandfather. His friends got upset by his suggestions of suicide and told the guidance counsellor at school. Then his parents got summoned. I was sorry to hear about his pain, but glad to know her kids might lead her to a place of honesty by admitting they were affected.

On June 20, while preparing the final draft of my dragon story to send to the editors of the proposed anthology, I got the call. Wendy had started labour.

I mailed it off, picked up movies for Bradley, and tore into the city. When I arrived at 1:30 p.m., the hospital staff surprised me by refusing to admit me to the delivery area. Bill came down and explained the attending doctor had approved me.

The three of us walked arm-in-arm around the ward. Because of back and hip injuries from two car accidents, Wendy insisted she would only squat during delivery. So Bill and I ran interference with the hospital staff, who repeatedly asked her to lie down. For most of the early labour, she panted and sweated on a toilet in a tiny washroom. Bill leaned against the tank and rubbed her back while I wiped her face with cool cloths, and fed her ice chips.

By 4:30 p.m., her contractions increased. The nurses begged us to come out of the washroom. The doctor checked on her and said he would return. We walked a bit more.

Wendy and Bill told me they wanted to be alone; I left for a meal. When I got back, she had gone into the bathroom again, for what I call the "trance stage" of active labour. The nurse panicked. After we helped her back to the room, Bill and I customized the hospital bed so she could keep squatting. She knelt and leaned against the head of the bed. We removed the bottom half of the mattress, since the bed could be split in two.

I almost laughed out loud when the nurse returned. She looked puzzled but didn't mention the bed. She asked Wendy, "Could you avoid pushing just yet? The doctor is not here."

I leaned and whispered to Wendy, "The doctor may not be here, but your baby might be coming. Listen to your body. You don't need a doctor to have a baby."

I knew this to be true because I had delivered Bradley, by myself, in a hospital washroom. I wanted to urinate, but he appeared. I grabbed him and walked back to the bed, holding his head. I knew about the efficiency of squatting on a toilet.

The nurse exclaimed, "The baby's crowning. But the doctor is not here!"

Wendy snarled. "I don't care. Bill, keep massaging. Donna, keep your hands on my head."

Bill and I jumped around the bed, switching hands to get water and ice while one of us kept rubbing.

The woman in the adjoining bed shouted, "What's going on? Is she having the baby right here?" She sounded scared to hear what lay in store for her.

Then things happened fast. A delivery room became available, the young doctor showed up, and Bill and I scrambled into surgical wear. I never had time to slip on those sterile booties. We followed our altered bed into the delivery room.

Wendy muttered, "Keep your hands on me. I do *not* want to lie down."

Then she was gone, down into the dark hole of primal concentration, panting like a winded horse. Bill stroked, caressed, and murmured; I stood guard.

The doctor looked at the job we had done on the bed and scratched his head. "I admit I have never delivered a baby in this position. It will be a new game for me."

He knelt on the floor to check on developments. Wendy had not taken any drugs, or epidurals, or gas. And she never did lie down, a real accomplishment, considering how many authority figures had told her otherwise. Five minutes later, the baby's head popped out. I leaned over to catch a glimpse. The doctor caught the gray-blue body sliding out in a blood-streaked gush. He suctioned the nose and mouth, and the new arrival turned pink.

The doctor lifted the bundle up and Bill cut the cord. The nurse snatched the baby and wrapped him, then stuck him under the heat lamps.

While Wendy delivered the placenta and the doctor pulled out a huge needle to stitch her, I said, "This hurts. I know it hurts."

Bill stared at me.

I said, "When I had my kids, the worst part was people telling me it didn't hurt."

I picked up the baby, unwound his wrappings, and stuck his nose near the breast.

"What's his name?"

"Patrick."

I held him close to Wendy's bosom. Tears came to my eyes.

Bill looked on in awe at his child, and kissed Wendy. "He's perfect! I love you so much! What a team!"

The doctor grinned and shook hands all around. The intern thanked us for teaching him about birthing in the squatting mode. The nurse looked reluctantly impressed. In the recovery room, Wendy wilted after the euphoria but kept smiling. Bill left for some food while the new son learned how to eat. Alert and watchful, he latched on strongly.

Wendy said, "I wanted a girl, but he's gorgeous. And he knows what to do."

I said, "My shirt is soaked. Thank you, Wendy. I was glad to be part of this."

They whisked Patrick away to be examined in triage and moved Wendy to the regular room. They wheeled her roommate's baby in, with a bottle tucked beside it. When the young woman staggered into the washroom, Wendy said quietly, "She's giving her baby up for adoption."

While waiting for Bill to come back from eating, I offered tips on breastfeeding. "Ignore the rule about switching. Breaking suction is hard on boob and baby. Besides, the hind milk, which comes out later, is the meat and potatoes, not just the thirst-quencher."

A nurse popped into the room. "How many minutes has he been feeding on that side?"

Wendy smiled and winked. "Maybe five."

The nurse replied, "Don't forget to switch every fifteen minutes."

We burst into laughter. Bill returned and I stayed for a while longer. The last thing I saw was the two of them staring at the bundle. I did not feel the least bit tired in the car on the way home. It was 12:30 a.m. when I turned up our driveway, more than half a day since I had sped out of the yard. The best twelve hours I had spent in a long while, maybe in a lifetime.

It made up for the other shit.

64

A FRIEND CALLED TO TELL ME CLAUDETTE'S mother had died. I went to the funeral and saw many of my former teaching colleagues. I hadn't seen most of them since my father's crime went public in the media, and I couldn't help but wonder how many knew.

I wrote to my cousin Eleanor to ask her to meet with me at Karen's office. I mailed the letter, and then packed up my canoe and left on a four-day whitewater paddling trip, ignoring signs of a potential cold. That night, in the tent, I couldn't sleep because of violent coughing. I worried I wouldn't be able to keep up. But my paddling partner, an army captain, carried a selection of pills in her first aid kit. She dispensed painkillers and even bandaged my blisters with duct tape. We travelled through 100 kilometres of unbelievable scenery. The wilderness setting forced me to accept physical care, without protest. On this expedition, I was the rookie, learning from competent adults.

When I returned, a week's worth of laundry greeted me. Not only that, Warren had not been eating properly and had developed an anal fissure. His tolerance for work and family life dwindled.

Despite this problem, on August 15, our fourteenth anniversary, Warren surprised me. We had planned to leave on a short holiday, but he could not sit for long-distance travel. He disappeared; I assumed he was working in his office. His mother arrived, unannounced. Around 11:00 a.m., he returned from town with wine and food for a picnic. We spent the day at a beach, without children. I kept looking out at the water, expecting to see a wet, blonde head emerge. He had never done anything like this, and I had never gone to the beach, without children, since having them.

We picked up the mail on the way home. Jean had written, saying she hoped the court dates in October were final. I wondered if she would attend.

I called Karen, who had been working all summer as a minister at West Hawk Lake, and asked her if she'd baptize Wendy's baby in the United Church there. I called Barb and asked her to talk to the local women about hosting a baby shower on the same day. Then I called Wendy to let her know. She agreed to our plan and then mentioned Jean planned to tell Joan how stupid she was about the whole issue.

I said, "So who gets to tell Jean how stupid she's been?"

"Just so you know, Jean asked me if I want a baby shower at her cottage."

"I don't think it's a good idea. First, there'll be too many people. Second, her cottage is hard to find. Third, it's easier to stay at the church and go into the basement. And it's a more neutral space."

Wendy's baby shower provided a small payback for the many ways she had been cheated since her wedding. Eva phoned to reassure me all the food and decorations would be looked after by the church women. Some collected money for a high chair, while others presented toys and clothes. Esther, Karen, Margaret, and Hettie drove out. An assortment of friends, neighbours, and relations, staying at cottages, attended. Joan did not show up. Jean came, but looked down at the floor, and did not say much to me, or anyone.

During her service, Karen spoke on the parable of seeds falling on different soils, drawing an analogy to parenting. After the shower ended, Wendy thanked the women for coming and giving such generous gifts.

I stood up, once again groping for words. "We all know why one mother is not here. She died. And we know why the other mother is not here. But I'd like to thank all of you for the mothering that you are doing today, and the mothering you've done in the past."

Some of the women started crying. After the shower ended and the dishes got washed, Barb invited people back to her house. In her spacious dining room, Karen raised a glass of wine to toast the women of West Hawk. "May you keep telling your truths."

Barb toasted. "Here's to hurdles. If you run up and fling yourself over, they can't stop you. Wendy, I commend you."

When a few of us gathered in the foyer to bid farewell to Eva and her husband, she recounted an incident from my mother's funeral. "I've never told anyone. At the end of the service, I felt so sad for all you children. I was crying, and I walked up to Jock to offer condolences. He grabbed me. He actually fondled me. In the midst of so much pain. My pain. His children's pain. All he saw was a chance to feel me up. I was shocked. I never told anyone."

Under the protective arch of Barb's entranceway, we huddled together and hugged each other. Karen stared at the ceiling as if reciting a silent benediction. Later, she said to me, "It was as if we all sensed the icy fingers of his palpable evil, and needed to cling to each other for protection and solace."

Second Crown

65

ON THE LABOUR DAY WEEKEND, DONNA P AND her children, Margaret and her children, Melanie, Paul, and their daughter came out for a "summer's ending" barbecue. After the big meal, Melanie and I went skinny-dipping. When the sky darkened, the mosquitoes swarmed, so we moved the singalong indoors. This evening of family fun almost pushed the grim prospect of what was supposed to happen in the next month out of my mind.

On the Monday, another friend asked Warren to go fishing. He arrived with his two daughters and everyone except me got into the boat. While I handed out life jackets, Allison got mad at Bradley because he sat in the front seat. She grabbed him. "I'm gonna push you in the river, you little worm."

Staying up so late had affected us. I said, "No, you won't. Get out of the boat!"

Bradley yelled, "You are so mean to her. I'm not coming fishing!"

He jumped out and ran into the house. I tried to lift Allison out of the boat, but almost ended up in the water. She jumped up and ran into the house. They locked themselves in our bedroom, chanting, "We hate you. We hate you."

After five minutes, I said, "You can stay or go fishing. They haven't gone far."

Sniffling, they followed me down to the water. After we called the fishing crew back to the dock, they jumped in the boat. I felt drained by their allied anger, and once again, totally inadequate as a parent.

The next week, Bradley started kindergarten. Whenever he played or coloured, he hummed. Allison warned him, "Don't sing like that at school. Everyone will think you are weird."

That first morning, he was almost levitating. Because of the "B" in his name, he got to bring the first snack. When I arrived at 3:30 p.m. to offer a ride home, he chose to go on the bus. But he came home crying. "The big boys in the back teased me and stole my hat."

I resisted the urge to judge, warn, or interrupt, and we snuggled on the couch with a book.

The next day, I visited Karen and discussed using drugs to handle the feelings. She reminded me, "Sure, you could get Prozac to even yourself out, but where would you be? You'd miss the joy, the passion, the aliveness, the insights. Would you want to miss that?"

～

I HADN'T HEARD from the Justice Department since my final conversation with Lynne Kohm so I phoned the new Crown attorney to find out what was happening. He returned my call almost immediately, speaking in a crisp, low voice, "The defence and prosecution held a pre-trial meeting at the end of the summer to find out what was happening. Mr. Pollock informed me that Mr. Tod's condition had worsened over the summer. He intends to apply to have the proceedings dropped."

I gritted my teeth and gripped the counter.

He continued in the same flat tones. "Pollock has not submitted a medical report. And he has not let us know what medical backup, if any, is needed if this trial proceeds. As Justice Hanssen stated in his judgment, I cannot understand why these charges were not stayed."

I gasped and tried to remember what part of the judgment he was citing. I said, "Lynne Kohm never voiced that opinion. I only recall Hanssen insisting the Crown could continue, if the right medical safeguards were provided."

"I cannot comment on what interpretation Ms. Kohm shared with you. Also, I do not understand why she subpoenaed almost every member of your family. It is not even worth talking to Jean, Robin, or David."

"I thought they were already summoned to appear."

"It is not necessary."

"Well, your opinions are certainly different from what Ms. Kohm told us."

"That may be true, but . . ."

After fourteen years of living with a lawyer, I recognized the diversionary tactics.

At length, he lectured me on the importance of a lawyer's impartiality. Then he said, "I plan to consult with the senior Crown and director of prosecutions shortly to decide whether or not to drop the charges."

I almost choked but kept asking questions.

After a few more reminders that lawyers should not get emotionally involved in their cases, he asked, "Would you consult your siblings and ask what order they'd like to appear?"

I gagged—astounded that he expected me to do his job.

He ignored my noises. "This is a simple sexual assault case. The only complicating factor is the health of the accused."

I recovered my voice. "How soon will we know?"

"Maybe the end of the week."

"How long do you think he'd get for a sentence?"

"What did Ms. Kohm tell you?"

"I don't remember. I want to know what you think."

I tried to use humour to loosen our conversation, but he did not respond. Most sickening of all, he repeated several times, "It is most disturbing to be accused of sexual assault by one's daughters."

This sympathy for the offender, especially coming from a Crown attorney, troubled me. I said, "Look, we have been told repeatedly during the past three years he was going to die. And he is still here. I want to see this through."

He reiterated his main points. I recognized this second legal tactic, persuasion through repetition. The other party gives up, not because anything makes sense, but out of boredom. It can backfire if the listener gets upset with such condescension. After saying the same things, over and over, different ways, he ended the conversation.

I burst into Warren's office. "Can the Crown be sued for screwing up a prosecution? And causing damage to the witnesses?"

"I seem to recall instances of such a position. Why?"

"I just talked to the new Crown attorney. He doesn't want to even put his toe in this shit, let alone walk through it with us."

After supper, I caught my horse and galloped along the gravel road, into the twilight, cursing the insanity of the legal system. It was no small wonder sexual assaults were so under-reported.

The rhythm of the horse calmed me and the smell of freshly soaped leather soothed me. My saddle was over twenty years old, moulded to my legs and buttocks, but still in good shape. Then I remembered—Jock and Joan had given it to me for graduating from university. It was the one physical reminder of my life with them.

With a sigh, I wondered if a newer saddle would fit the mare better. Or fit me better. Then I thought of the old saying—it's stupid to change your horse midstream. Perhaps the same could be said of donkey Crown attorneys.

I swatted a swarm of mosquitoes on the mare's rump and muttered, "Where is Lynne Kohm, now we really need her?"

The horse spun on her hindquarters. She wanted to gallop home. For once, I let her follow her head; I did not have the energy to control the speed. She ran flat out through the darkness back to the corral.

66

ON SEPTEMBER 14, I SPENT HOURS PHONING back and forth between siblings, explaining the stance of the new Crown attorney, and encouraging them to tell him their opinions. Because of a late meeting in town, Margaret decided to sleep over at our house.

When she arrived, I asked, "Do you want to go for a swim?"

"No, it's too cold. Would you like a massage?"

"Okay. Just do my shoulders and back."

The tensions of the past few days unfroze and slid a bit.

At 3:00 a.m. I sat at the kitchen table with my guitar, singing a simple, quiet chorus.

"Feelings come like a wave; I get tired of being brave . . . again."

I went outside. The air scarcely stirred. Wisps of lazy fog rose from the river. I let the dog out of her kennel and we crunched together through the mist-shrouded, gleaming pasture. Startled by nocturnal visitors, the horses snorted and bolted a short distance. Their snuffling noises echoed in the silence.

The mare sidled up to me and touched my face with her nostrils, nibbling and nuzzling in my hair. I threw my arms around her neck. I wanted to ride her in the moonlight, without saddle or bridle. When I attempted to swing up onto her back, she jumped sideways. I turned and walked toward the lights by the front door. She followed. Every five steps, I stopped and she shoved her nose into the collar of my jacket and nibbled my hair.

"No, horse, just do my shoulders and back."

Her foggy, warm breath made me realize how cold it was. The temperature had dropped; my tomatoes would freeze. In the moonlight, on my knees, I scooped up handfuls of them and piled them in the wheelbarrow. The exertion warmed me. After the vegetables were in the garage, I said goodnight to the mare and fed her the small pile of leftover green tomatoes.

I wandered down to the dock and dipped my hand in the liquid silver. Compared to the air, it felt warm. I stripped and dove off the end of the dock. My breasts, nipples, stomach muscles contracted. The outline of the dock disappeared in the mist. My head floated through a hazy world of reflected moonlight and shadows stretching from the trees along the shore.

I trembled, making small ripples as I swam. The resident beaver slipped through the water just metres away and whacked her tail on the surface. Dog-paddling to keep my head on the surface, I felt acutely alive, and lucky to be the only person enjoying this moonlit river. Every noise was magnified. A radio played country music on the opposite side of the river. I could hear every cheating word.

After fifteen minutes, I climbed onto the dock and grabbed my jacket. Still dripping, I didn't bother putting on the rest of my clothes. I thought about visiting

Margaret, to touch her with my frigid hands and to tell
her what she missed. I decided to spare her. Warren
gasped when I climbed into bed. It took an hour and
three extra blankets before I warmed up.

In that shivering hour prior to sleep's arrival, I concluded I needed to do something about Neil Cutler—just
exactly what was not clear.

67

THE NEXT MORNING, AFTER MARGARET LEFT,
Warren called Cutler. I listened on the extension. Cutler reiterated his concerns in another winding explanation. He said, "I'm not certain how to arrange medical
supports, and furthermore, Pollock has not indicated
what they need."

At intervals, Warren said, "uh-huh," "no," and "yes."

Once in a while, Cutler paused long enough for him
to ask a question. Meanwhile, I bit my lips and screamed
in my head, "Blah! Blah! Blah! Why don't you say something real?"

Cutler described at length how Pollock insisted
the charges be stayed because of the deterioration of
Jock's health. He said, "I seriously question the value of
proceeding."

Warren asked, "Would you agree to a meeting with
Donna, Wendy, and me?"

"I do not want to meet with family. It becomes too
emotional. I will decide with the senior Crown and

the director of prosecutions whether to continue with the process."

After Warren finished talking to Cutler, I went for another ride on the mare to dissipate my anxiety. Then I began calling siblings. Wendy was incensed.

David asked me, "Doesn't Warren know anyone?"

"I'm not sure what you mean."

"You know, the political route. He must know some good Conservatives."

"He does. But I expect people to do what's right because it's their job. Obviously, there are exceptions."

"Who's the Attorney General?"

"I don't know."

I found out later we were between Attorney Generals.

"I campaigned for the Justice Minister," he said.

"Then you could phone her."

"Yes. I could."

He sounded determined, but I knew he would not phone. He saw the dying father, where I saw the latest screwing we were getting.

The following morning, Wendy called to say she had asked Cutler if we could be present when he met with the senior Crown and the director of prosecutions. He refused, but he phoned me later to ask what points we wanted brought up at this meeting.

"I need specific information about Jock Tod's health and habits," he said.

"You could ask Jean or John or Ernie. I haven't seen him for three years."

"I do not want to start up another police investigation."

I sighed. I could not think up compelling legal arguments while baking banana bread and listening to kids fighting, without the added pressure of coming up with a list of informants in West Hawk Lake.

On September 17, at 11:10 p.m., Ernie called.

"What's going on?"

"Haven't you heard?" I loved answering his questions with questions.

"No, you're the only one who tells me anything."

"John never told you? Has he received a subpoena?"

"I don't think so. He doesn't talk to me."

"Does anyone talk to you?"

"I went to visit Joan last night but she didn't say a thing. She looked upset, though."

"We're not sure if it's going to happen. There's a different Crown attorney now."

"It's not that female?"

"Why do you keep calling her 'that female'? She has a name. Or, if you can't remember, she has a job title." I exhaled loudly. "She's not working on this case or even in that department anymore. She's in Toronto. The new Crown is Neil Cutler. Do you want his number?"

"Maybe I have it already. If he's called me, it's around somewhere."

"I'll give it to you. You can phone him. You have lots of questions. Do you know why Tom planned his wedding the week after his father is scheduled to die?"

"No, I don't. It is kind of weird timing."

"It's like he counted on this file being stayed or delayed. In the eyes of the law, is fitness to host a large wedding equal to fitness to stand trial?" I forgot to ask if Ernie was invited, or planned to boycott the nuptials. Instead, I said, "Look, I haven't seen him for three years. What's it really like with him?"

"He's incoherent and doesn't listen. He shifts to different topics all the time, and it's never what you are talking to him about."

"Just like always. Where's the change?"

"He had a couple of strokes."

"I urge you to speak with the new Crown and tell him what you know."

"I don't think he'll last."

"We've heard that line. Will he last for the wedding? Besides, he's hurt so many people, who cares?"

"It sounds like you experienced the worst of it."

"Maybe so. But I'm referring to the past three years. Look at the costs—emotional, physical, financial. If he had admitted what he had done, right at the start, his sentence, if he even got one, would probably be over by now."

I pictured the old man with the shrinking heart: the smaller it got, the less he cared for anyone.

Ernie changed the subject. "How's Bradley?"

"He's fine. He's in school now."

"And how's . . . uh-h-h-h . . . what's her name?"

"Her name is Allison," I said.

He said, "Today is my birthday."

"Happy birthday. How did you celebrate?"

"I worked. Later on, I played broomball."

"Sounds like fun."

"Yeah, it helps get rid of frustration. I was wiring at Pollock's cottage today."

"You're a real professional. I'd be tempted to cross the wires so it would burn down."

"It was kind of awkward."

"Maybe you should ask Pollock what's going on."

I could not talk to him anymore. After I hung up, I went to the bathroom. I wanted to throw up, but nothing appeared. I came out and said to Warren, "You know, I was just talking to Ernie. He worked at Pollock's cottage this afternoon. What do you think of that?"

"Please, I'm trying to sleep."

I went into the living room and collapsed on the couch. Then I returned to the bedroom.

I said, "Earlier today, you listened for two hours to your manic-depressive friend, and then spent an hour telling me what a mess he is. I haven't heard from Ernie in six months. I mentioned one thing."

"I'm tired. I was up at six."

"I was up at six, too. I still listened to you. How do you think I feel?"

"Probably pissed off."

In the morning, Barb and Fran called for updates. They both restated their support and I asked them to keep phoning Cutler. I took the dog for a run and sent the children out to the bus. Then I attempted to contact the new Crown's supervisor, Saul Bernard. At precisely the same time, Wendy was trying to call him. Despite the sprinkling rain, I cycled to town for mail.

At 10:30 a.m., Mr. Bernard's secretary called me to ask if we could meet with him after lunch the next day. I felt relieved to finally be in touch with someone with an understanding of the case. Bernard had worked with

Ms. Kohm from the beginning, and although I had not spoken with him before, he sounded willing to listen. I called Wendy.

She said, "I can come, but I'm going to find out if Bernard met with Cutler yet."

A few minutes later, she called back. "I talked to Bernard's secretary. They haven't held this other meeting."

On September 19, I dropped Bradley off at our neighbour's house. I'd have liked to get to Winnipeg an hour before the meeting to talk to Wendy, but Warren wanted to finish up some work before we left. As I sped into the city, I ranted, "Jock is counting on us to back down! He wants to force the whole Justice Department to cave."

The legal tussle might well be terminated by the end of the afternoon. I felt exhausted from the stress of waiting, but losing a fight finishes it, at least.

We rushed to Bernard's office in the Woodsworth Building. Wendy carried Patrick, and a few women commented on him in the elevator. It seemed babies were an oddity in this building.

I told Wendy to watch for Cutler. "Look for the little gelding."

Saul Bernard appeared—tall and well groomed, with a full head of hair and glasses. He led us to a boardroom, and sat down, facing the four of us. He said, "I acknowledge the seriousness of the assaults. There's a very strong case against the accused. I admit I don't believe a word Mr. Tod says, but I feel obliged to listen to the doctors, who are presumed to be more objective."

I said, "What are you worried about? Do you think you might get sued?"

"I don't believe so. We haven't done anything."

"Could I be charged with murder if I ran around in front of his kitchen window and he got upset and died?"

He smiled along the edges of his mouth. "The Crown must be seen to treat the accused fairly. His crimes do not warrant the death penalty."

Bernard listened carefully and answered carefully for the rest of the afternoon. It made sense he was senior to Cutler.

I asked, "Can we switch Crowns?"

"At this late date, it would only delay the process."

"What is the worst case scenario, in your opinion?"

"He dies and the Crown's office gets blamed."

"What is it with Cutler?"

"He is thorough and conscientious."

"How would you feel about staying the charges?"

"I'd be frustrated because of all the time we've spent on this. Looking back, there was nothing we could have done differently. Although you may think otherwise, Pollock is just doing his job. He cannot be faulted."

"Why did Cutler refuse to see us?"

"He didn't actually refuse. It must have been difficult to be phoned by so many people."

"What about the fact that Jock is not hospitalized? Why hasn't his driver's license been pulled? What do we tell those people in our family who insist the justice system does not work and they use that as a reason not to come forward? How do we convince them it does?"

Even though we talked for over two hours, he responded patiently, and avoided lecturing us. But I had to bite my lip to keep from laughing when he glanced up and realized Wendy was breastfeeding. The professional facade slipped; his eyes darted from her chest to a point high above our heads. Then he turned his chair at an angle and directed his conversation at Warren. Yes, babies were not part of Justice Department culture.

We stood up to leave. Bernard emphasized they had not yet decided to drop the charges. I felt more positive as we walked to our car. However, I wondered—did Bernard think if he acted concerned, we would be more acquiescent to being let down gently? Perhaps it was time to "accept the things I cannot change."

I said, "This is typical. Jock wants us to fold, say we are sorry. Nothing is ever his fault."

On September 22, at 11:00 a.m., Cutler's secretary called to warn me. "You are on standby. You should be ready just in case the trial starts as planned. We are awaiting a doctor's report."

"Which doctor?"

"I don't know."

"Thank you. Goodbye."

Why in hell was I thanking her? I hated the waiting. I called Wendy, Barb, and Karen to update them, but avoided phoning Belle. It would take too much energy to explain the convoluted mess.

68

THE WEATHER TURNED WARM AGAIN. MY FRIEND Lorna joined Bradley and me for a boat trip up the river to admire the fall colours. When Allison came home from school, we all went for a quick swim. After Lorna left, Warren called from his office to tell me he wanted supper ready because he had decided to go on a four-day business trip to Toronto. Bradley told him he was very angry at him for leaving for so long. I was also angry but did not say much. Instead, I called Karen. We discussed the meeting we had with my cousin Eleanor.

I said, "I was grateful she could do it. But she had trouble listening to the hard parts."

"You're right. At times, she could barely stop herself from clapping her hands over her ears. She wasn't ready for your reality."

I said, "My anger surprised her. She can't get past her memories of good-hearted Uncle Jock and his happy tribe. Oh yes, speaking of that, I wonder if she'll attend Tom's wedding."

Minutes later, Shelley, Warren's youngest sister, phoned to ask about the legal situation. We talked about the confusion regarding whether it would actually occur. Then she said, "I'm not prepared to go to court with my father."

"I wouldn't recommend due process to anyone."

"For me, it's my pain and my right to decide who knows."

"But why protect the abuser? What about other victims?"

"You cannot tell me how to handle this."

"What obligation do you have to warn people? Your sister can't watch him twenty-four hours a day. Your mother spent her life trying, but she didn't stop him.

I ran into a woman who grew up near you and she told me how he masturbated and exposed himself to her every time he saw her alone. Your mother said she knew nothing about it."

"My mother minimizes. It was constant and it went on for years. I could never relax when he was around."

After she hung up, I mused on the contradiction. She offered comfort for my disclosure of my father's abuse yet refused to tell about her own situation. And her father was my daughter's grandfather—just like mine. Their crimes affected Allison, and every child they encountered.

The voice of author Craig Hollingshead on CBC radio interrupted my musing. He said, "We are raised to be innocent bystanders, feigning ignorance so as not to get involved."

His comments especially applied to my last two calls. There was Eleanor, the decent Christian, who refused to admit the damage of her uncle's crimes, and Shelley, the molested daughter, who refused to warn people about her father. Hollingshead talked about how strong words could be, although it finally dawned he was talking about racism. But the same principle applied in the unspeakable and murky world of incest.

The next day, I got sick with a sinus headache, aching body, runny nose—the works. Maybe it was better to have a fuzzy brain—and not be able to think.

Several people called. One of the West Hawk women phoned to ask what was going on. She promised to phone Cutler and to urge other concerned neighbours to do the same. Margaret called for an update and I requested she ask Cutler what was happening. Fran called; I told her to phone Cutler again. Barb called and promised to contact Cutler. Because of the cotton candy in my head, I drank a beer and flopped on the couch. The principal called to tell me Allison had gotten into trouble at school. I did not tell him to phone Cutler.

On September 30, we travelled to the city for another orthodontist's appointment and went to an open house at the CBC studio. I ran into a woman I met at Hecla Island. She had submitted poetry for the anthology where I sent my dragon story.

"Have you heard yet if your story has been accepted?"

"No, I haven't."

"Well, they sent mine back and asked for revisions, so I decided to forget it. My work stands on its own."

I hadn't thought about my dragon story since Patrick's birth.

On October 2, Anne called to tell me that Shelley had confronted her and the rest of her family for not supporting me. She said, "Ben is planning to visit Karen."

"I'll believe it when it happens. How's it going for you? Are you still seeing Karen?"

"Oh, I only went twice, and once to talk to Esther. What's going on with your case?"

I gave her the Cutler hotline number.

A friend called to talk about her recent birthing experience and breastfeeding difficulties. Then she said, "I heard a blurb on television about the adult children of an elderly man. It implied that they're conspiring to harm him by accusing him of abuse. I'm not sure if the word 'kill' was used. I couldn't hear. They said the full report would be on at noon."

My stomach flipped. The details sounded too similar to be coincidence. We didn't get that channel so I asked her to tape it. However, at 11:45 a.m., the mass media announced the O.J. Simpson verdict. For the entire noon-hour, every television and radio station in the Western world commented on the jury's ruling. Our little news was bumped by the big news. When I went to pick up the *Globe and Mail* at the gas bar, the manager was conducting an informal poll. Sixty-six believed O.J. was guilty; thirty-seven found him innocent.

I drove home with mail and newspaper, listening to the radio, thinking about the doubtful results of the justice system.

I recalled our meeting with Mr. Bernard. I had asked him if he believed it worked.

He said, "It does, at least in enough situations to keep me involved in it. Otherwise, I wouldn't be doing what I do."

His words offered scant comfort.

Two days later, Jan phoned and began to lecture me. Once again, I wondered why people who said they loved me chose to dump on me so often. She vacillated between revealing snippets of her own abuse, saying she did not give a shit about me, protesting that she loved her mother, and telling me I wasn't honest.

I asked, "Why are you so upset?"

She replied, "I'm not. You always respond with your head. Why can't you respond from your guts?"

"I'm not angry with you. But I do feel really criticized."

"What are you, some delicate flower?"

In my entire life, I had no such image of myself. I laughed and said I couldn't take any more. She seemed relieved, but disappointed by my lack of rebuttal. After Jan hung up, the woman in charge of the anthology phoned to ask for revisions on the dragon story.

On October 5, I managed to get through to Cutler.

He responded curtly. "We have already gone over this. I cannot tell you anything more. I am no longer making decisions. I am a messenger. What you are telling me is not a real argument. I could not use it in court and be found credible. I don't care if Jock was seen in Zeller's and looked fine."

Our differences of opinion frustrated me. The predictions of Jock's demise had rattled him. Because there was no case law to refer to, he was not willing to take risks.

Margaret phoned. When I told her about Jan's call, she said, "Jan really has some issues."

"Yes, she does. To change the subject—I want to go to Tom's wedding and glare at people who walk through the doors. I want to take pictures to prove to that donkey Crown just how ill Jock is. We're trying to play by the rules. And where does it get us?"

The following day, Cutler phoned to tell me the Crown was protesting the motion to stay the charges. He sounded friendlier. He said, "I tried to get two cardiologists to look at Mr. Tod. One did not want to get involved. The other knew him and refused."

"Is it relevant to any cardiologist that he is happily shopping at Zeller's?"

"I do not have time to launch a police investigation. Could you get any people to testify, or even write letters with the details?"

"I could try," I said.

The next weekend was Thanksgiving.

Warren had only two more council meetings in his term of office. He had been elected just a couple of weeks after Belle contacted the police in October 1992. I hoped that the end of his political career would coincide with the promised conclusion of our legal odyssey.

I dreaded another holiday weekend, especially this one, with Tom's wedding coming soon. His marriage highlighted my feelings of loss and exclusion.

Robin phoned after supper. He sounded animated, almost cheerful.

"I still haven't got my invitation."

"I haven't either. Maybe there's a mail strike in West Hawk."

"Even if he doesn't want me in person, I am going to phone and offer best wishes."

"We could send jokey messages. Warn him the police have staked out the reception."

Wendy called to inform me old Aunt Jean, the financial backer of Jock's defence fund, had asked Wendy if she planned to attend the wedding.

Wendy said, "I told her no and told her the reason. She seemed surprised. I also talked to Rena last week. I was glad to hear she decided not to go. She said she did not want to listen to them saying hateful things about people she cares about."

Warren's sister Shelley called immediately after Wendy's call.

"I did not ream anyone out. My mother gets so mixed up. I simply phoned Allan to tell him what was going on."

The flood of communication from the "see-no-evil, hear-no-evil, speak-no-evil" monkeys astounded me. Being on standby for a trial was definitely not an ideal way to spend time. But, despite being snubbed by my brother, waiting for the Justice Department to make a decision, and suffering from unknown intestinal and sinus disturbances, I felt reasonably strong.

A person could only hide behind monkeys for so long.

69

MY YOUNGEST BROTHER'S WEDDING WAS SCHEDuled to start at 3:00 p.m.

Jean told Wendy that Jock would be there, but "only for a little while."

I thought about Wendy's wedding in 1992, and all that had happened. And then I thought some more—why did siblings who said they supported the court case still plan to attend the wedding? Why couldn't they boycott in solidarity? Would any relatives notice our absence, and at least ask questions?

For the whole morning, I struggled with the notion of crashing the party. But my stomach ached so much. I decided I wouldn't bother driving to West Hawk.

Robin called. He had phoned Tom the night before and asked him, "Why am I being excluded? I've been a good brother."

Tom had replied, "I don't want to ruin it for Joan. She wouldn't come if you guys came."

Belle also called. She said, "I guess I should get Tom a wedding present."

I said, "Are you serious? If Tom lacks the balls to invite his sisters, you have no obligation to send presents. Why reinforce such rudeness?"

"You're right. What was I thinking?"

"We've been conditioned. Someone shits on us and we smile and thank them for the warm feeling. We don't mind the smell, we don't mind cleaning it up, and we act as if the mess is our fault."

On October 25, I received a note informing me my dragon story would be included in the proposed anthology. It was my forty-first birthday. Bradley caught whatever virus I had been fighting and threw up for a few days.

Wendy called and told me she had just spoken to Cutler. Turned out, the motions court, pertaining to Jock's health, had been hearing all week. Cutler had told me it "might" happen.

She sounded desperate. "Tomorrow might be the last day. It may fall apart and we won't know why. What can we do?"

"I'll phone Beverley, and ask her to tell the Crown what she's seen. She lives next door to Jock and she sees things—like watching him walk over to her store every day. The thought of asking her upsets me. But the thought of Pollock swaying the judge with high-priced cardiologists' opinions upsets me even more."

Right away, I called Beverley.

She said, "I miss seeing all of you. At Tom's wedding, I talked to lots of people. Everyone agreed how sad it was." She hesitated. "I've seen him at Zeller's without his wheelchair and oxygen tanks. He was talking and walking. His colour was good."

"That's right. Didn't you used to be a nurse?"

"Yes, before we moved to West Hawk. At the wedding, Jock had the wheelchair and oxygen. Joan hovered around him all night. Not like at Zeller's."

"Would you be willing to testify or write a letter about what you just told me?"

Another hesitation. "I feel sorry for you girls, but I just couldn't . . ."

I gave her the Crown's phone number, in case she changed her mind, and then ended the conversation. I left a message for Cutler to contact me. Beverley's refusal hurt, but I had no time to react. Warren sent me to pick up some documents for a client. When I came home, Bradley began to vomit again.

Cutler called shortly after the puking stopped. Whatever else I thought of him, I admired his promptness at returning calls. I wanted to let him know what I had done. After all, he had requested that I ask people in West Hawk to come forward.

"Has any person other than doctors given testimony?" I asked.

"Yes, Mrs. Tod was on the stand."

"How did that go?"

"I refuse to speculate. I can assure you all of the doctors, and Mrs. Tod, were cross-examined thoroughly and efficiently by myself and Deborah McCawley, the Crown responsible for the constitutional arguments."

"I only wanted your opinion."

"I told you. They were dealt with in a competent and professional manner."

"Can we watch these proceedings?"

"It's an open court. You may do as you wish. I advise you not to appear. It makes the judge think the witnesses are overzealous. It is not worthwhile."

"We are overzealous, with good reason. Why shouldn't we be there?"

"It is not useful. We are conducting this as competently and thoroughly as possible."

Similar words had been thrown around at the meeting with Mr. Bernard, when he described Mr. Cutler's style.

"Is it going to go on for much longer?"

"I refuse to speculate. The judge probably wishes to settle this matter. Personally, I do not see the point of continuing. The doctors have abundantly proven Mr. Tod is seriously ill. I do not wish to discuss this any further."

"What about the trips to Zeller's?"

"Are these people willing to come forward?"

Beverley's refusal to testify finally and fully hit me. I began to shake.

Cutler said, "You have no evidence. I asked you to get these people to testify."

I knew it was not my job to gather evidence; I had lost control of my voice and could not reply.

Cutler's voice oozed disdain. "I asked you to get them to write me."

When he said that, my mind jumped. He had asked last Friday. Even if I had talked to Beverley immediately and she wrote immediately, her letter wouldn't have reached the city yet.

"I have received no letters. There is no evidence. I have nothing to discuss with you."

I felt beaten, blamed, incompetent, useless. I choked; my voice cracked out of my throat.

"Do you have . . . any idea how difficult it is to ask people to do that?"

I cried. I hated showing this surge of emotion, especially when speaking to Cutler.

"Have you any idea?" I repeated loudly.

"This is ridiculous! I refuse to discuss this further!"

"I have one more question, Mr. Cutler, have you ever been . . . sexually abused?"

"That's enough!" He slammed down his receiver.

Disclosing sexual abuse was futile and crazy. Here was the proof.

The ugly, familiar wall I had been struggling to hold back collapsed. Cutler's reprimands and Beverley's refusals combined with the bitterness at being excluded from Tom's wedding. The pent-up feelings poured out.

Allison came home from school. Bradley came out of the bedroom where he had been asleep. They huddled round and embraced me.

"We'll take care of you, Mommy. Bradley, go get Dad," Allison said.

Warren appeared and made tea. I attempted to explain the gist of the two conversations, but I had been transported to an airless, barren planet, cut off from humanity.

I had to stop crying. A neighbour up the road had recently organized a 4-H light horse and pony club, and I had offered the use of our house for a meeting, scheduled to start in one hour. It was too late to cancel or shift it. Parents and kids arrived. To our surprise, the woman who had arranged the meeting sent along a resignation letter with one of the girls. The kid read the message; heads turned in my direction. I gulped. My tongue needed to be unrolled.

I said, "I might seem a logical choice to replace her. I've been a 4-H leader before. And Allison is interested in horses. But I can't handle anything . . . "

I sketched the details. I wanted to be honest with the children and their parents, but I also noticed the look of terror on Allison's face—a frozen mask of suffering, like the one on Wendy's face two years ago at Hecla Island. Here I was, telling a group of people I knew, but not well, who lived close to me.

After the meeting, Wendy called. Between sobs, I tried to explain what Cutler had said.

She waited until I could speak normally. "I had trouble with him, too. When I called Ms. McCawley, the constitutional expert, she told me the room number and the time, without any lectures. It could end at any moment. And we won't know a thing."

"Cutler told me not to appear, under dire threat of insubordination."

"It's a free country. But . . ."

Simultaneously, we knew we needed to be in the courtroom. We did not trust Cutler. He wanted the file to quietly slide away. I promised to get into the city as early as possible in the morning. Let others attend weddings; we would attend court.

70

THE NEXT MORNING, I SPED INTO THE CITY AND searched for parking near the law courts building, a nerve-wracking procedure that was getting to be a habit. It made me late, but I assumed from our previous experience in the Victim Assistance room that not much would have happened. I was wrong.

I walked into the courtroom; no one was talking. Wendy and Bill, with Patrick asleep in his car seat, sat beside Karen and Esther in the back row. In unison, they looked up at me.

Four lawyers in black robes faced the judge. It was a small room; they all turned around when I burst through the door at the rear. I sat down to assess the situation.

The row of lawyers refocused their attention on the judge. I stared at the backs of their heads, figuring out the identity of each person. Cutler was short, mid-fifties, with glasses and dark hair. I recognized Pollock from the lake. Older, slighter, and impeccably groomed, he sat with his nose pointed at the ceiling. Doyle, his partner, was much taller, but a less imposing presence. He wore glasses and appeared to be around Cutler's age. Next to Cutler sat Ms. McCawley, the Crown's constitutional expert. She looked to be in her late thirties; she had red hair and an intense gaze. Doyle and Pollock ignored us. A younger man in a tailored trench coat sat in the first row.

"They're deciding what to do next. They just called for a break," Wendy said.

During the time out, Deborah McCawley walked to the back and introduced herself. Cutler remained at the table and made no attempt to acknowledge me. I had never met him in person.

Ms. McCawley leaned toward us and whispered, "We're thinking of asking the judge to allow you and Wendy to take the stand. Would you be willing to speak to the court?"

I said, "Yes! I've been waiting three years!"

"Okay, good. We'll see if he allows it."

After she left, Karen, Esther, and Wendy started talking at the same time. Then they stopped and let Karen explain.

She said, "One of the doctors said he had asked the accused to name his children. Jock could not remember all eleven. The judge asked the doctor which children's names he could recall. The only ones were John, Jean, Ernie, Valerie, Tom, and, with effort, David. I felt a thrill go up my spine. You could see light bulbs going off above the judge's head."

"Yeah, the bad children do not exist," I said.

I turned around and saw a boyish face smiling back at me.

"You're Donna."

"Yes. And you?"

"Martin Pollock."

He looked just like his dad, Harvey. "Oh . . . I see."

"How are you?" He ignored the descending chill.

"Not great, considering."

"Do you still have horses? Do you have children?"

"Yes. And yes."

Wendy frowned at him, as if to shove his eager presence away. With a snap, I regained focus. "I don't want to talk to you. I need to pay attention."

"I understand. I wish we could have met under less difficult circumstances."

He rose to leave, and put on his fancy coat.

I thought—fuck off, spawn of Satan!

The black robes swooped back into the courtroom. Cutler sat down and gazed at Pollock. Ms. McCawley nodded at us in the back row. Somehow, she had found a precedent during the break. In this similar case, victims were allowed to speak to the court. When proceedings got underway, she cited it at length.

Doyle stood up. "I object. We are dealing with the assumed innocence of our client. Victim impact statements are heard after, not before a judgment. The accused has not been found guilty."

Justice Clearwater said, "That is not the entire issue. We need to take this a step further."

"Yes, M'lord, but we don't want to take it a giant leap forward." Doyle giggled at his own attempt at humour.

Clearwater ignored it. "What is the effect on these witnesses of not having the trial?"

"The effects on the accused could be quite devastating," Doyle said.

Clearwater nodded. "But the victims' rights are important as well."

With dramatic solemnity, Doyle said, "This man is innocent until proven guilty."

Ms. McCawley rose. "We are not arguing about guilt or innocence. This situation affects the victims and members of the wider community. Medical evidence can be weighed against the public interest." She quoted from the precedent again.

"I will adjourn until 2:00 p.m. I need to think about this," the judge said.

Just as he was about to rush out of the room, I stood up. Startled by my movement, he looked straight at me for the first time.

I said, "I have a letter summarizing the effects of waiting. I could read it or give it to you to look over during the break."

"No, thank you."

After I spoke, the lawyers swung in my direction again, and stared at me, like I was a wild ferret let loose. Whatever I was doing was apparently not allowed. I sat down and a vivid image came to me. I was Alice in the Queen of Hearts' court, trapped in a serious-looking game, but a game nevertheless. The players did not appreciate spectators and we could not question their moves. We only served as game pieces and we did not matter. They could stop the game or change the rules at whim. It did not count that the game was being played right on top of our lives and we might get trampled.

We all stood as the judge exited. I felt exhausted from staring at him; my eyes had scarcely blinked or left his face. I wanted my laser focus to sear into his soul; I wanted him to be ignited by the injustice of what we had endured.

Pollock rose, threw his arm around Cutler, pulled him to his feet, and said, "Let's go for a walk down the aisle and discuss this."

Karen, Esther, Wendy, Bill, and I smiled at each other as the two of them left the room.

I said, "They really do look like they'd like to take a stroll down the aisle. Good thing there's a woman of the cloth here. In case they want to exchange wedding vows."

Karen nodded. "You're joking, but it is interesting to observe the body language. Cutler is either watching Pollock, or inspecting his nails."

"Yeah, he pays no attention to McCawley, and she's working with him," Wendy said.

Karen said, "She's on her own out there. He doesn't look at her or talk to her. Meanwhile, Doyle and Pollock are constantly whispering."

"Doyle reminds me of a sheepdog, waiting to lick his master's boots," Bill said.

"Pollock needs a cape and a moustache. He makes the judge watch him, flinging up his arms, flopping in his chair, slamming down his briefcase," I said.

Karen and Esther left to catch up on some errands. For an unknown reason, Pollock and Doyle returned, without Cutler. He approached me. "You're Donna."

Like father, like son. I did not speak. He knew who I was.

Wendy spoke quietly, but with steel in her voice. "Yes, she's one of Jock's forgotten children, one of the babies abducted by aliens at birth."

Pollock sneered. "You just want to see him dead."

Wendy's words came out clear and level. "No, we want justice."

"Hanging justice. That's what I call it."

I walked over to Pollock and stopped a half metre in front of him. I was pretty sure he wasn't supposed to be talking to us. I stared into his eyes. "I plan to write your comments down. I think they're extremely relevant."

"You're trying to intimidate me. You'd like to hit me."

I moved closer. "You're right. I'd like to punch you. But I won't."

I examined every vein in his eyeballs and the lines snaking around his tanned face.

"I'm not your husband . . . I'll charge you with assault. You're impeding me."

I stared harder. "I'm not stopping you."

"I'll have you charged."

Wendy interjected, "You *can* walk around her."

Doyle sprang into action. He shouted, "Call security! Call security!"

Wendy said, "We don't need security. You can walk around her."

Pollock glanced at the floor tiles and saw that she was right. He had enough space to walk around me. He gestured to Doyle; they disappeared into the marble hallway.

Three minutes later, two guards arrived. One asked, "Where's the altercation? Is this the right room? What's going on?"

Bill, kneeling to buckle Patrick in his car seat, looked up and smiled. The guards scratched their heads, bewildered. Two women watching a dad bundling up a baby did not pose much threat.

Out in the parking lot, I told Wendy, "I hope you weren't worried I'd poke him."

"He wanted you to push him around or hit him, to cause a scene, if only to discredit us."

"He was ready to sacrifice his body to win a case."

Bill said, "You could have wiped the floor with him."

We climbed into their car and laughed. Karen and Esther had promised to join us for lunch, so we hurried to Wendy's house. In the next 105 minutes, we had to compose ourselves and capture in words the effects of an abuse-filled childhood and the repercussions of waiting three years for a trial to happen.

71

WHEN WE RETURNED AFTER LUNCH, MS. MCCAWLEY invited me to sit down and talk with her, on the hard bench outside the courtroom.

"Don't get involved with Pollock. He's trying to provoke you," she said.

"Did you see any unreasonable anger from me?"

"Not really. But I saw anger from him. Don't talk to him."

"Okay, I'll stay away."

She obviously knew Pollock and knew Jock and knew what we were up against. As much as she could in the time available, she briefed us for questioning and cautioned us about the defence lawyers' tactics.

A distinguished-looking man walked past. She looked up at him. "Maybe you'd like to come and watch. It might prove interesting. It's a case you are well acquainted with, one of your favourites."

The man did a double take. "Not again. Did they get him to show? I'd like to see him."

"No, they're still arguing. Saying he is sicker than ever."

They both laughed. The man continued on his way into a nearby office.

Wendy said, "Do you know who that is? I saw his name on the door. That was Justice Hanssen, the one who gave the previous judgment."

We filed back into the room. The judge appeared through a different entrance; we stood up. He said, "I have considered the application to hear the complainants speak. When viewing the interests of the public versus the rights of the accused . . ."

Doyle stood up. "It is not in the public interest to hear the victim's impact statement prior to conviction."

They lobbed precedents back and forth. Finally, the defence, the judge, and the Crown agreed. We could speak, but we could not talk about the actual abuse.

We could only mention the effects of justice delayed. This notion seemed absurd to me. How exactly could the two be separated?

Doyle insisted, "We must limit the questions only to the circumstances which followed from the date the charges were laid, up to the present time."

Justice Clearwater said, "That will be difficult to do."

After more quoting of case law, they agreed we could be called to the stand. Wendy went first, so I exited the courtroom, to wait out in the hall. Karen hoped she might also be allowed to address the court, so she came with me.

During the discussions, Bill had left to find a washroom and change Patrick. When he returned, he handed the dry baby to Karen. Patrick was awake, and squirming, after exposing his bare bum on the cold marble floor. I made faces and blew raspberries on his hands; he got the hiccups from laughing.

Karen watched me fooling around with Patrick. She said, "Your story is worth telling."

I made arm curls, rabbit-punched the air, bounced on my toes. "I can do this, coach . . ."

Inside, I was so terrified I couldn't think.

Karen said, "Wendy went first. She might show her pain. You can use your intellect. The judge needs to see both. Ms. McCawley knows what she is doing."

"Right."

I gazed at Patrick and almost burst into tears. "Look at him. That's what this is all about—protecting children."

The minutes dragged; I realized I was shaking. Then, without warning, the attendant called us into the courtroom. Ms. McCawley removed the summary letter from my hands. I nodded; I could not be allowed to read a prepared text.

I walked up to the witness box. I imagined Pollock and Doyle smirking and spewing weird dialogue. "Looks like she wants to hunt someone. What a lumberjack."

Time slowed almost to a halt but random thoughts zipped around in my brain. I fought to shepherd these ideas into lucid sentences.

The court clerk addressed me, "Do you want to swear on a Bible or affirm to tell the truth?"

"Affirm," I said.

"What is your name? Spell it completely, please."

My tongue felt wedged in my mouth. But, after telling the clerk my name, words slipped out more readily.

"Is your husband an attorney?"

"Yes."

"Are you married?

"Yes."

"Do you have children?"

"Yes."

"Their ages?"

"Five and eleven." Why was he asking these questions? Ms. McCawley rose. "Do you work?"

"My husband runs his practice in our house. I help out. My son is at home part-time."

"You have two jobs then."

I appreciated her acknowledgement. Then the real questioning began.

"Please state some of the effects these delays have had on you."

"I am not supposed to talk about the sexual abuse but . . ."

Doyle popped up at the "s-word." He opened his mouth, looked at the judge, and sat down without speaking.

I continued. "But the combination of dealing with the sexual abuse, openly, for the first time, and the breakup of the family, and the delays, has been very hard. There are physical side effects. Like headaches, backaches, nausea, insomnia, anxiety attacks, chest pains. My husband drove me to the hospital to check out a pain in my chest, just to make sure I wasn't having a heart attack. Counselling and massage have relieved some symptoms. I've been going to counselling for three years."

Then I noticed Ms. McCawley staring at me. She leaned forward, her whole body radiating encouragement, like a rider urging a horse in a race. I focused on her bright blue eyes. I told about no longer wanting to attend church or teach Sunday school.

The judge perked up. He said, "Where did you teach Sunday school?"

"In the town where I live."

From where I sat, it was difficult to see the judge's face. He was seated so much higher. The setting instilled a sense of isolation and frustration. How would a child react to such intimidation?

I wanted to stand up on my chair, look into Clearwater's eyes and shout at him until he recognized me as a human being. But, if I stood, one of the sheriffs might pull a gun or cart me off. These two sheriffs were much larger than the ones who had been in the room in the morning. They must have been warned about the rowdy women.

"Oh, yeah, I have sexual problems . . ."

Doyle jumped up again, triggered by the "s-word."

I noticed all of the male robes had stopped listening and squirmed. They did not want to hear how a deviant man could damage a child. Given the context, a sexual abuse case, I found their reluctance to pay attention disconcerting.

Before I could describe the problems, Justice Clearwater interrupted me. "Why do you want to see these charges pursued?"

I was stumped. Why didn't a judge with years of experience know the reasons why police laid charges and offenders got punished? It was his job to weigh the facts and sentence appropriately. I stared at him in disbelief.

He continued, "Isn't it enough that the people who love and care about you believe you?"

I was speechless, unable to respond. He had just asked me to justify the centuries-old concept of lawful punishment. Why report any crime if it only mattered that people who loved you believed you? Did he make the same comments to owners of stolen cars? The police officers and Crown attorneys had never told me the charges would be dropped if my husband believed me.

I spoke slowly, "Sexual abuse is a crime. I have met hundreds of women who have been sexually assaulted and have not reported. However, as a child, I did not identify it as a crime. I believed I deserved it. I know differently now."

Doyle twitched but did not get up.

Clearwater said, "What do you mean 'hundreds of women'? We are constantly dealing with troops of offenders in these courtrooms." Then he glared at me, almost as if it were my fault.

"Well, that's only a small percentage."

I could not believe his digression. Here I was, arguing with a judge about the purpose of the legal system and the numbers of unreported sexual assaults, neither of which had anything to do with the personal effects of the court's delays. Was he toying with us, allowing us to vent our rage, so he'd feel justified doing what he had already made up his mind to do?

"You mentioned 'validation' earlier. When did you first hear this word?" he asked.

"What? Do you mean in my whole life?"

This must be a trick question. I had read thousands of books, graduated from university with an honours English degree, and taught language arts.

I said, "I don't remember. I have known that word for a long time."

"Well, let me put it this way, when did you first feel 'validation'?"

"If you are referring specifically to this case, I felt it when I reported the sexual abuse . . ."

Doyle rose at the mention of the "s-word."

I finished my sentence. ". . . to the police."

Doyle sat down.

The judge heaved a mammoth sigh and said something unintelligible like "Right!"

I thought—does any of this matter? None of them want me to finish a sentence. The judge interrupts and pulls the questioning all over the map. That jack-in-the-box Doyle can't contain himself.

I had barely started to explain the effects. But the judge was already calling on Pollock or Doyle to cross-examine me.

First off, Doyle asked, "How long did your post-partum depression last?"

His question confounded me. I had never suffered post-partum depression with either child and I had just stated my children were five and eleven years old. I couldn't make any connection between his odd question and the sexual assault charges. They had openly agreed to only discuss events that followed after they were laid.

He was using the old "nuts or sluts" tactic, trying to portray me as a hysterical woman at the mercy of her hormones, who could not handle birthing babies, let alone reality. Maybe Pollock preferred not to sully his image with stupid sexist insinuations, so he let Doyle do it.

Then Doyle got up and read a list of people I had not called since the charges were laid. He did not ask why I hadn't called any of these people.

"And you haven't picked up the phone to call your sister Valerie?"

"I sent her letters. She did not reply."

Doyle made a pained face.

I thought—was letter-writing inappropriate?

"What about your stepmother?"

"She made arrangements to visit me. She did not come. I wrote letters to all of my siblings about this issue. Most never wrote back."

I forgot to mention the court order that was issued after the charges were laid, which stated the offender should not have contact with witnesses. I forgot to explain how it eliminated the urge to "just pick up the phone and call" as Doyle suggested.

He was looking for a place to set a wedge. But his tactics had faltered. When I answered so quickly, it didn't appear that I was making anything up. He decided to settle on a new line of questioning. "Would you want these proceedings to take place if you were told by a credible physician there was a high probability that they would have a catastrophic effect on your father's health?"

"I don't believe they would."

"I will ask you the question again." And he did, same question, four times, with slightly different words, but always with "catastrophe" emphasized.

"I don't believe it," I stated, to each altered query.

Then I said, "I had a bladder infection diagnosed. One week later, I was near dead from a ruptured appendix. My mother was told, by a credible doctor, she was having a bad menopause. She died shortly after, from a brain tumour. I do not always believe doctors. The first time they said Jock's heart was not functioning, he was out deer hunting."

The judge did not appreciate my diatribe. He said, "Answer the question."

"I don't believe it."

Clearwater decided to come at it from a more direct angle. "Would it matter to you if your father died as a result of these proceedings?"

I paused. "No . . . it wouldn't."

(Later that night, I rehashed the scene in my mind. I wished I had shouted, in answer to this last catastrophe question, "No, but it might matter to Mr. Pollock—a real catastrophe. Jock's wife would get the bill and she has no money.")

The judge beamed at Doyle, like a proud father, proving that I could be managed, if only the proper firm approach was taken. "You see, she answered the question," he said.

Wendy could not contain her umbrage. "Well, you reworded the bloody question . . ."

All the black robes swung around in unison and glared at her. The sheriff shifted his weight and crossed his arms. According to courtroom decorum, spectators could not speak. Wendy stopped mid-sentence and swallowed the rest. Satisfied she was under control, the judge returned to an earlier theme.

"You say you'd like to get your father to admit his wrongdoing. I want you to know that I cannot make him admit anything. And the police cannot, and his lawyers cannot, either."

Clearwater had stated the obvious, but it shocked me how easily he relinquished the authority of the court. On the one hand, Pollock argued the pressure of appearing in court would kill his client. On the other hand, this judge insisted the court had no power.

After they asked me to step down from the witness box, I was reeling, mentally beaten up. Bill gave me thumbs-up from the back. I stumbled to the chairs and sat down. The judge ended the session. He would not decide right there if the trial would proceed. He would not allow Karen to speak.

Then it was over. I walked toward Ms. McCawley to thank her.

While she spoke with us for a few minutes, Pollock muttered loudly. Bits of his sentences drifted over to us. "Can you believe it? . . . A women's issue . . . They have made it into quite the feminist thing."

He had labelled five women talking as a "feminist conspiracy."

I had learned my lesson about falling for his provocation. We all ignored him.

Cutler left the courtroom without speaking to any of us.

72

PRIOR TO FINDING OUT THAT THE MOTIONS COURT might hear our testimony, I had signed up for another weekend workshop with Karen and Esther. I appreciated their presence during much of the day at the law courts building, especially since the workshop started the same evening.

After a pizza and a cold beer, I sped to Karen and Esther's offices. Hettie, from last summer's support group, greeted me when I entered. I sat down and faced the circle of women. I tried to gauge my emotional state, questioning if this was a good idea. We did a check-in, but I was too scrambled to listen. Words. Words. Words. I had been rubbed raw by words all day.

Karen placed a box of objects in the centre of the room. She asked us to pick up a relevant thing and talk; I grabbed a beanbag. My turn came; I chucked the bag as hard as possible at the opposite wall. It slid down and plopped on a woman's head. The participants stared at me as if to say, "Is this part of the program? I didn't pay to have this woman throw things at me."

I apologized and wanted to leave.

After the break, Esther asked us to draw a picture. I drew jagged lines with blood dripping. A blindfolded statue of Justice stood with a sword stuck in her heart. Nazi symbols oozed red fluid. When my turn to speak came again, I choked out a summary of the day's events.

The session ended at 10:00 p.m., and Hettie and I went for a drink to catch up. Two other women came with us. Hettie wanted a detailed report of the court scenes. When I got back to their house, Wendy was still up. She said, "I would have liked to see Hettie. I could not get to sleep."

I knew what she meant. We were both running on adrenalin. For two hours, we talked about what she said in court and what I said and what we both wished we had said.

After I went to bed, memories of the day's events spun around in my head. I flipped and groaned, thinking I had blown my one chance to tell the truth, to convince the judge. When sleep came, I dreamt I was wedged inside a small box. I wanted to smash its walls, to punch the demons beating me while I was trapped.

I got up around six and rumbled around in the kitchen. Wendy joined me and we rehashed Pollock's tactics and the bizarre exchanges in the courtroom. We laughed so hard I forgot to watch the clock. I brushed my teeth in the car, and then exhaustion hit me. I wanted to pull over in the intersection and doze.

At the workshop, Karen asked us to recall a time when it felt safe to be creative. I described writing a poem on a flat rock in the bush, and bringing it to my mother. It was about the English grandmother I had never met. It made my mother weep. I had never seen her cry, except when she got hit.

Karen had asked us to bring, and share, something creative we had made. I read my dragon story. I wanted to read it quick and sharp, like a razor slice, so I wouldn't feel it. I gulped a big breath and started. Until I finished, the air moved so little in my lungs it felt like I was under water. The room got quiet. Had I committed another faux pas, like smashing a beanbag on someone's head?

Hettie wept. "I am in awe."

I looked at her and remembered the daughter she had lost to suicide. A part of me wanted to take out her sad eyes, wash them, and put them back. She began to sing. She said it was her only creative outlet. I sang with her.

We chanted the chorus of the spiritual. "A-men, A-men, A-men." We changed it to "Wo-men, Wo-men, Wo-men." The rest joined in, quietly, then with fervour, improvising verses. After the song ended, the workshop was over.

Hettie and I went for another beer. We talked in the parking lot before getting into our cars. She said, "I want to take care of you."

I realized she was probably thinking of her daughter and remembering not being able to save her. She stared with such intensity, I was embarrassed.

"I'll be okay. I'm sure of it."

"I know you want to get home to your children. But you need to allow yourself to be nurtured."

This woman, almost old enough to be my mother, held my face in her hands and kissed both cheeks. I wiped a tear off the ridge under her eye and gently broke away.

73

THE JUDGE HAD DECIDED TO CONTINUE HEARING the unfinished motion on October 30, in the evening. I phoned Wendy to explain my plan. I wanted to load the courtroom with spectators. She agreed to call some people. I spent the morning and afternoon contacting people. I did not want to have to persuade anyone. But most of them said, right away, "I'll be there. I think it's important."

Late in the afternoon, I called Barb. Her husband, Craig, answered. While we waited for her to come to the phone, I described the courtroom escapades.

He said, "Isn't Pollock a champion whistler? You could've grabbed his balls, yanked, and said, 'Let's hear you whistle now!' I'd have loved to have seen his face."

"I could have knocked out his teeth and said, 'Let's hear you whistle now.' But I didn't."

We laughed at these fantasies. Then Barb took the phone from him and promised to carpool with several others from West Hawk.

Before I knew it, it was time to leave for Winnipeg.

The court employees moved the hearing to a larger room because seventeen people had showed up: Sharon, Fran and Dave, Barb, Shelley, Hettie, Wendy, Bill, Warren, women from West Hawk, and me.

Pollock glowered at everyone who walked into the room. Cutler still did not look at or speak to Wendy or me, but Ms. McCawley appeared encouraged by the group. When the judge entered, he appeared somewhat taken aback. But there it was—the community he kept referring to when he talked of "the community's interests."

Wendy had invited our cousin Sharon, the other lawyer in the family. She told us she had articled with Clearwater. Her comments on the procedures and his habits proved invaluable. Doyle was first up, citing the case of an ill man who molested his daughters; the charges were stayed. Pollock twitched in his chair while Doyle droned on about Jock's health and then quoted at length from the now-familiar doctors' reports.

The judge summarized the content in one sentence: "What you are saying is that the accused has good days and bad days."

I got excited. Clearwater seemed to get it.

Doyle looked frustrated and repeated the "catastrophe" term.

Clearwater said, "I realize the accused has suffered a stroke. But Justice Hanssen said the trial process could be adapted to accommodate his condition without exposing him to too much risk."

Doyle reiterated his points, and inserted "catastrophe" several more times.

I smiled when Doyle said, "Mr. Tod can respond coherently when questioned in a cool and sympathetic manner."

All our lives, we had been trained to talk to him in "a cool and sympathetic manner," or he went berserk.

With his chair turned at a forty-five degree angle, Pollock continued to glare at the audience. Cutler did not pick up a pen or touch a paper except when Ms. McCawley addressed him. He buffed his fingernails and cleaned his glasses.

At 8:00 p.m., Ms. McCawley got up to speak. She reflected briefly on the longevity of the case and referred to the first stay of proceedings in November 1993. She called this episode "take two." She noted the extended period of abuse and violence and "the courage and emotional strength required" to come forward.

A surprising exchange occurred when Ms. McCawley used the legal term "sidebar" to direct the judge's attention to a relevant section of a precedent.

Clearwater said, "I don't know what that term means exactly. It reminds me of that television show where the lawyer says the 'sidebar' is the little pub across the street where they meet for drinks after court."

The male robes chortled, loudly and long.

Ms. McCawley waited for the noise to subside. "Now to return to the serious matter at hand . . ."

The judge interrupted her. "I want you to know, Ms. McCawley; I do indeed appreciate the seriousness of the matter before me."

Ms. McCawley talked about "opening old wounds" and how the failure to report was often caused by the offenders.

The judge said, "The offenders will always be older than the victims. Because of that factor, they will be more likely to suffer ill health."

I was baffled by his statement of the obvious.

Cutler seemed mesmerized by Pollock. When Pollock polished his bifocals, Cutler cleaned his lenses. When Pollock stroked his face, Cutler rubbed his ear.

Ms. McCawley cited Hanssen's judgment and emphasized the section that referred to the accused "attempting to manoeuver his way out of his legal predicament through manipulation and malingering." She said, "Mr. Tod should not be allowed to use his worsening health as an excuse. The delays were entirely his choice."

Clearwater got excited. "Why was he permitted to malinger? Everyone knew his age and health. This particular case has had twenty-five consecutive adjournments. This is an egregious waste of time and resources. Why wasn't he committed to trial? Why wasn't he treated like someone who was in custody?"

Ms. McCawley blushed to match her hair, as if she were the cause of the department's failures, despite all her attempts to expedite the case. (Warren explained the concept of "speedy justice" to me later. If the person is in jail, the system moves quickly so he or she does not have to languish in custody).

The judge calmed down and mused out loud. "These assaults took place over a long period. What caused them to come out now?"

Without thinking, I said, loudly, "He was doing it again. That's why."

It was a rhetorical question. I forgot we weren't allowed to speak.

The judge stared at me. "One more outburst from you and you will be watching these proceedings from somewhere out in the hall."

Then he turned back to the robes. "Yes, it seems he was doing it again."

I chuckled at his choice of words. The audience murmured and nodded.

The judge said, "And I can see by the expressions of these people, they are not in agreement with these delays."

Ms. McCawley attempted to rationalize the delays from the Crown's perspective. Clearwater dismissed her explanations with a wave and told her she was not responsible.

Ms. McCawley quoted from another case and noted, "Unreasonable delay is an abuse of process. Mr. Tod must have been aware of the possibility of his health getting worse."

Pollock shifted his chair so we could not see his face. Cutler alternated between staring at his cuticles and looking at Pollock. Ms. McCawley, encouraged by the judge's growing grasp of the situation, spoke more firmly. "The Charter must not be used as a shield to avoid facing justice."

Pollock tented his fingers in the prayer position. Cutler continued to watch him.

Ms. McCawley continued, "The accused was not at any time ready to prove his innocence. The stress must have indeed taken its toll, but Mr. Tod chose to take this course. None of the experts could point to anything more than a probability. The trial process can be flexible enough to accommodate the proceeding."

She mentioned the wedding, the trips to Winnipeg, and the shopping excursions.

She said, "Much of the testimony on his health is based on information gathered from Mrs. Tod. I question her credibility. I believe her fears are exaggerated. For example, she insisted on bringing or giving oxygen when a doctor deemed it unnecessary. Mrs. Tod states he is never home alone. This is not the case. She leaves him for hours at a time. He still has a driver's license. Why is this allowed if he is so ill? The neurologist concluded that even if he misnames objects, he would be able to participate. As far as 'cool and sympathetic' questioning, I believe the judge could control the proceedings so he would not be badgered and stressed."

Cutler massaged his ear.

Ms. McCawley said, "It is not appropriate to re-argue Justice Hanssen's judgment."

To me this seemed a no-brainer, but Warren pointed out later it was an important point of law. Hanssen had decided, given the evidence he had at the time, and his conclusions could not be rehashed willy-nilly. Clearwater agreed and referred to specific statements in the judgment. Pollock contemplated his hands; Doyle scribbled madly.

Clearwater said, "The court must focus on accountability, and consider Hanssen's opinions on malingering and avoiding. The court must consider the seriousness of the charges."

He grew more adamant. "This will not be delayed again! I will decide at once to stay the charges or go directly to trial. I will not worry about juggling schedules but will go ahead with or without you present!"

Ms. McCawley stood and dropped her head. "I am grateful to hear that, M'lord."

Doyle jumped to his feet. "I take issue with the term 'malingering.'"

Clearwater said, "I cannot argue with Hanssen's opinions. He said it is not fair to those involved. This man has put himself at risk."

Pollock stood up. "Well, the proceedings . . . just went on, M'lord."

The judge burned a look at Pollock, who sat down, sputtering.

Clearwater continued, as if he had not been interrupted, "We all recognize he is sick, but how much worse is it? His heart output was 20 percent. Has this changed?"

The audience stirred, moved by the growing realization that someone had finally clicked onto the inconsistencies of this farce and its convoluted history.

The judge talked about Mr. Tod being a "gambling man," banking on the odds of the charges getting stayed. I assumed we would be told his opinion before he left the room, but he wanted to think about it on his own time. He promised to let us know "as soon as possible." Because it was evening, no court officer was present.

Pollock leapt up and shouted, "All rise!" and Clearwater disappeared in a billow of fabric.

Now we were free to move about, I said to Ms. McCawley, "We appreciate all your efforts. Could you please let us know as soon as you know?"

Cutler still did not speak to any of us. Pollock stood by the door, arms crossed, as we filed out.

Barb walked past him and said, loudly, "My name is Barb Hamilton and I live at Falcon Lake."

She knew he would be offended. He liked to think the lake people admired him. Others walked past and made similar assertions. Everyone streamed out into the marble hall, erupting with laughter and exclamations of astonishment.

"Could you believe the antics of that prancing fool?"

"Did you see how he scowled at us? Well, I just glared right back."

"Donna, you must have known the judge would allow you one kick at the cat. He even repeated what you said."

"I almost peed myself when he threatened to throw you out!"

"Did you notice Cutler? His nails must be perfect. I hope he doesn't get paid for this night's work."

"I loved it when Pollock almost squirmed out of his chair. It looked like he might rub a hole in his pants."

"This really helped me understand what you girls have been up against."

Wendy departed with Bill to feed Patrick. The rest of the group gathered at a nearby restaurant. Jokes about Jock, Pollock's histrionics, and the judge's remarks flew around the table. People asked Sharon dozens of questions about court procedures and Clearwater's personality.

The next day, Warren attended his last council meeting. For my birthday, he had given me a harmonica. Margaret gave me a massage. On the weekend, we hosted our now annual Halloween party. Allison and Bradley rated it as "fairly successful, given the lead-up time." About thirty people showed up, half adults, half children, almost all acting like children. It helped shift my mind off the comedic legal drama.

The editor of the anthology sent back my story for revision. I was relieved to see how little it was altered. When I mailed the new copy back to her, I promised myself I would tell the complete story. The dragon tale was just a beginning. The longer version was funnier, especially the part we were at now.

74

SHORTLY AFTER THE HEARING, ONE OF MY AUNTS died. Seeing the last name of Tod in the obituaries shocked me, until I read the notice and figured out it was my father's sister-in-law.

In the morning, before the funeral, I visited Karen; she urged me to attend. I wouldn't know who might show up, but this aunt had tried to make life easier for us. Every summer, she invited my sister Valerie and me to her home for a week. I remembered tiptoeing across her polished floors, afraid to poop or pee in the toilet. The spotlessness impressed me; the feeling of safety impressed me even more. I wanted to honour her passing.

I left my car at a muffler shop and Bill and Wendy picked me up there. At the chapel, we sat near the door so Wendy or Bill could exit if Patrick started fidgeting. But this meant everyone who entered passed in front of us.

A few minutes after we sat down, Joan made her entrance. With the heavy makeup, lacquered hair, and stern expression, her face reminded me of an ancient mask. Wendy told me that Joan's sister and husband had walked in with her. I wondered if they knew.

When Jean walked to the front of the chapel with her husband and a group of cousins, I was dumb-founded. Wendy had invited her to the hearing and she had insisted she could barely move. The rest of the clan moved to the reserved seats, heralded by a sympathetic murmur. I looked at the cousins—what about us? What about our losses?

My cousin Eleanor and her husband, Cliff, came in late and sat beside us. She smiled at me. "It's so good to see you."

Another latecomer burst into the chapel—my oldest brother, John. I hadn't seen him since our first family meeting. He slid in beside Wendy. To make room, Bill jumped up and placed Patrick, sleeping in his car seat, on the floor. John peered into the bundle of blankets. I remembered he had not met Patrick.

John grunted. "Thank God, he looks like Bill's side. Not too ugly."

I started to say something in rebuttal, but my aunt's only daughter entered, and stopped by our pew. She hugged me and said, "I'm glad you came."

"She was . . . my aunt."

The funeral proceeded. The service didn't last long. However, by the end I had decided I wanted to send an obituary to the newspaper and hold a ceremony for the father who never existed.

Wendy and I hung back while Bill struggled with Patrick's snowsuit. Joan passed us without a word or glance. I wanted to tackle her, to turn her head, and make her look at Patrick. John ignored me and kept insulting Wendy.

I walked out the side entrance where the hearses had assembled and leaned against the wall. A few cousins spoke to me. Joan approached, but spun on her heels and disappeared when she saw that I was standing near the exit.

Eleanor came out and stood beside me. She waved at Jean and invited her to join us. Then she grabbed both of us by the shoulders and pushed us together. She said, "I know you aren't seeing eye-to-eye these days, but I know there's still a lot of caring."

I tried to keep my voice level. "It's a bit more than not seeing eye-to-eye. She has given up on people who are doing the right thing. Can you imagine how that feels?"

Eleanor and Jean never got a chance to respond. Old Aunt Jean, the one who had bankrolled my father's defence, stepped between us.

She asked me, "Where is your baby?"

"He's in school today," I said.

"What? Your baby is in school?"

Old age had solidified her features. Her faded blue eyes stared wide-eyed, without a trace of pain, intellect, or pity. She looked at me and said, "I hope you'll all be at my funeral."

I stifled a giggle. How would she know?

Jean's oldest son, Trevor, joined our cluster. Another older woman walked over, introduced herself, and asked him, "Where's your grandfather? Is he not feeling well these days?"

Neither Jean nor Trevor answered. They mumbled and turned to other mourners.

I stared at all of them, huddled by the hearses in the frosty sunshine, and realized I felt more clear-headed than I had for a long time. I pictured my toxic clan gathered down in a big valley, calling up to me, "We don't like your stance! Change back! Come down."

FOR THE NEXT few days, I kept busy with 4-H, yoga, ringette, art lessons, work on ski trails, and company. It was almost two weeks since we had been in court and we still hadn't heard from Justice Clearwater. Fran and Dave got married at her mother's home. Karen performed the service. Karen, Warren, and I were the only people present who were not family members.

During the meal, Karen spoke to me. "I've called that Crown prosecutor so many times. I told him I wanted to see this madness stopped."

A couple of days later, Belle called to find out about the judge's decision.

I said, "I don't know and I don't have the energy to ask Cutler. He's patronizing and dismissive. The people who came to court all commented on his lack of interest, especially when compared to Ms. McCawley."

On the evening of November 20, while playing ringette, I tripped over my friend's skate, flew through the air for a few metres, and landed hard on my left shoulder. She skated back to check on me. This teammate worked as an ambulance attendant. I answered her questions about how many fingers, got up, and stumbled to the dressing room. Once there, I realized I couldn't drive home; my left arm hung useless. After struggling out of my jersey, I stared at my laces and tried to suck back the tears.

My friend drove me to the emergency ward and waited with me. The doctor said my shoulder wasn't broken, but I had damaged the joint. By now, I was in shock from pain and she offered to take me home. During our trip along the cold and dark gravel road, I blathered about past romances. For a week, I could not sleep properly, or drive.

75

WENDY CALLED TO TELL ME THE DECISION WOULD be heard on November 24, a Friday morning, at 9:00 a.m. For the rest of the day, I called people and asked them to be present at the reading of the judgment. I felt unusually calm. But I was gulping painkillers for my injured shoulder.

We asked Warren's mother to stay with Bradley so we could drive to Winnipeg to hear the judgment. He was sick again, from another bug passed around in kindergarten. That morning, I had booked the farrier to trim the horses' hooves. They had to be captured, haltered, and put into a small corral, in case we were not back when he showed up. This took longer than expected, and then it started snowing.

We did not pull up to the courthouse until after 9:00 a.m. I felt uncomfortable wearing my sling, so I left it in the car. I rushed inside to find the assigned room while Warren circled around trying to find a parking spot. I sat down in the front row with Hettie, Irene, Karen, Wendy, Barb, Bill, and Sharon.

Wendy poked my good arm and spoke quietly. "He's not going to allow Pollock's motion."

It was only 9:10 a.m. I knew we were late, but I didn't expect it would be over so soon.

Pollock stood and flung his hands up. "I'm going to withdraw, M'lord. I cannot, in good conscience, be a part of this. I will not continue. I do not want to kill this man."

Clearwater looked at him. "I appreciate that, Mr. Pollock. This is an exceptionally difficult case. If I had my way, I, too, would withdraw. However, these choices are not ours to make. I refuse to allow you. It would only delay the matter further. We must proceed, with all haste."

Pollock blanched.

Clearwater asked, "Will you be speaking to Mr. Tod in person to discuss his defence?"

Pollock blushed, noticeably red after his previous white.

"Actually . . . I haven't seen Mr. Tod for several months."

Hettie nudged me and whispered, "I see. He doesn't care much for the real person, despite his outrage. How can he trot out that self-righteous shit?"

Pollock said, "M'lord, I am going away for a few weeks. I will not be available."

Clearwater replied, "I will start next week, if you want."

Pollock pointed to a side door. "M'lord . . . I would like to meet with you and Mr. Cutler to discuss this privately, in your chambers."

"I decline. These matters can be decided openly, right now. I am ready to accommodate you, even though I will be in Ottawa next week."

Pollock said, "Oh, we cannot decide right now. We dare not impose on you, M'lord."

Clearwater would not be shaken off course. "I will take your phone numbers and contact you at a prearranged time for a conference call."

Pollock still sat upright, despite his setbacks, but Doyle had slumped forward and was hunched over the table. Pollock whispered some instructions and then lifted his foot onto the seat of Doyle's chair. He shoved his boot under his assistant's butt, and leaned on his own leg. It was an odd pose, especially when Pollock turned and half faced the audience. It looked as if he might fall over at any moment and twist his ankle.

Cutler looked interested, and yet stunned, by Clearwater's responses to Pollock. Despite his lack of effort, he might actually win this case. He sat up straight and participated in the discussion on how to physically get Jock into the courtroom.

Clearwater said to Pollock, "Your client does not have to be present. Phones, televisions, and doctors can be utilized. I will even come into the comfort of Mr. Tod's home to take his deposition, if required."

The audience chuckled; Pollock looked buffaloed. He spoke in a low murmur. "I would like to remind the Crown it is obligated to provide the necessary medical supports."

"Mr. Pollock, it is your responsibility to find out what that entails," said Clearwater.

Pollock opened his mouth. Clearwater interrupted him, "Read the evidence."

Mr. Pollock could not miss Clearwater's point. Perhaps the time had come to plead guilty. Clearwater had dismantled every one of his prevarications.

Clearwater shouted, "Read the evidence, Mr. Pollock! Read the evidence!"

I could not believe what I was hearing. The audience murmured and exchanged glances. Pollock would be motivated to end it, and leave on his holiday.

I noticed that no one asked us if we were available or had any Christmas vacations planned. Our needs and wants had long since receded into minute insignificance.

Mr. Cutler said, "I have other cases booked this next week. I will not be able to be present."

And no one would notice, I thought, but refrained from saying it.

Clearwater asked Ms. McCawley, "Could you take over the case if Mr. Cutler is not available?"

I curbed my impulse to yelp in excitement. She knew the major players and she was present to us, mentally and physically, every time we saw her. She may have nodded but I couldn't see her.

Then Clearwater spoke to the defence team. "I'll arrange the conference call during lunch hour."

Pollock said, "Oh, M'lord, we could not impose on you . . ."

Clearwater interrupted him again. "I am willing to do this, any time, day or night."

They wrangled some more about dates and schedules. Clearwater mentioned December 11. Someone shouted, "ALL RISE!" and he disappeared.

Pollock shot all of us a look of disdain. Cutler sprang into action. He said, "Where's Donna? Which one of you is Wendy? I might as well talk to you right now, in my office, about your statements."

I couldn't believe this was the same guy who had disowned what we were doing, hung up on me when I cried in frustration, and ignored us every time we entered a room. He opened doors for us, pushed elevator buttons, and pulled out chairs.

I settled into his office chair—this wasn't the Cutler I'd come to know and dislike.

On the wall in his office, he had a portrait of himself with another robed figure. I asked Cutler about his companion; he gave me the name of a well-known legal personality. Then he dashed off to tell Saul Bernard about the judge's decision.

Wendy returned to the courtroom to tell the rest where we were. Cutler had herded us away from them quickly, without saying what he wanted with us or for how long.

After he came back from Bernard's office, he helped me remove my jacket. He noticed I struggled to lift my left arm but he didn't ask why. He went through my statement and informed me of the line of questioning Pollock might take. His drone made me sleepy, but my stomach started to heave when he asked about specific details.

I could not recall feeling so embarrassed speaking with Ms. Kohm. I said, "I know you were very reluctant to see this through."

"You can rest assured, when I am told to prosecute, I will do so to the best of my abilities."

I was not assured—resting or otherwise. I stared at his mouth moving and moving, and tried to remember what Mr. Bernard had said about something in Mr. Cutler's "history" that would cause him to take our case seriously. It was too late to change horses, but I also knew I did not like dealing with skittish and stubborn donkeys.

After Cutler finished, he sent me out to call for Wendy. I followed her back into his office. That's when I realized how messed up I was from the painkillers. She turned me around and pointed me to the right door. I joined the others downstairs in the cafeteria.

Everyone, except Bill, had stuck around, even my busy lawyer-cousin, Sharon.

Karen spoke first. "I thanked Ms. McCawley for you."

A newspaper reporter, who had attended the morning's court session, ordered a coffee, and watched us from across the room. I looked at him and realized it was the same guy who had been hanging around the aborted preliminary hearing in the spring.

Someone passed me a copy of Clearwater's written judgment. Sharon, who had already skimmed through it, said to me, "You won't like some of his opinions. He says the victims wrongly view the court process as part of treatment."

"I never said that! He came up with that idea on his own."

She asked, "Who's been subpoenaed?"

I told her the names I knew for sure.

Her next comment surprised me. "I think it'd be a good move if Jean was brought in. A reluctant witness who tells the truth would be very effective."

"I know that. Ms. Kohm knew that. Cutler doesn't."

Just then, Cutler strolled through the cafeteria, with the Acting Attorney General and another suit in tow. He waved as we got up to leave.

It took two and a half hours to drive home through the swirling snow. Bradley jumped with excitement when he saw us. Anne reported he was angry when he got out of bed and we were gone. The farrier had phoned and said he couldn't come because of highway conditions. After Anne left, I went and released all the horses.

I came back inside, flopped on the couch, and cried.

Warren asked, "What's wrong? Is it your shoulder?"

I started to explain how much I had been holding in all day. That night, I dreamt, once again, of mutilation and death.

Early the next morning, the phone rang into my fogged-up consciousness. Wendy said she was on her way to West Hawk, to attend the funeral of a husband of one of the women who had supported us in court. For a couple of hours, I contemplated going to the funeral, but decided against it; my arm still felt too sore to drive.

After she hung up, I stared into my coffee cup and mused about what would happen. Jock's choices were limited. He could: (a) die, (b) plead guilty, or (c) participate in a real trial.

76

DURING THE LAST WEEK OF NOVEMBER, BARB told me that a young man whose father ran a business across the road from Jock's new house had shot himself. I couldn't stop thinking about him. Then Linda called to ask about the decision. She urged me to start writing about the entire legal process and asked if I could handle death threats. We joked about Salman Rushdie.

My short-term memory wasn't working. I took Allison to the 4-H Christmas sleigh ride, but hadn't bought a present for the exchange. I raced back to town for a gift, but forgot the stores weren't open on Sunday. I forgot to arrange another visit from the farrier.

On the Monday, Bradley's kindergarten teacher called to ask if I could bake cookies with the class on the starting date of the trial. I laughed and told her to go fuck herself. She knew me and knew about the situation and laughed when I explained how I would be occupied that day.

Perhaps inspired by the suggestion planted by Doyle, I called my sister Valerie. I had not spoken to her since Wendy's wedding.

I said, "I want to tell you something you might not know. I'm not sure if you realize what is going on, but . . ."

"Shut up, you stupid little bitch. I hate you. Don't talk to me!"

She hung up. Without thinking, I dialled her number again.

"Before you hang up, please listen," I said quickly.

"I don't want to talk to you. The fact you are my sister is the worst thing in the world."

"I just want to tell you . . ."

"You call yourself a Christian! You are the sickest, most hateful person in the world! A Christian would never do what you are doing. I hate you!"

"I don't call myself anything. Jean has made a statement to the police. Of the six of us, you're the only one who has refused. This is your last chance, this week."

Her volume and pitch increased to a full scream. "Do you *really* expect me to do that? I've dealt with this shit long ago! This is your problem! You have all these hateful feelings! You are a terrible, sick person!"

To my surprise, my voice came out clear and even. "This is not just my problem. It concerns all of us. You can tell your part now, before it's too late."

"Leave me alone! I'll call the police! You're harassing me! I'll have you charged!"

"You'll live with it for the rest of your life."

"And you'll live with this, you hateful mean-spirited bitch! Get over it!"

"I wanted you to know about Jean's statement. That's all."

"I don't give a shit!"

"Okay, I'm hanging up now. I hope you call the police. I'd like to talk to them. Goodbye."

After the call ended, I started to shiver, yet dripped with sweat. It felt like she had been kicking me in the stomach. I wanted to shower and change. Why had no one in my family spewed rage, like Valerie's profane venom, at the offender?

I stripped and ran the water. Then I chuckled when I recalled Doyle's theory about "picking up the phone and calling your sister."

Although I was still shaken, I wanted to attend a vigil for the women murdered in Montreal. After supper, I drove to the high school in a neighbouring town. About thirty people watched a video of an interview with one of the victim's mothers. The other video featured my friends Melanie and Margaret, and the woman who was sitting beside me. They had been interviewed for a television program on their reactions to the massacre. The woman sitting next to me and Melanie had organized the vigil.

In the sharing circle, Melanie asked the audience to respond to a single question, "Why hold a vigil?"

My gut reaction reminded me of all the other times, other places. Finally, after what seemed like hours, the sharing stone landed in my shaking fingers. I said, "I want to . . . answer Melanie's question. But it's hard to speak. Has anyone here seen the news reports about the old guy who is too sick to stand trial?" A few hands went up. "I believe in these vigils because of the violence done to women, to myself, to my sisters, to my mother. "

The woman next to me placed her hand on my shoulder. I wanted the floor to slide open and consume me. When I removed my glasses to wipe away tears, I left them off. It was easier not to see the reactions.

The next day, my throat swelled in response to a virus, cold sores erupted around my mouth, and my shoulder had still not stopped aching. Despite feeling shitty, I decided to take Bradley skating. When we got home, Cutler called. He said, "Pollock has suggested a guilty plea but wants a guarantee of no jail time. I need input from you and your sisters on the sentencing . . ."

His request upset me so much I couldn't answer. After a long pause, I said, "I need to think about this."

"Yes, you might want to contact your siblings." He hung up.

I wondered why he had saddled me with his work again, and why we had to decide what was appropriate sentencing. There must be some standards that applied in similar cases. After he ended the call, Wendy phoned to warn me about what Cutler had already asked.

She said, "I didn't know what to say, either. I have something else to tell you, but it will take a while to explain. I'll phone again when I have time."

Because of the pain in my shoulder, I did not go to yoga or ringette.

The following morning, Wendy called for the promised conversation. "David phoned me last night. He was very upset. Sandra's having an affair with her professor."

"She wrote her thesis years ago. Has she been screwing him since then? Why is she telling her secrets now?"

"I'm very worried about David. It was hard enough on him with this trial going on. He promised he'd call me back."

I could not fathom Sandra's sense of timing.

The next morning, it stormed again and schools were closed. I felt like crying all day long. Everything was too hard, too sad, too unfair.

Wendy phoned again and did not sound so upset. "I called to see if David was all right. Sandra answered and listed all of his many faults. David called me back and told me that Sandra's mother drove him to Shannon's place. He said he curled up in her arms and bawled. Sandra said David was lighting fires. Turned out he sat on the sidewalk and burned the lingerie she wore on her dates. Her mom called the cops because he shouted, asking Sandra to leave. The cops wouldn't do a thing. In fact, they said they understood."

After we discussed the situation for an hour, I decided to phone David. The instant I began to dial, our phone rang. He was calling me. I strained to hear his voice; he explained that he did not want Sandra, his mother-in-law, or his daughter to wake up.

I said, "I'm worried about you doing violence to yourself. However strong the feelings are right now, they will pass. She's not worth one drop of your blood."

I told him Karen's hints on what to do when considering suicide. He talked and I listened until at least 1:00 a.m.

In the morning, another blizzard, and my period, started. My shoulder still hurt to move. Almost constantly, I longed for someone to rescue me. But, as I said to David, there was only one surefire way to stop all the pain and I had promised not to do that.

I phoned Karen. She said, "No one older was willing to fight back. You carved a space for your younger siblings. You really are a gentle person. It just wasn't allowed to come out."

We talked about Wendy.

"She's broken away and dug in. She's not taking care of anyone or trying to fix people," Karen said.

"You're right. She reminds me not to drive, or get in the wrong elevator, or punch out Pollock. And she can do it even when she has Patrick to think about."

A reassuring image appeared to me. We were a new family being born. It had been a long labour, over three and a half years.

On December 11, 1995, the two-week trial was scheduled to start.

Trial?

77

THE WEATHER TURNED BRUTALLY COLD AFTER the storms.

Despite the temperatures, Warren accompanied Allison to the kids' cross-country ski club and a bonfire, and then to the city for her orthodontist appointment. I decided to take Bradley to visit Margaret's son. We followed a snowplow all the way to their house. The boys played happily together and Bradley asked to stay for a sleepover.

Warren and Allison returned, and we got a movie—not the usual cartoon: one advantage of not having Bradley with us. Nightmares and cold sweats woke me during the night. In spite of the minus thirty-two degrees temperature, I went for a night ski, to get rid of the tension, to tire myself enough to sleep.

In the morning, Margaret invited Allison and Bradley to watch her children in their United Church Christmas play. I welcomed the opportunity to forget what was supposed to happen the next day. Warren did not come with us. In the car, the girls turned the radio to a heavy rock station and chatted about teachers and school.

I walked into the church and stared at the minister. She had been at the second women's gathering at Hecla Island. After the service ended, I went out to start the car. Although I planned to go directly home, I wanted to tell her what was happening—meeting her again seemed really important, some kind of sign.

I returned to the warm sanctuary. "Maybe you don't remember what I shared at that women's gathering. But I wanted to tell you, it's going to happen, tomorrow, after three and a half years. Strange, I run into you the day before it starts."

She looked into my eyes. "You can stand proud and speak your truth."

"Thanks, I appreciate that."

Margaret invited us for lunch at her mother's place. I decided to forget about going home. When we got there, Allison said it gave her a memory of the house at West Hawk. It had the same dark wood walls, rough basement, multitude of rooms all connected like a rabbit's warren, and immense meal spread out on the kitchen table. The impending trial seemed to spur Margaret's mother to speak about her memories of my mother. She said, "I knew she had a horrible lot. Her face told it."

After lunch, we went outside and I tried to catch a horse, but couldn't. On the drive home, I was struck by how numb I felt, and how relieved I was to fill the day with people and activity.

Margaret had asked me to drop off some movies. When I walked into the convenience store, I picked up the Sunday paper. One headline stood out: "Accused's weak heart puts court in hospital."

Allison read the article as we drove home. When I asked her how she felt about it, she would not answer.

Warren's mother had agreed to stay overnight so we could leave right after supper and not worry about driving for an hour and fifteen minutes in the morning cold. Warren left to pick her up. I still felt foggy, but we needed to pack clothes to stay in the city, and I had to prepare stuff for the kids. In a burst of panic, I yelled at Allison to help.

She yelled back, "You hate everyone! Leave me alone!"

I felt saddened by her anger and overwhelmed by the things I had to arrange. I found Bradley to explain what was going on, and reminded him how we might not be around for a few days. I cleaned up the kitchen table and Warren returned with his mother.

The phone rang.

An accented voice came on the line. "Hello, Donna. I saw the newspaper today. I am outraged! I meant to call sooner, but I was preparing to go to Denmark to visit my son."

"Yes, it is an outrage . . ." I could not place the voice.

"I wanted to tell you I saw your father in the big mall in Kenora two weeks ago. He was walking around, eating by himself—no oxygen, no wheelchair, no Joan. I was with two other people. They had heard all the stories. They were just as amazed as I was, to see him there."

Finally, I realized who it was. It was my friend's mother, Mrs. Jenson. I had talked to her about our crisis when she came to see Warren about a legal matter and had stayed for lunch, so many months ago.

"Are you willing to make a statement to the Crown or the police?"

"Yes, I would. But I am leaving soon. I'm sure the women I was with are willing, also. They were very upset. Not only for you girls, but about all the money spent on this foolish old man."

"Could I give the Crown your number?"

"Yes, that would be fine. I feel so sorry for you girls."

"Thank you. This means a lot."

Her revelations jolted me. For so long, I had fretted about asking people to step forward. My first thought—I need to tell Cutler. But I did not have a home phone number for him. My brain had stopped working. I sat down at the table and attempted to make small talk with Anne.

"Oh, my, it's cold out there," she said.

"Yes, unusual for so early in the winter."

"Our car wouldn't start."

"Yeah, they do that when it's cold."

The phone rang again. I jumped up from the table.

It was Cutler. He said, "Pollock just called. Mr. Tod has decided to plead guilty. There will be no trial, if he sticks with his decision."

"What does this mean?"

"He will not stand trial. The judge will hear his plea and decide about sentencing."

Then I remembered the previous call. "A woman just phoned me, not more than five minutes ago. She said she saw Jock in a shopping mall, two weeks ago, alone, unassisted, no oxygen, and no wheelchair. It may not matter now, but she agreed to make a statement. Here's her number."

"If I call her, I will have to let Pollock know. Her statement will become evidence." He paused. "Since you were scheduled to testify first tomorrow, you do not need to show up."

"I intend to be there, no matter what. You know, of course, that Shannon and Belle have already flown to the city. They'll want to be there, I'm sure."

He promised to call Mrs. Jenson and ended the conversation. I turned to Anne and Warren. My voice quaked. "He's pleading guilty! Why did it take three years? I can't believe all the pain he inflicted."

The familiar wall of emotion dropped on me. My legs collapsed. I sat on the floor and stared at the phone.

Warren helped me up. "He had no way out. There were five of you. I'm just surprised he waited 'til the last minute. Maybe he doubted the judge would go through with it."

"Now we don't even get to tell what he did. He took that away from us."

Much later, I learned this tactic was common. Offenders, faced with the inevitable, plead guilty, saying they want to spare the witness the agony of testifying, but in reality, they want to avoid having the judge hear the specifics or witness the injured party's pain. Juries who hear the details usually respond with more severe sentences. It also works to the offender's advantage, especially if they are related to or known by the victim. Judges almost always take close relationships into account. This somehow reduces the horror, instead of increasing it, as might be expected. The sentences reflect the lessened impact. If a stranger commits a similar assault, it is deemed more reprehensible.

I called Wendy to tell her about Mrs. Jenson's message and her willingness to testify.

We discussed Cutler's news for a few minutes.

"See you tomorrow." I couldn't think of anything else to say.

78

IT WAS DECEMBER 11, 1995.

The mercury had stalled at minus thirty. The pressure to arrive at the proceedings was gone, so Warren and I decided to drive into the city in the morning.

The Justice Department had opted to hold the "trial" in a hospital. They had asked a few facilities, and they had refused, but finally the Misericordia Hospital, an older teaching institution in the downtown area, accepted.

Five sisters and an assortment of friends and spouses assembled in a large, empty "witness room" across the hall from the "courtroom." Three nursing mothers were present: Wendy with Patrick, Shannon with her two-month-old son, Aiden, and my friend Melanie with her daughter, Emma, who had been born around the same time as Patrick.

I relished the black robes seeing babes at the breast in their courtroom during a proceeding that involved child sexual abuse. Jean showed up with her oldest son, Trevor. She was technically not a witness because she made her statement too late.

"Are you girls thinking of civil litigation?" she asked.

I snorted. "First of all, we're not girls. Second, as I keep reminding you, we were all abused. This includes you."

Despite the tension, we joked about the offender trying to elude justice by walking around in a shopping mall.

"An obvious suicide attempt," Wendy said.

"Yeah, the cops should have taken away his credit card, like they do with shoelaces and neckties for guys in lockup," I said.

Jock arrived on a stretcher. A SWAT team of ambulance attendants rolled him into his specially arranged facility. A guy in a uniform told us to stop watching the arrival of the medical entourage.

Before we had a chance to discuss anything else, court was called into session. We filed into the makeshift courtroom. The court reporter's table faced the witness table. The judge's table sat at the front, facing the defence and prosecution tables, and the audience. An artist sat off to the side, sketching the scene.

When I saw Ms. McCawley sitting with Cutler, I murmured a prayer of thanks. The last I had heard from the Justice Department, she had finished her part, the constitutional argument, and her attendance at these proceedings was deemed unnecessary. She nodded at us as we found chairs.

The faithful women from West Hawk and Falcon Lakes occupied the rear seats. I sat down and recognized the person beside me as a reporter from CBC television. Right away, the judge issued a ban on publication.

A large video monitor stood on a tall stand beside the judge's table. The camera in the medically fitted-out adjoining room pointed at the accused, seated in a chair. The judge read the charges, which had been reduced to four counts of indecent assault, and the single counts of sexual assault and sexual exploitation. The charges of physical assault against my mother, bestiality, and possession of an unregistered weapon had been dropped.

I thought—how could decades of repeated attacks be reduced to such inconsequence? If only he had assaulted us on just six occasions.

Despite the piles of electronic equipment and cables snaking back and forth, someone ascertained they had "technical difficulties." The video transferred the pictures two-way, but the sound only went one way. The accused could hear us; we could not hear him.

The judge needed to hear Jock's response to the charges, so he offered to go into the other room. Pollock wanted to monitor the responses, so he offered to accompany him. The court reporter also had to hear the words "guilty" or "not guilty" and make sure they were recorded, so she also offered to go with them. Unfortunately, her large pile of equipment could not offer to get up and walk into the other room. Cutler offered to listen on Pollock's headset, and repeat whatever the accused said into the recorder. The insanity of so many people leaving the room to accommodate the accused didn't seem to occur to any of them.

I wondered—what would have been so wrong about asking the ambulance attendants to wheel him in for two minutes, feed him some nitro while the charges were read and answered, and then take him out for the remainder of the proceedings?

It would have satisfied a deep emotional need to see and hear him say the word "guilty." What we got was Cutler speaking into the headset and echoing a second-hand version of the accused's pleas. "What's that you said, Mr. Tod? Can you hear me? Can you speak up? What do you plead? Guilty? Is that what you said?"

Jock might have said, "I'm thirsty!" Cutler may have heard him wrong.

While the charges were read, we could see Jock on the monitor. He shook his head, cried out, and clutched at his chest. Small wonder Cutler could not hear him.

I sensed sympathy rising amongst the non-involved spectators, responding to the weeping old man on the screen. If he were in a real courtroom, he would have never been allowed to wail and beat his breasts. I wanted to believe the judge would have ordered him to shut up, just as he ordered me to shut up. In the background, we could also hear the whispers and murmurs of Joan, anticipating his every twitch and yelp.

We started to hear a few accounts of what he did to Belle and Wendy, and then the sound to his room was turned off. I couldn't figure out a reason, except to guess the judge got alarmed by the moaning. We had entered a nonsensical zone where even the bizarre regular court procedure did not apply. At the same time they said they recognized the years of anguish caused by the admitted offender, the officers of the court catered to his every whim.

In the morning, before we began, Cutler had warned us the judge might go directly into a sentencing hearing.

And that's exactly what happened. Usually a month or so elapses before sentencing is decided. During that period, the accused is incarcerated. The victims are given a month or so to prepare impact statements and are allowed to read these statements to the court at the impact hearing.

Given that we wouldn't be allowed time to do this, I asked Cutler if he could read Karen's letter of assessment of me, submitted to the Criminal Injuries Compensation Board. Karen heard me ask him and volunteered to take the stand. She said she'd also give her opinion of the effects on Wendy and me, and on all the family members who had come to group sessions during the past three and a half years.

When Cutler asked the judge if Karen could do this, Pollock stood up. "I object, M'lord. This letter is not an impact statement. Plus I have not had the chance to read it. The Crown is not entitled to call this person as witness. I have a problem . . ."

But you're the ass who let this fool dangle until the last possible minute. We heard the plea at five o'clock last night. And now you're complaining about not being prepared.

Clearwater interrupted Pollock. "I want to sentence the accused as quickly as possible. This has gone on long enough. Are the witnesses, as individuals, willing to speak to the court about the effects of the sexual assaults?"

Wendy, Belle, and I agreed. Shannon declined. The room spun around me; I couldn't believe what was happening. Once again, Clearwater had asked us to collect our thoughts quickly and sum up years of abuse.

Up until now, Joan had remained in the medical room with Jock, switching between kneeling in front of him and asking what he needed. At one point, he pushed her face into his lap, like a man demanding oral sex.

Despite the frigid temperatures, the courtroom was at least twenty-eight degrees Celsius. Someone opened almost all the windows. During a break, we joked about how appropriate the extreme heat was, given the proximity of so much evil. The CBC reporter beside me panted and dripped sweat. I couldn't tell if he was overcome by emotions or dehydration. The bathroom was on the next floor so I entered the stairwell to get to it. By accident or design, Melanie's husband, Paul, followed me.

I said, "I hate this shit. How can anyone look at that pathetic old man and not feel sorry? And we get blamed. What happened to us is never going to seem bad enough to justify this!"

I slumped against the open window's sill and sobbed. The cold air froze my tears and numbed my face.

Paul said, "You're wrong. No one in that room can look at him without being disgusted. He did what he did. No one's blaming you. This hellish scene is not your doing."

They chose Belle to speak first, and asked Shannon, Wendy, and me to wait in the witness room so our stories wouldn't be contaminated. Belle told me later she explained how her overall personality was affected and how marrying an abuser had affected her. Pollock asked many irrelevant questions. She said she didn't think he was allowed to do that since it was no longer a trial and he shouldn't be cross-examining her. But the judge didn't stop him and Cutler did not object. The friends who watched said Belle showed emotion but presented her story strongly.

I was not in the room so I didn't hear why Jock was allowed to stop listening. They took him to another, cooler part of the hospital.

When I was summoned back to the "courtroom," I could only focus my eyesight on a band about one metre wide. I walked to the witness chair and sat down quickly, facing the court reporter and her barrage of hardware. Off to one side, Clearwater asked me to address the effects of the sexual assaults.

I thought—I've done this before with this guy! Only now he's sitting at the same level.

I began slowly, staring straight ahead. "We were affected as children and now again as adults. The whole process has been about admissions. I have been forced to admit things about myself, my life, my family, and, mostly, my father. So much had been buried, pushed away. So much energy, throughout our entire lives, went into protecting the perpetrator. He was not only sexually violent but physically violent. We all had a fear of punishment and retaliation. The revelation of the past abuses has affected my husband and children. They've watched me going through emotional and physical hell. I've experienced panic attacks, sleep disruptions, eating problems, anger. I have recurring suicidal ideations. I wake up often, trembling and sweating. I have stopped going to church. It's like I don't know what to believe, or why, any more. I'm tired of the whole mess, and furious it has been allowed to continue for so long."

Tears dripped down my cheeks. Although I was conscious of wetness, my speaking voice did not break. In fact, I was surprised at how easily the words came out, despite the clenching and unclenching of teeth. I guessed it paid off to practise. While I spoke, I closed my eyes or stared at the court reporter's apparatus. I barely looked at the judge's face, even when he addressed me directly. In my peripheral vision, I noted Pollock squirming in his chair. I continued to talk with my eyes half closed.

A shadow draped across the table. For a second, I imagined that Clearwater had ordered one of the sheriffs to toss me out because I was taking too long. I smelt a familiar perfume; two large arms enveloped me.

It was Joan. I had waited three and a half years for her to hear my story. She had come into the room and had been sitting beside Pollock all along. I hadn't noticed her. She said something. I was so stupefied it did not register as human speech. She pulled my head toward her rigid brassiere. Her face frightened me, so stiff, so white. Her lips looked like fresh wounds, gaping and closing. Words I still could not fathom erupted from the two slashes.

"Oh, Donna . . ."

Every person in the room sat immobilized, speech-less, even the judge—as if they were waiting for sobbing and forgiveness, the happy ending, like that moment in a tear-jerking movie when the dog returns or two lovers lunge at each other after running across a field of flowers.

Trapped underneath her arms, I fought to regain my equilibrium. This woman had chosen father over daughters, marriage over truth, and status over protection. And she wanted to silence me!

"Don't, Donna . . . don't, don't, don't."

I scrambled to collect my thoughts and wondered—don't what?

I shoved her arms away, mumbling, "No, please, no . . . " and then spoke louder, "No! No!"

All of this took place in less than a minute. But it seemed like an hour before I was able to struggle out from her clutches. Neither Clearwater nor Cutler nor Pollock asked the wife of the accused to step away from the witness. The sheriffs stood, transfixed. It was a display of courtroom insanity gone completely over the top, and it took place under the supervision of the same judge who threatened to remove me for answering his rhetorical questions. Why was Joan allowed to approach a witness? What if she had a gun?

Her tactic, planned or spontaneous, worked. After she released me and returned to her chair, I could not resume the flow of my testimony. Flustered, I said a few more words and asked to be excused.

"I want this to end. I don't know how much more we can stand."

The judge looked me in the eyes. "You have my solemn promise. It will end."

I stepped down and was allowed to listen to Wendy. Belle had listened to both of us. Wendy began talking about our mother.

Pollock stood up. "I object, M'lord. I don't think this has any bearing on the matter at hand."

Cutler concurred. "Please restrict your comments to the effects of the sexual assaults."

Clearwater dismissed both comments with a wave. He looked genuinely interested. "Please continue. It's all relevant. You do not have to restrict your remarks."

Wendy told about the physical attacks on our mother and siblings, and the verbal attacks on our stepmother. She spoke of the sexual abuse after our mother died, and described her difficulties coping with sexual issues, dating, and finding a partner she could trust.

I remembered her wedding; we had come full circle. The story began with her marriage, and now it might finally end with her talking about it. I was amazed how calmly she spoke. Perhaps because she seemed less emotional, the judge questioned her more.

"What caused you to suffer more? The original abuse? Or dealing with the justice system?"

"Both caused a lot of pain."

After Wendy finished, the judge declared, "I want to discuss sentencing now."

Cutler stood up. "I have heard evidence that contravenes what the accused has said about his health. Three individuals, whom I have personally spoken to, saw him in a shopping mall with no oxygen, no wheelchair, and no companions. The court might be mindful of these facts when considering sentencing."

Pollock bounced to his feet. "It was . . . ahhh . . . a small shopping mall, M'lord."

The spectators roared with sharp, bitter laughs. Pollock blushed and sat down.

Clearwater mentioned the issues of rehabilitation and detention, both individual and general. He insisted the conduct of people like Jock would not be tolerated.

Cutler surprised everyone by rising and speaking. "I have contacted the corrections department. They have assured me they can accommodate prisoners with complex medical conditions."

Clearwater said, "Why not? People have been sent to the penitentiary for much less severe infractions. Our number one purpose is to send a message to the broader community. No matter how old the events. No matter how old the perpetrator."

I looked at my sisters and we all nodded. This judge certainly talked the talk. But I could not help thinking— it's not bad enough.

Emboldened, Cutler rose again. "The Crown recommends a jail term."

Pollock, although still sulking, resumed his shopping defence. "M'lord, we do not know how far he walked in the mall. We do not know how large the mall was. We do not know how long he had been walking."

Later, I learned he'd phoned Mrs. Jenson and the two other witnesses to harass them into recanting. I don't believe this is legal, but I was not surprised.

Pollock continued, "I submit, M'lord, the book of similar sentences." He cited decisions dealing with ailing prisoners. Then he switched to a different tack. "M'lord, I request the ambulance attendants who were with Mr. Tod be allowed to comment."

I couldn't understand how the opinions of people who had sat with Jock for two hours took precedence over an ordained minister and counsellor, who had known and advised the family for years.

Cutler agreed. "This is not relevant."

Clearwater asked Pollock, "Why do you want their comments? I have done everything in my power to make this as least stressful as possible."

"Putting someone in jail is at least as stressful as this," said Pollock.

Despite his reluctance, Clearwater agreed and called for the two men who had been looking after the accused.

After inquiring about his experience, Pollock asked one of the attendants to summarize his observations on Jock Tod's medical condition. The young man said, "He was fully alert, but complained of chest pains. He had an elevated heart rate. We administered ten nitro doses. He was on oxygen throughout."

"Ten times? Isn't that a lot? What are the normal doses of nitro?" asked Pollock.

"Three is usual."

Later, Wendy, the nurse, told me that three times was usual, but not for a man who has been taking nitro for more than twenty years. And just because he asked for nitro, it didn't mean they were obliged to give it.

But Cutler had finally caught on to something. "Isn't an elevated heart rate consistent with increased anxiety? Even in healthy individuals?"

The judge glanced at his watch. It was past noon. He adjourned until 2:35 p.m.

Wendy rushed home to relieve her aching breasts. The rest of us followed her, and joined Patrick for lunch. While we mulled over the morning's events, we discussed the folks who had come out to support us. Carol, from Falcon Lake, had come even though her husband had died only a couple of weeks earlier. Wendy and I agreed we were hurt by the absence of brothers. Robin had decided not to drive from northern Saskatchewan. Like the rest of us, he did not expect a sentence to be handed out so soon. David, out in British Columbia, was too shaken by the mess with his wife. As for the others, we had no contact so we couldn't even speculate.

At 2:35 p.m., Clearwater called the court back into session. Pollock launched into a lengthy submission about the health of Jock Tod.

He said, "His wife feeds him, dresses him, and bathes him."

I harrumphed—nothing's changed!

Then Pollock listed all the post-secondary education obtained by Jock's offspring. For some, he added years of schooling or university degrees. For example, Ernie, an electrician, became an electrical engineer. I wondered if all his other "facts" were as accurate. All of us exchanged looks of bewilderment. We couldn't understand why he was doing this, instead of asking the court for mercy. When he came to my name, Pollock stood up straighter and puffed up his chest. "And then there's Donna. She married a lawyer . . ."

The audience catcalled and hooted, so loudly that no one heard about my titles and degrees. Pollock stopped reading his list.

The judge shouted, "What is this all about? Why this laughter? Are these facts not accurate?"

Like schoolchildren being lectured by a teacher, we all stared at the floor. No one dared answer, for fear of being expelled. Some merely shook their heads. Pollock, Cutler, and the judge looked genuinely baffled, unaware of the sexism of Pollock's implication that marriage to a lawyer was an exalted status.

Pollock finished the list of achievements and then quoted from my 1993 statement wherein I wished Jock not be incarcerated. He didn't ask if my opinions had changed after three and a half years. He mentioned that our father had forfeited his right to a preliminary hearing and spared us the agony of testifying at the trial. He did not ask if it was our choice or if we viewed this omission as positive. Pollock stressed the absence of penetration. He did not ask if a penis mattered more than fingers or masturbating on a child's legs and anus mattered.

Pollock cited Jock's clean criminal record, stature in the community, work habits, carpentry skills, and war history. While he praised our father, I almost choked— why doesn't Cutler object? So much is inaccurate; all is irrelevant.

Doyle stood up to read a long list of precedents regarding sentences for invalids. As he droned, the sexual proclivity of these paraplegic and physically challenged perverts astounded me. He repeated his line about cruel and unusual punishment at least ten times.

When Doyle emphasized the age of the offender, I fought the urge to jump up and yell—that slime bucket did not take our ages into account!

Doyle insisted Jock was no longer a threat and requested a suspended sentence. Ms. McCawley rose and pointed out numerous inconsistencies in the Doyle arguments. The clock was running out. We all hoped that Clearwater might end the afternoon with a pronouncement on sentencing, but he declared, "We will reconvene tomorrow morning, in the same place, at 10:30."

This meant we faced another long drive home and long drive back, in arctic conditions.

After the adjournment, Karen stomped up and down the hallway. "I'm so angry with that man! He could've apologized or asked for forgiveness! But no! He trots out that trumped-up list of degrees, which weren't even his achievements! He took away all your accomplishments in one fell swoop! I cannot believe the gall of that bastard!"

She grabbed her forehead with both hands. "Do you know what he was saying when he was grimacing and wagging his head? I went out in the hall. He was yelling he didn't have to take this and he should be let go! He wasn't in pain. He was defiant, despite the guilty plea—not exactly contrite."

I wished the judge had heard him.

79

AFTER A LONG, SLEEPLESS NIGHT SPENT THINKING about Clearwater's intentions, I got up to feed the horses and prepared to leave for the city.

When I hugged Bradley, he frowned and asked, "Where are you going, Mom?"

"Back to court. We aren't finished yet."

"Well, you tell that judge-man I don't like this court stuff. It takes too much time. I want you here with . . . me," he broke off, crying.

I hugged him again. Warren went out to start the car. He planned to drive into Winnipeg, later, with his sister and the children. I raced into the city and joined my four sisters and the rest of the supporters assembled in the witness room. We discussed possible outcomes and the judge's choices. Some were impressed by his handling of the defence and his hard-line stance. Others repeated their doubts about the legal system, which seemed designed to fail at even its most basic functions. I did not comment. A couple of people reported seeing a drawing of the courtroom scene on the previous night's CBC television news. Because I sat at the front, my head and shoulders were included.

Someone said, "Don't worry. You had your face in your hands. Didn't you see the news?"

"No, we were still driving home."

We returned to the boiling hot courtroom and looked up at the monitor. Joan had returned to her same position, kneeling by Jock, who was wailing and flailing his arms.

The judge entered and got things rolling right away. He said, "Although Mr. Tod may have been generally respected, it is now obvious that life in the accused's home was not what it seemed."

The judge was wrong, twice in one sentence. Jock was not "generally respected" and he was not the "accused." He was now the "convicted."

"His actions caused many long-lasting effects. His daughters suffered and continue to suffer. Their own inner strengths and the strengths of their relationships have sustained them so far. In 1989, he apparently ceased to offend, not by his own inclinations, but rather by his declining health. There is no perfect justice. Perhaps capital punishment would be appropriate."

The believers in justice got excited.

"If not for the state of his health, he would be looking at three to five years in the penitentiary."

We sucked in our breaths.

Clearwater hesitated. "But we have to remember, this man is eighty and not in perfect health. Only 20 percent of his heart is functioning. This cannot be faked, whatever else he has faked."

The cynical faction let out a huge sigh. It looked as if they were to be proven right. No judge would send Jock to jail.

"First of all, I prohibit Jock from driving. If he is as disabled as he claims, with diminished mental capacities and a barely functioning heart, he should not be operating a vehicle."

Jock got more agitated, the most upset he had been so far. It looked as if losing his license meant more than being convicted of sexual assault against his daughters.

The judge continued, "He is sentenced to two years of supervised probation. I order him to take part in enforced counselling for sexual offenders. I also prohibit him from contact with children under sixteen, except in the presence of another adult."

The judge banged the gavel and disappeared. Stunned silence hung in the sweltering air for a minute or two. Belle stood up and swore loudly.

One of the sheriffs said, "You can be charged with disturbing the peace."

She yelled even louder, "Can you believe this? They've just let this child molester free. And now we are treated as the criminals! I will yell as loud as I want! I'm not hurting anyone! He hurt hundreds of people!"

The sheriff shrugged and stopped chiding her. Anyway, by now others had joined in, loudly expressing their anger. Some clutched at each other, crying.

I turned to the CBC reporter beside me and pointed my finger at the door where the judge had exited. "I hope you tell this part of the story. This is insane. He got off, after over three and a half years of legal shit, and forty years of molesting."

The reporter spoke to me, for the first time. "You're right. But I have seen this ending all too often. This isn't news. The only real story here was the hospital angle. He could have died, but he didn't. So your story is no different than thousands of others."

After the yelling subsided, the sheriffs herded us back into the witness room and closed the door. They refused to let us out or watch the attendants trundle Jock out on his stretcher. Maybe they were worried that we might yell at him and cause him to do what he had promised to do for three and a half years—drop dead! The people in the witness room hugged each other, kicked chairs, paced from spot to spot, or yelled. Some did all four.

While Shannon tried to calm herself enough to breastfeed, I cried and apologized to Aiden. "Oh, baby, I'm so sorry you saw this. It is horrible, but life isn't always like this. Children matter in some places."

I expected Cutler and Ms. McCawley to appear and debrief us, or at least commiserate. But they had both left the hospital. After over three years of phone calls, trips to the city, wasted hours, letters, and endless efforts on our parts to be "good witnesses" and play by the rules, we were ignored, forgotten, discarded. We no longer served the Crown's purpose. As traumatized ex-witnesses, we remained barricaded in the sweltering, empty room.

Belle asked to be let out to speak to the CBC reporter, hoping he could raise a ruckus that night on the television news. They said he could enter the room to talk to us for a few minutes, but he declined to conduct an interview, even if all the victims promised to sign releases regarding the publication ban.

Slowly, with more hugging and tears, the group broke apart. We stumbled down to the hospital's main entrance. One of the sheriffs, a young woman, followed us into the foyer.

I thought—did she want to make sure we didn't damage anything?

She stepped toward us. "Look, I know this has been terrible. I've seen the worst pain both days. You did the right thing. I wish all of you women luck. And I know you may not believe it, coming from me, but I really mean it."

It was already past 2:00 p.m.

Wendy invited everyone to come for drinks and food. Belle, Jean, Shannon, and Aiden got into Jean's vehicle and headed to their house. Paul had left the court to visit someone, but Melanie and Emma caught a ride with me.

I was parched from the heat in the makeshift courtroom. Partly because I had an empty stomach and partly because I did not want to feel any more, I chugged five glasses of wine. Then I spent the rest of the afternoon apologizing to people and telling them I loved them.

Except Jean. I could not.

When Warren and the children showed up around 3:30 p.m., Allison informed me I was drunk. I wondered how she knew, since she had never seen me drunk. With the heaters going full blast, I slept most of the way home. To the rhythm of the tires clunking on the rigid asphalt, I murmured, "It's over! It's over! It's over!"

The judge promised he would finish it and he did, for better or worse. Jock had eluded us all, and left a path of destruction in his wake.

December 13, 1995—Tucked away in a back corner of the paper, the final headline about my father's prosecution read "Man Sentenced."

Epilogue

ON JANUARY 6, 1996, I DECIDED TO WRITE ANOTHER letter—to Aunt Iris, my mother's only sister, in England.

I wanted to write before Christmas and thank you again for your unequivocal support. But this is the first chance I've had to sit down and think. Due to the court proceedings and the resulting upheaval, we barely did any Christmas preparations. I'm not sure if it was lack of time, or energy, or Christmas spirit—maybe all three combined.

I have enclosed some newspaper clippings; they summarize what happened. Because we had been told, at the beginning, not to exchange details of our assaults, I did not fully realize that I was the one Jock abused the most often, until the "trial." This was the first time in this province someone had been tried in a hospital. But they kept Jock in another room and we could only see him on a video monitor. So he didn't have to face us. I did not realize it when it was happening, but the judge had no intention of sending Jock to prison. Usually, victims get a few weeks to prepare impact statements. During that interval, the convicted person is in jail. The judge did not wait. He asked us for our statements right away and sent Jock home.

Speaking of Christmas, we had a quiet one, but Robin, Wendy and her family, and my friend Barb and her family came to visit. Wendy's baby is gorgeous. I don't remember if I told you I was there when he was born. Joan still refuses to acknowledge his existence.

While I wrote this letter, I listened to CBC radio. A journalist reported on riots at the federal penitentiary. A group of sexual offenders had been attacked and mutilated. The fear in the voice of the sexual offender in the interview clip intrigued me.

I wondered if Jock was listening. I wanted him to know that fear.

Call me Incested.

Acknowledgements

TO CREATE THIS MEMOIR, I HAD PLENTY OF HELP and support.

First of all, when people ask if writing the book was "good therapy," I tell them, "No, good therapy gave me the awareness and determination to write it." Thanks go out to the many caring counsellors I have visited over the past twenty-five years.

I thank my friend, Gerard Beirne, the Irish author. Like a literary godfather, he appeared in my part of rural Manitoba exactly when I needed him. He read my work, showed me what a writer's life looked like, and, along with his amazing family, hosted unforgettable St. Patrick's Day parties. Also, I thank Winnipeg writer and book reviewer Joan Thomas, who encouraged me in all the best ways. At Sage Hill Writing Experience, Denise Chong taught me the unstoppable power of true stories and the writers in her creative nonfiction sessions inspired me with their kindness and enthusiasm.

I thank the Canada Council for the Arts, Access Copyright Foundation, and Manitoba Arts Council for various grants and travel funds. Thanks go out to the Manitoba Writers' Guild for their ongoing support for writers and to *Prairie Fire Magazine* for publishing my stories. When I participated in *Prairie Fire*'s Boreality Project issues, it helped me to self-identify as a "boreal writer."

Also, I value ongoing collaborations with local arts champions Winnipeg River Arts Council. I strongly believe in their motto, "Connecting People through Art," and have served as a board member for more than ten years.

In addition, I am deeply grateful for my lifelong friend, Barb Hamilton, mentioned often in these pages. She offered emotional buttressing, hosted my writing workshops, and sold my first stories to her guests at Falcon Trails Resort. Her support has been consistent and unwavering.

Words cannot capture my boundless gratitude for my women's circle (inadvertently known as "Whimsicals"). This band of feminists has been getting together to share food and friendship, once a month, for almost thirty years. Present members include Melanie Whyte, Donna Pierce, Wendy Boyd, Nancy Greenaway, Dorothy Parker, Sandi Fitzmaurice, and occasional adjunct Susan Detlor. With generosity and compassion, they have listened to hundreds of my traumatic disclosures and validated my writing habit.

I am further blessed to share potluck dinners, lively conversation, companionship, and singalongs with another group of long-time friends. Members include

Caroline McIntosh, Paul and Laraine Lussier, Grace Kost, Kathy Picard, Scott Buckboro, and occasional adjunct Beverley Richmond.

Thanks go out to writing groups in Lac du Bonnet and Pinawa, where I learned to write better. I am also grateful for all the readers, writerly gatherings, book clubs, and students who have welcomed me in various settings. As well, I feel nurtured by writer-friends Sally Ito, Sharron Arksey, Lauren Carter, Sue Sorensen, Joanna Lilley, Erna Buffie, Ariel Gordon, and numerous colleagues who have supplied commiseration and community.

I feel forever indebted to my family, who still provide abundant material and inspiration. I am grateful for my former husband, Warren, who struggled with a similar history of childhood adversity. His unexpected death gave clarity and seclusion, creating a perfect Petri dish to grow a writer. And I thank my beloved children, Allison and Bradley.

PHOTO: KRISTEN SAWATSKY

DONNA BESEL loves writing of all kinds and does presentations for schools, libraries, universities, conferences, and retreats. Her work has gained recognition from CBC Literary Prizes and won national contests. Her collection of short stories, *Lessons from a Nude Man,* earned two nominations for the Manitoba Book Awards and a spot on McNally Robinson's annual bestseller list. Recently, *Prairie Fire Magazine* awarded her story, "A Bay Filly," first place in their annual nonfiction contest. The forests of eastern Manitoba, where she has always lived, provide endless ideas and settings for her "boreal stories."

A NOTE ABOUT THE TYPE

THIS BOOK IS SET IN MINION PRO. Designed by Robert Slimbach, it is inspired by classical, old style typefaces of the late Renaissance, a period of elegant, beautiful, and highly readable type designs and is intended for body text and extended reading.

Minion's name comes from the traditional naming system for type sizes, in which minion is between nonpareil and brevier, with the type body 7pt in height. As the historically rooted name indicates, Minion was designed for body text in a classic style, although slightly condensed and with large apertures to increase legibility. Slimbach described the design as having "a simplified structure and moderate proportions." The design is slightly condensed, although Slimbach has said that this was intended not for commercial reasons so much as to achieve a good balance of the size of letters relative to the ascenders and descenders.

THE REGINA COLLECTION

Named as a tribute to Saskatchewan's capital city with its rich history of boundary-defying innovation, *The Regina Collection* builds upon University of Regina Press's motto of "a voice for many peoples." Intimate in size and beautifully packaged, these books aim to tell the stories of those who have been caught up in social and political circumstances beyond their control.

To see other books in *The Regina Collection*, visit WWW.UOFRPRESS.CA